GRAND EXPECTATIONS

GRAND EXPECTATIONS

The Joys and Dilemmas of Being a Grandparent

CELIA DODD

GREEN TREE

GREEN TREE
Bloomsbury Publishing Plc
50 Bedford Square, London, WC1B 3DP, UK
Bloomsbury Publishing Ireland Limited
29 Earlsfort Terrace, Dublin 2, D02 AY28, Ireland

BLOOMSBURY, GREEN TREE and the Green Tree logo are trademarks of Bloomsbury Publishing Plc

First published in Great Britain 2026

Copyright © Celia Dodd, 2026

Celia Dodd has asserted her right under the Copyright, Designs and Patents Act, 1988, to be identified as Author of this work

For legal purposes the Acknowledgements on p. 256 constitute an extension of this copyright page

All rights reserved. No part of this publication may be: i) reproduced or transmitted in any form, electronic or mechanical, including photocopying, recording or by means of any information storage or retrieval system without prior permission in writing from the publishers; or ii) used or reproduced in any way for the training, development or operation of artificial intelligence (AI) technologies, including generative AI technologies. The rights holders expressly reserve this publication from the text and data mining exception as per Article 4(3) of the Digital Single Market Directive (EU) 2019/790

Bloomsbury Publishing Plc does not have any control over, or responsibility for, any third-party websites referred to or in this book. All internet addresses given in this book were correct at the time of going to press. The author and publisher regret any inconvenience caused if addresses have changed or sites have ceased to exist, but can accept no responsibility for any such changes

A catalogue record for this book is available from the British Library

Library of Congress Cataloguing-in-Publication data has been applied for

ISBN: TPB: 978-1-3994-1694-8; eBook: 978-1-3994-1697-9

2 4 6 8 10 9 7 5 3 1

Typeset in Adobe Garamond Pro by Lumina Datamatics Ltd
Printed and bound in Great Britain by Clays Ltd, Elcograf S.p.A.

To find out more about our authors and books visit www.bloomsbury.com and sign up for our newsletters
For product safety related questions contact productsafety@bloomsbury.com

For Lena, Gabriel, Luke, Justin, Jem and Rosa

Contents

Introduction   1

1. Becoming the Grandparent You Want to Be   10
2. Building a Close Relationship With Your Grandchild: Babies to Young Adults   27
3. Your Grandchild's Parents: Your Adult Child   65
4. Your Grandchild's Parents: Your Daughter-in-Law or Son-in-Law   89
5. Childcare and Babysitting   110
6. Grandfathers   138
7. Single Grandparents   155
8. Number One Grandparents? Paternal and Maternal Grandparents   164
9. Longing for a Grandchild: Supporting Your Adult Child Through Fertility Treatment   180
10. If Your Child Divorces or Your Own Marriage Ends   196

Conclusion   235
Resources   238
Bibliography   243
Acknowledgements   256
Index   257

Introduction

People say two things about being a grandparent. The first is that it's pure, unadulterated bliss. The second is that grandparents are exploited and hard done by. Although there's some truth in both, neither quite rings true to me. It's not that I disagree that being a grandparent is wonderful. It's one of the best things that ever happened to me; being a mother is the other. But that's not the whole story. These days, there's a third thing people say: 'It's complicated'. It's more complicated than anyone ever imagines. Becoming a grandparent is not just about the baby. It marks a seismic shake-up of family life, as the relationship with your son or daughter flips on its head. As one new grandmother says, 'The dynamic between my daughter and me has completely changed. She's in control now.' Many grandparents feel the same about their son- or daughter-in-law. They often feel they're treading on eggshells, and worry about saying the wrong thing. From now on, it's up to them how often grandparents see their grandchildren. Your happiness is in their hands.

Family relationships are rich and special *because* they're complicated and demanding, and they get even more complicated the closer families become. Many grandparents today want to be closer and more involved with their grandchildren than ever before, whether or not they are part of the grandparent childcare army. But that doesn't mean they feel hard done by; childcare is hard work but it's also a real privilege to be trusted with someone else's child.

Grandchildren are an unstoppable force. You just can't help falling in love with them. Suddenly, you're no longer in control of your life, and all your carefully laid plans and dreams are in danger of flying out of the window. Before my first grandchild was born, I felt apprehensive about this. I had finally made peace with my empty nest and was enjoying being selfish and single-minded. I wasn't at all sure about going back to being pulled in different directions. Now that I have six grandchildren, there are times when I feel torn between wanting to spend as much time with them as I can and getting on with writing and all the other stuff I want to do. I've discovered all over again that you can't have it all. I feel like Bill, whose four grandchildren range from 19 years to 3 months: 'There's a dilemma between being a grandparent and wanting to be there for the grandchildren all the time, and being a retired person trying to do everything you can while you can still do it. I'm trying to find a balance between the two, but it's not easy!'

As well as overwhelming love, there are times when grandparents feel ambivalent about so many things: wanting to pass on experience and wisdom but knowing they mustn't interfere; feeling that they're no longer at the beating heart of family life when they still have so much to give; being both a parent and a grandparent at the same time; feeling twinges of jealousy of the other grandparents but wanting to get on with them. The problem is that it's just not on to admit to mixed feelings, or indeed to feeling anything other than pure unadulterated joy and pride. Rosa, who has two granddaughters under five, says, 'So many grandparents give themselves a hard time for feeling ambivalent. It's so difficult to say how you really feel because there's always this fear of appearing to be ungrateful. Friends without grandchildren say rather accusingly, "It's all right for you, you're so lucky." But that denies grandparents the right to express ourselves.' As a result, many grandparents feel isolated and guilty for mixed feelings that are actually just par for the course.

This hardly seems fair: these days, new mums and dads have plenty of spaces to air difficult and contradictory emotions. But if grandparents say anything that sounds even remotely negative, they feel bad. They soon learn to preface remarks with 'I'm not complaining but. . .' or 'I love my grandchildren to bits, but. . .' That's not just because they get shot down by grandchild-free friends; they beat themselves up too. A friend who has been looking after her daughter's baby three days a week set me straight about this. 'I'm totally knackered,' she said. 'I can't go out in the evenings and I've got to cram my work into two days. But when I say I'm not complaining, I mean it. It's nothing to do with anyone else, it's because I've wanted this grandchild for such a long time and I feel so lucky. But that doesn't mean it isn't complicated!'

CHILDCARE

For many grandparents, the dilemmas are more acute with the new expectation that they'll do some childcare. Grandparents have always been the lynchpin of family life, and they have always supported their families in many different ways: practical, emotional, financial. But they are arguably more important now than at any other time in history. Many families have no choice when it comes to both parents working to meet escalating mortgage repayments or rent, not to mention the rising cost of living generally, and this is where the grandparent army comes in. Around one in four working parents rely on their parents' help, saving a fortune on the high cost of childcare. Grandchildcare makes life complicated because it's driven primarily by love, but also money, as the gulf grows between some comfortably off baby boomers and their adult children, who are often struggling financially. Perhaps there's even an element of guilt involved, or at least a desire on the grandparents' part to do something to redress the balance.

Grandparents respond differently to this new expectation. Some are clear about saying no. They feel that they've done their bit with their own kids, they don't particularly want to do it again and don't see why they should. This can create real resentment if adult children have been expecting them to step up. Other grandparents, like Ken and Anita in chapter 5, do five full-on days a week and love it. But most grandparents are equivocal about a commitment that disrupts their own plans. They might be happy to do a day or two a week, yet feel torn between time for themselves and time for their grandchildren. They veer between wanting to help more and wanting to do more of their own thing, and they end up feeling selfish and guilty as a result. They often find themselves juggling priorities – work, older parents, younger children, interests, friendships – in a way that takes them back to their own days of working parenthood.

So while there's a lot of talk of grandparents being exploited, that's not how most grandparents feel. The reality is much more nuanced. There's no doubt that some grandparents are taken advantage of by parents who assume they've got nothing better to do, and it's outrageous that successive governments take their goodwill for granted. The powers that be are short-sighted about the impact of state pension age rises on the pool of grandparents who are available to do childcare, and that's not just in the UK but in countries all over the world.

For individual families, it feels good to share out some of the responsibility of bringing up children, and not just for financial reasons. Many parents love looking after their grandchildren and the close bond that blossoms as a result. It's flattering to be asked, and it hurts when you're not. It feels fantastic to be needed in your fifties and beyond, especially if you've stopped work and retirement feels a bit aimless. But childcare can create friction with adult children, because it introduces formality to informal relationships. It is super-hard for grandparents not to commit the cardinal sin of interfering when they're in sole charge of a grandchild. At the same time, adult sons and daughters have their own mixed feelings about being reliant on their parents. I wanted to explore these dilemmas from

INTRODUCTION

both generations' points of view, so in chapter 5 grandparents and adult children talk not only about how to make the arrangement work well for everyone, but also about what they've learned about what *not* to do.

*

But this book is not only about grandchildcare. What's really noticeable, whether you're a grandparent or not, is the way so many people's lives revolve around their grandchildren these days, even if they don't look after the kids regularly. What's expected of grandparents, and what they expect of themselves, has changed dramatically in recent generations. Not so long ago, grandmothers and grandfathers might be kind and twinkly, but they were often slightly distant too, demanding respect and best behaviour. In most families, that just doesn't wash anymore. Grandparents today want to be friendlier and closer to their adult children's families than they ever were to their own parents and grandparents. It's inevitable that a generation who were full-on as parents have gone on to aspire to be full-on as grandparents too. Niall, who has four grandchildren, says, 'I've always thought that our parents, who had lived through the war, just wanted the world to calm down and to fulfil their civic duty. They didn't really want to have close emotional relationships with their children. We did, for some reason, and I think we want the same kind of close emotional relationship with our grandchildren.'

That makes it particularly tough for grandparents who are separated from their grandchildren by geography or by disagreements with their adult children or in-laws. Some grandparents uproot themselves and move across the country, or even the world, to be near their grandchildren. For others, it's just not possible. Pam, whose four grandsons live on the other side of the world, says, 'I can't help wondering, am I a second-rate older person because I don't have my grandchildren round about? Because these days so many people's time is involved with grandchildren, especially after they retire, and that's a whole chunk of life that I don't have. I have a really good friend who I used to go walking and do loads of stuff with, but now it seems that her whole life is taken over by her grandchildren, so she's just not available in the same way anymore. So I have the double whammy of not having my grandchildren nearby and seeing less of my friends who do.'

It's no coincidence that we've reached a moment in history when conditions are just right for close relationships between grandchildren and their grandparents to flourish. It's partly that parenting styles have become more relaxed and easy-going since the 1960s. At the same time, grandparents outnumber grandchildren for the first time in history, so they have more love to lavish on them and more time to develop close bonds. The increase in life expectancy is another bonus. My friend Sam is the first man in his family for a few generations to live long enough to become a grandfather. The over-fifties are healthier and more active than ever before; they can surf and ski and play football with their grandchildren. These days, many people are grandparents for over a third of their lives, and can expect to stay close to their grandchildren as they grow into adulthood, which feels like a real privilege. It also demands curiosity and willingness to change, so it's just as well that older people are more flexible than they're usually given credit for.

But it's swings and roundabouts. While half the grandparents in the UK are under 65, many people now don't become grandparents until their late sixties or seventies, and joy is tempered by concern that they might not be able to keep up with a three-year-old zooming down the pavement on his scooter. The age when people become grandparents varies hugely, and it clearly has an impact on how involved they can be. At a canoeing retreat last year I met a great-grandmother in her early sixties who had been a grandmother in her mid-thirties, while I recently congratulated a former colleague who became a first-time grandfather in his mid-eighties – that's a whacking 50-year difference. The trend for parents to delay starting a family has had a knock-on effect; in recent decades, the average age has increased to nearly 34 for fathers and 31 for mothers. A woman who had a child in her early forties might well become a grandmother in her early eighties, if her son or daughter does the same. This leaves many people wondering whether it will ever happen, with a growing anxiety at the passing of precious time (more on this in chapter 9).

Another major concern is divorce. This dread lurks in the back of many grandparents' minds, not only because of the effect it will have on their beloved child and their grandchildren, but because they know it could mean they'll see them less, or even lose contact altogether. Paternal grandparents are usually the ones who lose out most, because grandchildren end up living with their mother in the majority of cases. That's sad for everyone, because it's now widely recognised that both sets of grandparents can play a significant role in helping their grandchildren cope with the huge upheaval in their lives, just by being a stable, comforting presence. They offer respite and reassurance if grandchildren are sharing their lives with new step-siblings. That's no mean feat for grandparents as they build their own relationships with their new step-grandchildren and new son- or daughter-in-law, while at the same time trying to maintain a good connection with their adult child's ex. Becoming step-grandparents is a whole new challenge in itself (*see* chapter 10).

It can be just as devastating for the whole family if grandparents themselves separate, which is becoming more of a thing as 'silver' divorce in the over-fifties continues to rise. Grandparents need to find a way of managing their own emotional turmoil as well as their grandchildren's upset and their adult children's reaction. They're often just as traumatised as much younger children, yet more likely to take sides, and that's tough for everyone.

Meanwhile, grandparenting as a single person is very different from sharing the joys and stresses, as well as the physical care, with a partner. I take my hat off to all single grandparents, especially those with more than one grandchild, because I honestly don't know how they do it. Yet solo grandparenting hardly gets any attention. I've tried to put this right in chapter 7. It's a grim thought for couples, but most of us will end up being single, whether it's through divorce or a partner's death. Some grandparents I spoke to had been single parents for years before they had grandchildren. They don't just get on with it, they see huge positives as well as big challenges. Others, more recently divorced or widowed, find it harder.

GRANDFATHERS

'Grandparents' is often taken to mean 'grandmothers', but this book is about grandfathers too. Men often look after kids with their partners, yet they're still widely regarded as the B team. That's so unfair! Grandfathers have changed even more than grandmothers in recent generations, and they're finally coming into their own. The two traditional models, authoritarian patriarch and kindly old geezer pottering about in his shed, have had their day. The new dads who emerged in the 1970s have turned into enthusiastic new grandads, while fathers who felt they missed out with their own kids the first time round seize the opportunity to get stuck in with their grandchildren. They can no longer be ignored or seen as the support act. In fact, they make their own unique contribution that sets them apart from grandmothers, and that features throughout this book, as well as in chapter 6, which is devoted to grandfathers.

*

I wrote this book because I wanted to find out if other grandmothers and grandfathers found the whole thing as complicated as I did. So I spoke to grandparents who had all kinds of different experiences. But I also wanted to know what the middle generation think, so I

INTRODUCTION

spoke to adult children, sons- and daughters-in-law too, as well as the leading sociologists, psychologists and family psychotherapists who had the foresight to do some brilliant work on grandparents. Halfway through my research I got chatting to a woman on Whitechapel station as we waited for our train. She'd just left her granddaughter's sixth birthday party, and she seemed a bit deflated. She seized on an academic tome about contemporary grandparenting I was reading. 'I need that book!' she said. 'I feel so isolated. Parents can easily find other parents to talk to, but I can't find anywhere like that, and I would really like to know how other people are working it out, because I'm struggling. Everything's so new. It's all changed so much since my mum used to have my kids.' I hope that the experiences of the many grandparents I spoke to for this book, as well as their adult children, daughters- and sons-in-law, might help her. With any luck, her daughter might read it too…

1

Becoming the Grandparent You Want to Be

The transformation from parent to grandparent is one of the most significant transitions people go through in life. It's a joyous rite of passage that changes everything: the way you see yourself, your relationship with your adult child and their partner, your purpose in life, how you feel about the future. Grandchildren create new energy, purpose and meaning. They keep you up to the minute and in the moment. They're the best consolation prize for getting older. Above all, it's heart-achingly awesome to see the son or daughter who was once *your* baby cradling their newborn in their arms.

Yet it's not about you. The focus is quite rightly on the new life, and your adult child's even more mind-boggling transition to parent. So it's not surprising that grandparents don't usually think enough about the huge psychological and emotional transition they're going through themselves. Yet making the adjustment well, and coming to terms with this new stage in your own life, is the key to being a good grandparent and working out what kind of grandparent you want to be. That can take time and self-reflection, because there is a whole spectrum of different ways to be a good grandparent these days, ranging from full-on childcarer to devotedly distant treat-giver. Ultimately, it's about working out what suits you while at the same time helping your family in the best way you can. And it's about finding confidence as a grandparent, never mind how anyone else does it, and recognising your own special strengths. Because although a new grandparent is born every minute, it is an utterly individual experience, at the same time both miraculously special and run of the mill.

WHAT BEING A GRANDPARENT CHANGES

Your identity

Overnight, you've got a new name and a whole new identity: Grandma, Grandad, Nana, Gramps. Like 'Mum' or 'Dad', the title is at once universal and unique: the first time a grandchild can say their version of 'Granny' is pure magic. Yet it comes with baggage, not just of ageing, but of your own personal experience of grandparents. Suddenly, you've been bumped up into the oldie generation. I still do a double take when my son refers to me as 'Grandma' – surely he's talking about my mum, not *me*? 'I don't want to be called Grandad,' Darren says. 'It's nothing to do with being old, I'm fine with that. And I love my grandson, he's brilliant. I just don't like the whole thing of being a grandad.'

It's not surprising that grandparents mind a great deal about what they're called, and often go to great pains to find some other name they feel comfortable with, whether it's Opa or Yaya, although their grandchild may end up calling them something completely different! There may be a tussle if the other set of grandparents bag the name you've set your heart on. When her daughter was pregnant, Maxine came up with 'Mimi', because, she explains, 'I don't want to be Grandma or Granny. I feel the name fashions how you are and I don't feel like a grandmother. I'd rather it was less of a name that's attached to an older person, because the prospect of being a grandma doesn't make me feel old, in fact it's rejuvenating. I've been looking up names for Grandma in different cultures. I'm looking forward to having a grandchild, but I don't want to feel pigeonholed into that granny or grandmother sort of role: homely, fitting a bit of a stereotype. I hate the idea that once the grandchild comes along, your role has changed, and that removes your autonomy and all the things you want to do. You're supposed to shelve all that because you're a grandparent.'

One of the great things about being a grandparent is that it makes sense of getting older. You can't be a grandparent without reaching a certain age. And babies and toddlers see *you*, the essence of you, not grey hair and crows' feet, although sadly by the time they get to five they're more clear-sighted! Besides, it's the layers of experience, wisdom, knowledge, awareness and memory that give grandparents their unique understanding and strength. The journalist and author Angela Neustatter, who has four grandchildren, says, 'Getting older is hard. We feel something is being taken away from us and that it's not going to be replaced and we're not going anywhere we want to go to; all the negatives. But what I felt when Mai was born was that suddenly I didn't have to think about being older because grannies *are* older. You have to be older to be a granny so hey . . . I've got my new role and that's OK. I don't want to turn into a little grey crumpled-up old thing, but I do want to be the person I am as a granny, and that wouldn't be possible if I hadn't got older. It's like the reward for it. And as the grandchildren get older and grow up, you have to get older to watch them.'

The way you feel about yourself as a grandparent has a lot to do with how you feel about ageing and mortality. For many people, their own grandparents' passing was their first personal experience of death. Even grandparents who are in their forties or fifties seem ancient to a child. We like to think we look younger these days, but the uncomfortable truth is we probably look just as ancient to our own grandchildren as our grandparents did to us.

For Hilary, who is in her mid-fifties, it's been quite the wake-up call: 'Becoming grandparents has been quite a reality check: it's like OMG are we really that old? My husband and I rib each other a lot about being Granny and Grandpa. It's been quite good for me, because I have to come to terms with the fact that I am actually older now. Not that it means I have to behave like an older person, but it's like a little nudge every so often, a reminder that if someone offers you their seat on the train it's not because they want to chat you up!'

It's hard not to succumb to self-limiting beliefs about age. Thankfully, things are changing; it's almost cool to be a grandparent these days, with celebs, from Sandi Toksvig to Tom Hanks, more than happy to talk about having grandchildren. But what being a grandparent means is still bound up with outdated images of homely, grey-haired folk, pottering about rather than energetic and engaged in the world. Even grandparent emojis look past it. According to the psychologist Professor Peter Smith, former head of School and Family Studies at Goldsmiths College in London, some children's books are among the worst culprits. 'There's this stereotype about grandparents being very old, more like great-grandparents in fact,' he says. 'And they're not portrayed doing anything outside the home, they're domestic. Whereas in reality the average age of becoming a grandparent for the first time is about 50, and many grandparents of young children who are reading those picture books will be working. They're certainly not grannies shuffling about in slippers.'

Your position in the family

The birth of a grandchild changes family dynamics overnight. Each relationship shakes down into a new position: parents get shunted up a generation, a son becomes a father, brothers and sisters become uncles and aunts, while siblings' children become cousins. The crucial connection, both with children-in-law and their parents, who are now the other set of grandparents, takes on greater significance and is cemented for life. All these rebooted relationships need sensitive handling, because everyone can be a bit vulnerable as they feel their way into unfamiliar roles. And it's important not to ignore child-free adult children and how they might be feeling.

Grandparents no longer occupy the central role in family life that they did as parents. Adult children are in the driving seat from now on, and sometimes that can be hard to accept. 'It's on their terms now, and you just have to relax into that,' says Gary. I've heard grandparents talk about feeling irrelevant, that family life is going on without them; one blogger wrote that she feels like a spare part at family gatherings. Yet grandparents play a pivotal role in family life, perhaps more now than at any other time in history. Karen Woodall, a psychotherapist who specialises in family separation, says, 'Grandparents are the cornerstone of a healthy family, they are active players in a healthy family system. As a grandparent you have the capacity to see further in both directions, the future and the past. That can disconnect us from the ordinary everyday, and the busy-ness of being a parent, which seems so intense. As a grandparent you can't eradicate all life's challenges, but you can steer the ship with a wise hand and share the best of what you've learned in your life. Knowing when to step forward and when to step back is critical.'

Perhaps we should take inspiration from cultures where grandparents' importance is taken as read. A friend who lived and worked in New Zealand tells me that Maori elders play a key role in the lives of their grandchildren. In her research into Maori grandfathers, Dr Judith Davey writes about the strong relationships between the generations, and how grandparents are involved in decisions about their grandchildren: 'Grandparents have significant roles as decision-makers and leaders . . . as role models and preservers of good relationships.'

All grandparents, wherever they come from, have so much to offer. By this stage in life we've all built up a formidable emotional toolbox: resilience, experience, wisdom, patience, empathy, tolerance, flexibility, stability, a sense of perspective. Grandparents are perfectly placed to support the family, both emotionally and practically, because they've been through the highs and lows of parenting, and have the insider's unique insight and empathy. They can help, not just with the day-to-day stuff like babysitting, but in a more fundamental, enduring way as a rock of support, always there in the background. Young mother Molly says, 'I feel my mum does much more than just helping me out, she's providing stability for all of us. It's like we're sharing the responsibility that comes with having my own family. It's not like I'm suddenly on my own with this huge responsibility.'

Your priorities in life

Grandchildren give life new focus, an injection of new meaning, energy and purpose. That's true whether you see your grandchild once a year or once a week. It's a bit like being in love: the awareness of a rapidly developing new life lends everything a bit of a glow and creates new interest everywhere. Niall says, 'With my grandchildren I have this endless sense of continuity. It's like a movie that's always running: they're doing something, they're growing up.' Daily life gets busier and more eventful, particularly if you live close enough to babysit regularly. Looking after a grandchild is both energising and exhausting.

Grandchildren prompt you to reassess your priorities and make more careful choices about how to spend your precious time. This gains an extra edge when grandparents retire. There's more impetus to focus on activities that really matter to you and give you joy, and that may or may not involve childcare. If it does, a regular commitment introduces a new structure to the week as well as a powerful sense of purpose.

But a word of warning: grandchildren can be the nicest kind of displacement activity that can divert grandparents from fulfilling their own dreams. In their desire to help the family and spend time with their grandchildren, some grandparents put their own needs on the back burner. That's fine if it's a conscious choice. Many people find grandchildren so fulfilling that they happily put other things to one side. But it can lead to regret if grandparents just drift into it or feel like sitting ducks at the mercy of their adult children's demands.

How you feel about the future

Grandchildren not only transform the way life looks in the present, they carry you forward into the future. Don says, 'It's not just about the fun Lara is now, it's what she will be. Although of course that's tempered with gloom about the state of the world. And the grandchildren take my relationship with my wife into the future; they extend the continuity of 40 years of shared life.' There are so many milestones to look forward to: taking the grandchildren camping, and to *The Nutcracker*, having them to stay without their parents. But thinking about the future can be sobering too: when Lena and Gabriel are 15 I'll be 80. It's both comforting and sad to think that as your own horizons narrow, your grandchildren's lives will be gaining momentum. Natalie says, 'It makes sense of life, and it makes growing old more tolerable, because you're following other people's trajectories, not just your own decline.' It feels right to be in the autumn and winter of your life if the fresh growth you're making way for is right in front of your eyes, in the shape of young ones.

Consolation comes from the new link each grandchild creates between past and future generations; they affirm your place in the continuing stream of life. As people get older there's a natural interest in family who went before us, as well as those who will follow. It may sound a bit Victorian, even patriarchal, to go on about the family line continuing down the generations, but there's no denying the comfort in the idea of descendants who knew you and loved you. I have child-free friends who admit they feel the lack of life carrying on after them.

Health and well-being

Grandchildren are a powerful motivation to stay fit and healthy, so that you can keep up and live long enough to enjoy as much quality time with them as possible. They already give grandparents a head start health-wise. Research points to the benefits of a close relationship between the generations: better mental health, lower levels of depression, loneliness and isolation. Regular contact with grandchildren has been found to be good for brain health; it might also help people live longer, according to another study of 500 European grandparents over 70. It's not hard to see why. A grandchild's energy and sheer love of life just makes you feel better and keeps you on your toes, both mentally and physically. Interacting with children and teenagers and answering their brilliant questions provides a constantly changing stream of new interests to keep up with.

WHY IT'S IMPORTANT TO BE YOURSELF

If you can be yourself as a grandparent, rather than a version of what other grandparents do, or what anyone else expects of you, everyone benefits. You'll get the most out of the time you spend with your grandchild. They'll love being with you because you're relaxed and they'll pick up on the positive energy. And you won't feel resentful, which is key to harmony with the middle generation. Each grandparent has their own unique qualities, and it's confidence-boosting to recognise what they are and build on them.

If geography and circumstances are in your favour, it's largely up to you whether you're the kind of grandparent who does loads of babysitting or sits back and waits to be entertained. It's largely up to you whether you see your grandchild once a week or once every couple of months. There are so many different versions of grandparenting now, and they're all as good as each other. Social scientists have labelled a dizzying array of grandparenting types: fun-seeker, authoritative, formal, distant, detached, passive, indulgent, supportive, reservoir of family wisdom, caregiver. The American grandparenting guru Arthur Kornhaber adds nurturer, historian, hero, role model, teacher and mentor to the mix of roles.

At first you may not be sure what you want. I know one grandmother who was determined not to be 'one of those grandmothers who gives her life over to the grandchildren'. But since her eldest started school a year ago, she regrets not taking time to build a closer relationship in those crucial early years. When you're on unfamiliar ground, as new grandparents are, it's so easy to be swayed by what other people do, and feel guilty or inadequate in comparison. On the one hand, friends whose lives have been taken over by their grandchildren can make you feel wistful or guilty, while on the other, grandparents who take a back seat make you long to have more time to do your own thing.

It helps to reflect on what you honestly enjoy about spending time with your grandchildren. There's no right or wrong. Some people like fun outings, some people prefer staying at home. Some grandparents throw themselves into playing superheroes and building dens, while others would rather draw or do a puzzle or play chess or read a story or bake a cake. A friend of mine who's mad about jazz takes her eight-year-old grandson to gigs and now he loves it too. Other grandparents would rather take a back seat and applaud from the sidelines, and I'm sure their grandchildren love them just as much.

Your own grandparents' influence

Your own grandparents and parents inevitably influence what you're like as a grandparent. If a grandparent's childhood experience with their own grandparents was loving and joyful, you've still got an internal memory to tap into. But often there is not much to go on. Back in the day, grandparents generally demanded quiet and respect; they certainly wouldn't get down on the floor and play. If your own grandparents were forbidding or distant or dead, you can feel a bit lost; there's no playbook. My grandparents had all died by the time I was six, so I envy Lisa's happy memories of her grandmother: 'My grandmother is definitely a role model for me as a grandmother. She was young, just 49 when I was born, and we were often left with her, even when we were babies. She enjoyed doing things with us, which my mother didn't. She was great fun and loved to play games. She always had things we didn't have at home, like boiled eggs from the chickens and lime marmalade. I admired her enormously and I was really close to her all my life.'

When circumstances get in the way

Sadly, not everyone can choose what kind of grandparent they want to be: where you live plays a big part, and it's ultimately up to the middle generation when you see your grandchild and what you do together. (*See* chapter 2 on staying close if you live far apart.) Your age and stage in life plays a big part too: whether you're working or retired, have other commitments and preoccupations, whether you're single or share grandparenting with a long-term partner or someone new. Many grandparents, like Gabriella, regret not being younger. 'I wish I'd become a granny in my fifties and not my late sixties, because I've just rediscovered how knackering looking after a baby is,' she says. 'It's still delightful, but I think a lot about my limitations, although my children can't see them, thank goodness. I'm quite intrigued at what I can manage. I know I couldn't manage more childcare because I couldn't handle the tiredness. I'd like to be hands-on but I've got to be realistic.' Bill was 50 when his eldest granddaughter was born, and in his mid-sixties when his second arrived. He says, 'It's a lovely thing to be a young grandparent. One of the best memories was clambering up a haystack with my granddaughter and her taking a photo of me with my bum in the air. Obviously with this next lot of grandchildren I'm not going to be able to do the same things.'

Some grandparents have been longing for a grandchild for years, and throw themselves enthusiastically into the role. But for others it's too soon. They feel reluctant to give up their freedom because they haven't had time to enjoy their empty nest and explore all the new possibilities beyond parenting. Other grandparents have reservations about their child's partner or think they're not ready to be parents. Hilary says, 'I wasn't expecting any of this. My son and his girlfriend still seem like babies themselves! I've never had an empty nest. I feel like I haven't had any space between having my own children and having a grandchild. Now I've just got to roll with it.'

For lucky grandparents, like Maxine, the time is just right. Yet seven years ago she felt far from ready. She was working full-time, both her parents were suffering from dementia, and her daughters had all left home but still needed her around. 'If that had gone on I don't think I would have had room for a grandchild. I don't think I would have been able to cope very well with it all, and be available to help my daughter in the way I wanted to. Since then my parents have both died, and I no longer feel so responsible for my daughters, and that has freed me up. At the time you don't realise how much mental space these things take up. Then a couple of years ago it suddenly hit me that I wanted to be a grandmother. I really feel it's the right time for me now. I've got more to give as a grandparent now that I'm in a stable relationship, so I feel more anchored myself, and I've just stopped work.'

HOW TO BE YOURSELF AS A GRANDPARENT

- Grandchildren contribute so much to your personal growth, but other sides of your life need nurturing too. Make space in your diary for fulfilling activities that give you joy: time with friends, a walk, a wild swim, music, learning something new, holidays.
- Work out how much time you need in the week to commit to hobbies and courses to make them worthwhile.
- Take time out to stand back from your life: a retreat or a holiday can help.
- Make a list of priorities: grandchildren, friends, work, interests/passions, travel.
- Write down your dreams and ambitions. Make a rough plan of the next 10 years and what you hope to achieve in that time. Then work out the steps you'll need to take to get there.
- Childcare commitments can make organising holidays and long weekends more complicated, so nail plans down well in advance and get dates in the diary that work for you as well as the family.
- Pay attention to your physical health by choosing exercise you really enjoy: dancing, yoga and table tennis are just as good as the gym.

HOW BEING A GRANDPARENT IS DIFFERENT FROM BEING A PARENT

It's surprising how different grandparenting is from parenting. There's some truth in the old saying that at the end of the day you can give grandchildren back. Playing Pokémon for hours is bearable and even enjoyable because you know you can go home and read a book in peace and get an uninterrupted night's sleep. Grandparents aren't on it relentlessly, day in day out, in the way that parents are. It's why many people feel they make better grandparents than parents. Not being up close every day brings a different perspective. Lisa says, 'As a grandparent you have time to just observe in a way you don't have time to when you're a parent, and that's a real pleasure, a real gift. Also, because you're not seeing them all the time you're much more aware of how they change and how they're growing up, whereas when you're a parent you just notice when their shoes are getting a bit small.'

Grandparenting inevitably makes people reflect on the way they brought up their own children, and what they wish they had done differently. People often talk about being given a second chance with grandchildren. This willingness to learn and re-evaluate their parenting can have a really positive impact on the way they behave as grandparents. Relationships with grandchildren are not fettered by whether you're getting it right as a parent. You're freer to explore the kind of relationship you might have liked with your children. One grandfather said that in a way it was a more loving relationship than he'd had with his own kids. Angela Neustatter says, 'Being a grandmother is pure pleasure. I loved being a mother, but it's definitely in a different league. As a parent you're in the firing line, and that can be very difficult and very painful. Being a mother is so all-consuming in every way. There's the physical stuff which is wearing, but there is also the emotional bond – that tightness, that ever being vulnerable and never being off the hook with that. And feeling criticised because you don't do it well enough. The joys and delights of being a mother are very real, but they definitely come laden with these other things, whereas grandparenting doesn't in the same way. I can be exhausted at the end of the day but I don't feel that sense of responsibility.'

Having been through some gruelling times when they were parents themselves, grandparents can keep a sense of perspective about the issues parents understandably get obsessed about, whether it's school places or tantrums. They can see the wood for the trees, and their objectivity about what really matters in family life introduces a note of calm from the sidelines. Soon after his first grandchild was born, the late Scottish poet and novelist John Burnside hit the nail on the head in an essay for *The Tablet*. He wrote, 'My hope is that, as a grandparent, I can help my grandson see things that his parents might not be able to see, whether from inexperience, or from the sheer weight of being where they are.'

Finally, grandchildren don't take over your life in the way that children do; you don't lose your sense of yourself in the way mothers can. There is still room for you, and all the stuff that makes you *you*. Dr Reenee Singh, a consultant family psychotherapist and director of the London Intercultural Couples Centre at the Child and Family Practice, says, 'My own mother was a much better grandmother than she was ever a mother, and she was a much better mother to me as I got older. She was one of those women who liked doing things and liked her own space and there was something about being bound to being a mother that didn't agree with her very well. She wasn't a typical Indian mother in that way at all. She quite enjoyed a bit of separation and distance. And she could be a good grandmother because she could hand the children back, and really not interfere much at all.' (More about building a close relationship with your grandchild in chapter 2.)

Mixed feelings are natural

Many grandparents feel torn between their grandchildren and their other interests in life. Most of the grandparents I interviewed want to be close to their grandchildren and support their adult children. That's not merely because the parents make demands: grandparents want to help because they love it, and grandchildren are irresistible. But they also want to do their own thing after all the years of child-rearing; it finally feels like this is their chance for a different kind of fulfilment. So there's a tug of war between, on one side, love and wanting to be useful and closely involved, and on the other, a longing for agency, to rediscover the you that exists beyond the family. Dr Reenee Singh believes that's important for grandchildren too. 'Some of the most robust grandparenting relationships I've seen are when they have lots of other things in their lives, as many grandparents increasingly do. There is a place for different kinds of models, but I do think adventurousness can help.'

For grandmothers in particular there's often a resurgence of the familiar tussle between conflicting priorities, all of which they care deeply about, that can make for agonising choices. I think this goes to the heart of why many women have such complicated and conflicting feelings about being grandmothers. They feel it's their time, yet they feel guilty and selfish for putting their own needs above their family's. Besides, they get huge pleasure from their grandchildren and want to spend as much time with them as they can, particularly if they've longed to become grandmothers for many years. Grandfathers don't seem to wrestle with the same nagging guilt that they should do more for the family and less for themselves.

Ultimately, it's about finding a happy balance between grandchildren and the side of your life that has meaning and value beyond the family; all the things that contribute to your personal growth and fulfilment. I'm not suggesting that grandchildren don't contribute a huge amount to personal growth – of course they do. But there's still a powerful impetus to nurture another side of life so that the family doesn't completely take over. Angela says, 'I love these grandchildren and I'm here for them, but I also want my own life. Grandchildren don't interest every bit of me. Why should they? I need other stuff in my life, I'm primed to be a doer and to be occupied by things that interest me. And I'm sure the grandchildren are better off for that. I think it's important that they see that grandparents are not instantly available all the time, that we've got lives. I try not to have anything else on when I spend time with the kids but I'm not prepared to down tools or give up absolutely everything to be with them.'

'Be there, but don't interfere.' Really?

The conflict between the ideals that grandparents are expected to live up to and what they want for themselves has never been harder to manage. If you ask anyone for advice on how to behave as a grandparent, the chances are they'll say something like, 'You should be there, but don't interfere'. A study by the University of Manchester asked grandparents this question, and an overwhelming proportion, 85 per cent, gave this very same answer. It's good advice in theory, but when you really think about it, it's a pretty big ask. How is it possible to 'be there' without interfering, especially if you're a childcarer? And how does it impact on grandparents' need for agency and independence? Besides, 'being there' and 'not interfering' are utterly passive, and that jars with the mood of the times, when we're all exhorted to take charge of our own destinies and say what we think.

Mixed feelings are even harder to wrestle with now that grandparents are so closely involved. The sociologist Professor Vanessa May, who co-authored the study based on data from the London School of Hygiene and Tropical Medicine, says, 'The ambivalence some grandparents expressed was the result of a conflict between expectations of what a grandparent "should" do, and their wish to determine their own lives autonomously. My sense is that the expectation of not interfering has become stronger for grandparents, because the nuclear family has become more boundaried. There is also a sense that the parent generation, i.e. the adult children, should be independent of control by their parents, i.e. the grandparents.'

This points to another glaring contradiction: grandparents who feel they should be available whenever they're needed are also parents who have done their best to launch independent adult children into the world. The instinct to help your adult child is always powerful, but it's particularly hard to resist when parents are struggling to afford, or find, good childcare. Professor May explains, 'The difficulty is that grandparents are trying to parent and grandparent at the same time. The expectations attached to parenting and grandparenting are not the same, and that can lead to ambivalence. Grandparents are still parents to their adult children, but they also have to learn to let them live their own lives. However, there are some family situations where adult children have no option but to rely heavily on grandparents, particularly in the UK, where childcare is so expensive. Family relationships are difficult, and they involve various sorts of negotiations that often involve very strong emotions, particularly when it's down the line of parents, grandparents, adult children and grandchildren. There are these complex relationships of dependence and interdependence that have to be negotiated and managed.' Things may be beginning to change. In September 2025 the government introduced 30 hours' free childcare for children in England aged nine months to four years for 38 weeks a year. But some nurseries have to charge top-up fees, and in some areas childcare places are scarce.

2

Building a Close Relationship With Your Grandchild: Babies to Young Adults

'When I saw my granddaughter for the first time there was this incredible physical connection that absolutely took my breath away. I felt completely connected to her from the get-go. I wasn't expecting it, because I'm not a baby person and a grandchild is not like your own baby, it's one removed.'

The first thing I would say to any grandparent is, don't beat yourself up if you didn't feel like Iwona, who is quoted above, when you first held your grandchild in your arms. It's different for everyone and there is room for all kinds of emotions. Yet I am convinced that there is a unique closeness that exists naturally. It's partly down to the genetic link, to knowing that your grandchild has a quarter of your DNA. But it also flourishes with the right kind of attention. The first five years are crucial.

The notion of a direct emotional connection is backed up by a study of brain scans of grandmothers while looking at photos of their grandchild. Areas of the brain associated with emotional empathy were activated, which indicates that grandmothers were experiencing the same emotion as their grandchild. In an interview with the *Guardian*, Professor James Rilling, who led the research, said, 'That suggests that grandmothers are geared toward feeling what their grandchildren are feeling when they interact with them. If their grandchild is smiling, they're feeling the child's joy. And if their grandchild is crying, they're feeling the child's pain and distress.' Interestingly, it was quite different when grandmothers looked at photos of their adult children, which tended to activate different areas of the brain, associated with cognitive empathy. Rather than experiencing the adult child's emotions directly, it appears they were trying to understand their feelings cognitively.

The grandchild's bond with their grandparents is rather different from their relationship with their parents, and that's also its strength: it's calmer, less intense, and that allows for a different kind of closeness. An early cross-cultural study of grandparenting, in 1940, noted that grandparent-grandchild relationships seemed to be naturally easier and less tense than children's often more emotionally charged relationships with their parents. That makes perfect sense, partly because grandparents are one step removed, so they can be more objective and less reactive. Don says, 'One of the many things I like about being a grandparent is that you get a bit more distance. You've still got that relationship with the child but you're not running the show. So you can step back a little bit. And of course, that means being able to observe and enjoy more easily than when you were busy being an anxious, tired parent.'

Researchers have also suggested that grandparents and grandchildren have a special affinity because they're both on the margins of life, and see each other as natural allies on either side of a middle generation who are powerful and in control. This chimes with the saying that only the aged have the necessary patience for young children. I'm not sure today's grandparents see themselves as either marginal or old. Many are still caught up in life's cut and thrust. But what does ring true is that as people get older they appreciate the value of slowing down to a child's pace and being in the moment. One grandfather I spoke to, Niall, tells a sweet story about a neighbouring farmer. 'He used to walk around the farm with his five-year-old grandson while the middle generation were whizzing around in the Land Rover with the dogs. The parents said it was because they went at the same pace. They were great company for each other.'

NURTURING CLOSENESS AS GRANDCHILDREN GROW

Babymoons: grandparents and newborns

I've always assumed that a close relationship with a grandchild has to start when they're babies, and that it's hard to make up lost ground when they're older. Gabriella, whose grandson is a year old, agrees that these early bonds are important. 'I had a very strong relationship with all four of my grandparents, which lasted all my life. They must have put the effort in when I was little for me to want that closeness, and I'm hoping that I can develop something just as strong by putting that energy into my baby grandson now.' If babies are familiar with your smell and the way they feel in your arms, they will hopefully turn into toddlers, and eventually teenagers, who feel at ease in your company. Those visceral memories have deep roots. The psychologist Professor Peter Smith, who has done extensive research into grandparents, says, 'The easiest way of developing a strong attachment is from birth, or soon after birth, so the relationship is established right from the beginning, just by chatting and playing and doing nice things with the grandchild. That's not to say that you couldn't build it up later, when they're three or four or even five. And it's not just about what the grandparents do with the grandchildren directly, but also the indirect support they give them, by supporting the parents emotionally, practically and maybe financially.'

Most grandparents, including me, are desperate to hold their new grandchild as soon after birth as they can, but some experts question whether it makes any difference to the strength of the bond. I first heard about the idea of post-birth 'babymoons' from a grandmother who was desperately hurt when her daughter announced she was going to bubble with her wife and baby for the first two weeks and didn't want anyone else around, including the grandparents. This kind of 'babymoon' is the modern incarnation of what used to be known as 'confinement' or the 'lying-in' period. Sarah Johnson, a doula who runs courses for new grandparents, is definitely pro: 'I feel very anxious about grandparents' obsession with seeing a baby within days of birth. You won't have a closer relationship with the baby just because you're the first person to see it. The baby really needs to get used to its mother and father before getting used to other people, while the mother and baby both go through the incredible physical changes after the birth. Grandparents can protect that. In more traditional societies grandparents create a circle around the mother, and do everything for her, so that she can bond with her baby and get breastfeeding going. It will make her a more effective, confident mother and less likely to have postnatal illness. My experience with my own grandchildren bears this out. Having daily contact from day one with the younger one as a newborn made absolutely no impact on our relationship now, whereas living with her older brother when he was a toddler was a significant opportunity to get to know each other. I think the age of two to three is much more crucial if grandparents want to be involved.'

I was still sceptical about the idea of babymoons until I spoke to Iwona, who is quoted at the opening of this chapter. She waited a tantalising two weeks to meet her granddaughter for the first time, but it has made not a scrap of difference to the strong connection between them. She explains why she stayed away: 'I was happy to give my daughter and her husband space; I remember what it was like having a new baby. I felt that unless they needed me I didn't need to arrive until they had begun to find their way, and they knew I was on the other end of the phone. I thought that when I did arrive they would be so tired and so glad to see me, and sure enough I was like the fairy grandmother; I could just pick the baby up and suddenly make their world a better place.'

Building a close relationship in the early years

I saw a couple meeting up with their granddaughter and her mum in a seaside ice-cream parlour the other day. The little girl looked about four, and sat nicely with a huge sundae while they fired questions at her, took photos and then talked among themselves. It didn't look much fun, and I couldn't help wondering why they hadn't met on the beach with a bucket and spade where it would have been easier for everyone to engage.

Closeness can't be taken for granted. Grandparents need to be imaginative, open-minded, curious and willing to see things through their grandchild's eyes. Ada, a part-time lecturer at Buenos Aires University until she retired at the age of 72, says, 'As a grandparent you're growing all the time with your grandchildren. And learning to bond over very simple things, just sharing stories and the things they say. Being with the little girls and laughing at their jokes is something that's so very rich. It helps you to find out more about yourself. I used to feel that with my students too. Their curiosity and their needs and even their impatience and disagreements were helpful because when you processed it you learned something else about yourself. It makes you more open-minded.'

Some grandparents find it easy to tune in to their grandchildren's wavelength and get on to their level. But for others, children are a bit of a mystery. They may have lost the knack of being with young ones, or never had time to get down and play with their own kids, or perhaps had a difficult childhood themselves. 'I feel like I'm learning to be a grandparent; it's not a divine right,' Gabriella says. 'I've seen my brother-in-law almost in tears feeling so hurt that his grandchildren don't like him, but he doesn't know what to do about it. He thought it would just happen, I think. It's so surprising that this brusque man, who was a rather cold, hands-off father, just wants to be loved by these children, and doesn't know how to make it work. They find him scary because he shouts at them, and that fear turns into them keeping away from him.'

Many grandparents relish the opportunity to give their grandchildren the attention that they didn't have time to give their own children, whether they were working full-time or not. There are fewer distractions, fewer balls to juggle: most grandparents aren't trying to make a work call *and* help with homework *and* cook supper at the same time. From the grandchild's point of view, a relaxed grandparent who has time to play and answer questions and muck about is probably more fun than a frazzled, preoccupied parent. It helps explain why relationships between grandchildren and their grandparents can be so good. Even cool teenagers enjoy being with grandparents because they're calmer and they've got time to listen, and because things are less fraught than with their parents. Ada says, 'I'm more patient with my grandchildren than I was with my own children. I have more time just to sit down on the floor and play a game or read a story. With my children I was always in a hurry, and perhaps they would say that this was something they didn't like about me. I was always putting out one fire and then seeing about the next one.'

Enjoying the company of a young child is about being in the moment, slowing down to their pace and being patient. This doesn't come naturally to everyone, although most people have more patience as grandparents than as preoccupied parents. If you struggle with this then taking up a regular meditation practice, or doing yoga, can help. Don says, 'I can be infinitely patient because I'm only doing it one day a week. And I like young children – between the ages of 2 and 10, they're great! I regard their thoughts and their interests as every bit as important as mine. If that means I have to do the same thing over and over again for half an hour, I'll do it. That's what they need to do. And that underlies my view of children, and the pleasures and responsibilities of grandparenting. All the running around can be tiring, but talking to them about stuff, doing stuff, listening, that never drives me crazy.'

When I asked the psychotherapist Karen Woodall for advice on connecting with children, she came up with the brilliant idea of 'bewildered curiosity'. She recommends it for teenagers, but I find it works well with five-year-olds too! It's basically about asking your grandchild to explain something or teach you, whether it's the rules of a board game, or how the Lego fits together. Karen, who works with children and parents affected by family separation, explains, 'Just be curious, a bit bewildered, whether it's feigned or otherwise. Curiosity and openness to having the child teach you what they know triggers a shift in the generational relationship in that they feel pride at being heard and they feel competent. Then they're more likely to listen.

'This is where grandparents often get it the wrong way round. They want their grandchildren to listen before they've been heard. Once children have been heard grandparents can then share some of their own learning, and draw a link from the present to the past, and build respect through the child's recognition that older people have knowledge. I do this with kids I work with in a lot of different settings. It's also worked brilliantly with my teenage grandson, making links between gaming and what fighter pilots did in the Second World War. This is a boy who is usually either silent or horizontal because he's 13!'

Grandparenting older children

My two eldest grandchildren started school this week, and it's just hit me how precious the first five years are, and how quickly they pass. Seeing them stride off in their navy-blue uniforms marks an exciting new chapter. But it feels sad too, because something precious has come to an end and big changes are underway. From now on I won't see Lena and Gabriel so often, and when I do it will be at the end of the school day, when they'll probably be tired and maybe a bit scratchy. Kids grow up in a big leap when they start school: they'll soon be less interested in their boring old grandparents and more interested in their friends. Grace, who looked after her sons' children when they were growing up, says, 'My joy time with all my grandchildren was when they were little, until they were about five or six when they started getting a little cheeky. After that I would have to be more strict with them, although of course you're always more lenient than with your own. As a grandparent you have to keep changing all the time.'

A friend with older grandchildren has made me see that there's no need to regret the past because some new and often lovely phase emerges all the time. She talks about 'the golden years' between 8 and 11, when you can have a lot of fun with kids who are old enough to do stuff on their own, and don't need constant supervision, but haven't yet been sucked into the preoccupations of adolescence and secondary school. They can come to stay without their parents and may well like the same things that you do. They can learn how to mend a bike or knit or paint their bedroom. So as grandchildren get older it's up to grandparents to keep up with their lives, and find new ways of maintaining the connection that was established when they were younger. Ellen Glazer, a social worker in Massachusetts, is very conscious of this now that her oldest grandsons are 8, 10 and 13. 'When they were little, I was close with them. We went to parks, libraries, out for ice cream. These days they are off with their friends or doing sports and I have to find new ways to connect. My latest plan is to have an "investment club". I'll ask them to choose a stock or two and I'll buy each a few shares. I'm hoping we can follow the stocks together over time and hopefully have some fun and meaningful discussions.' The idea is to come up with a joint project, or a shared interest. Of course, there are all sorts of other ways to keep the bond between you alive, such as making things together, reading the books they like and talking about them, going to plays or concerts, or even playing computer games together. The best thing is when grandchildren want to get involved with what you love doing, whether that's canoeing or playing the guitar. But grandparents can also have a lot of fun if they're curious and prepared to explore.

As grandchildren grow older, the relationship gradually becomes less dependent on the middle generation. It's increasingly up to grandchildren how often they visit or call or come to stay. It's perhaps surprising, given the generation gap between grandparent and grandchild, but a close relationship can really come into its own during the turbulent teenage years, when grandchildren are often at loggerheads with their parents. The psychologist Professor Peter Smith says, 'A grandfather can be a good confidant, and that's particularly true for adolescent grandchildren. So where relations with parents may sometimes get a bit fraught, in terms of discipline and rules and so on, often teenagers can chat to grandparents in a way that they might not be able to so easily with their parents. And because grandparents are not in a disciplinary role it's easier.'

Grandparents offer a haven, and a cooler perspective, because they aren't caught up in the emotional maelstrom at home. That was true for Rita when her eldest granddaughter was a teenager. They've always been close since Rita regularly looked after Jude and had her to stay when she was little. She says, 'When Jude was about 15 or 16 she confided things in me that I think she couldn't talk to her parents about. She relied on me in a very close way for quite a long time, and I felt very close to her. We used to have good fun. I think that's where as a grandparent you come in, because you don't hold anything against them, and you don't have in-depth fights with them that they have with their parents, and things don't build up into dramas. And I think grandchildren respect that. It's an age thing as well. Grandparents have a different understanding because they've been through it. You know how to give kids the time and space that they need, whereas I think as a parent you're still learning, you don't quite know how to do that.'

In one study of 11- to 16-year-olds, over a third said their closest grandparent was the most important person in their life outside the immediate family. Reassuringly, the grandparents' age doesn't appear to come into it: other research found no evidence that teenagers and young adults feel closer to younger grandparents. It's also been found that adolescents who have a good relationship with their grandparents are more helpful and co-operative, and have fewer emotional problems. Some teenagers, like Rita's granddaughter, confide in their grandparents about things that they feel uncomfortable discussing with their parents. Pearl has spent a lot of time with her maternal grandparents since her parents divorced when she was a baby. She's now 14. Her mum, Kate, says, 'Because my mum is so close to Pearl she's better than I am at putting boundaries in place if she's being difficult. If Pearl is ever rude my mum just says, you're not rude to your mum here, and she immediately falls into line. My mum tries to play a bit of a parenting role in that way. Pearl might find it easier to talk to Grandma about something to do with grieving for her stepdad, who died a year ago, that she didn't want to say to me.

And I think they had a conversation about periods recently, which is funny, because when I was a teenager my mother would not have had that conversation with me very easily. I've seen quite a lot of that. Things my mother wouldn't have done for me she does for Pearl. I don't feel resentful about it, it's fine.'

While it's clear that grandparents can be close with their older grandchildren, the child and adolescent psychotherapist Ryan Lowe advises grandparents to tread carefully, because it's natural if parents find it painful that their child is able to confide in somebody other than them. She says, 'Sometimes children use their grandparents as confidants to say things they wouldn't say to their parents, because they feel like a safer option. That can be helpful as long as grandparents are in collaboration with their adult child rather than undermining them, or being in competition. Collaboration doesn't mean the grandparent telling the parent everything the grandchild said, and breaking their confidence, it just means saying, "they're talking to me". It's equally important for the parent to be able to admit that it's really hard to know that their child is talking to their grandparent, and not to them. If grandparents can see their role as supporting the person who's supporting the grandchild, there will be less competitiveness.'

Ryan Lowe believes that grandparents are well placed to help both the grandchild and their parent when it comes to serious teenage problems, including drugs and alcohol, depression and eating disorders. 'One of the things that grandparents could be really good at, not only because they are older and wiser, but also just because they're one step removed, is being less reactive to things that are anxiety-provoking for parents, like self-harm, for example. A parent is going to freak, and that's an appropriate reaction. A grandparent is in the perfect position to support the family because they can understand the feelings without being quite as consumed by them as a parent might. If a grandparent is able to contain the anxiety I think that's really helpful both for the grandchild and for their parent.'

Grandchildren in their teens and twenties challenge grandparents in all sorts of ways, whether it's by burying themselves in computer games and refusing to engage, or questioning ideas about gender, or getting arrested for drugs or at demos. Rita's eldest grandchild is now in their twenties and non-binary; they recently had an operation to remove their breasts and are taking hormones. 'I find it difficult to call Jude "they"; I try hard but sometimes "she" just comes out of my mouth,' Rita says. 'When Jude was planning to have the operation I did speak to them, but not in a bossy grandparent way. I just said they really needed to consider it quite carefully. They weren't really listening to me; like anybody that age, they're so focused on what they're doing that they can't really see the outside. Also, I'm not a counsellor. Too much of my own thoughts and feelings get involved, and that's not helpful for anybody.

'I find it very painful when I catch a glimpse of Jude's scars. I'm not as close as I feel I should be, and as close as we used to be, because of the gender thing. I don't understand it and I don't want to upset Jude by talking about it too much. It's a weird one for me, because I always thought I was very open and quite radical about things; it's never worried me if blokes wear skirts or make-up, but for me this is something quite different. I try not to think about it, but very often it does come up at 1.30 in the morning. Although my son wouldn't talk about it to begin with, he's now accepted it. So that makes me feel a bit isolated, but that's fine, it's not my life. As I grow older it feels like my grandchildren are less in my life, but I guess that's because they're getting on with theirs. And what more could you want than that?'

Older grandparents who won't see their grandchildren grow up

One of the most painful things for older grandparents is knowing that they won't be around when their grandchild graduates or gets married. Ellen Glazer, who is in her late seventies, has started a project that makes it easier to bear: she writes essays for her grandchildren to read when they're grown up and perhaps have children of their own. Two of her grandchildren were born through surrogacy, and she wants to pass on her memories of their special births. She says, 'Although I spend a lot of time with my youngest grandchildren, who are four and seven, now I'm aware that our time together is limited. Just as their older cousins prefer to spend time with their friends, I know the little ones will soon move on as well. I'm keenly aware of my age and the ways it will inevitably limit my future time with my grandchildren. I'm very active now but doing the math, I know that can't last very long. I may make it to a high school graduation or two but there is no way I will be at their weddings. Writing helps ease the sadness of this realisation. My essays are about things I think they may be interested in in their thirties, perhaps when they're becoming parents themselves, like the story of waiting for them to be born, and advice, like "Always be frugal, never be cheap". Sometimes I'm simply preserving a memory of something that was very precious at the time that they won't remember. I get a lot of pleasure from it, both because I like to write, but also because I feel like it's a way of passing something on.'

MORE THAN ONE GRANDCHILD

Being fair

When I told a fellow grandmother I was expecting my sixth grandchild, she said, 'That's a bit greedy!', while other friends looked slightly aghast. You certainly don't get the congratulations you did with your first. Although it's not unusual for grandparents to end up having more grandchildren than they have children, it's still quite a thing to get your head round. For me, just remembering all their birthdays is a challenge, let alone finding time in the week to be with them all. Maintaining a close relationship with each grandchild gets more difficult the more grandchildren you have, just because you have less time on your own with each one. Dividing your time and attention equally, not just between siblings but between cousins and perhaps step-grandchildren, is impossible, particularly if one family lives nearer than the other. Izzie, who has seven grandchildren in their teens and twenties, says, 'My 13-year-old granddaughter counts the number of days we stay with her family compared with her cousins, and she'll say things like, "Which grandchild is your favourite?" I don't bother too much about spending equal amounts on their presents. If one of them wants something expensive that seems like a good idea, fair enough. It usually evens out in the end.'

It's probably more realistic to aim for quality time and fairness rather than equality. So while it's hard to give a three-year-old the attention he wants if his baby brother is screaming, you can make up for it when things calm down. It helps to take each grandchild out for a special treat on their own, or even to set up a regular date where you take them to an art session or to the library, for example. And rather than worrying about spending the same amount on presents, tune in to each child's changing obsessions so that you can choose something that really hits the spot. A child won't care that his older sister's present cost more, although he might well be put out if she has more to unwrap.

Dividing your time fairly is equally challenging when it comes to babysitting and childcare. Families have different needs: it could be that in one both parents work full-time, while in another, one parent looks after the kids full-time and the other travels frequently for work. One family may be able to afford more childcare than another. Or if there's a new baby and four-year-old twins, a growing family will need more support than if the kids are all at school.

If one family lives close by and you babysit regularly, it should be possible to look after the more distant family's children for a night or two when they come for the weekend. And the bottom line is that you'll drop everything to help in an emergency, wherever they live.

A new baby

For a grandchild, the arrival of a younger sibling is a huge emotional upheaval, and grandparents can help by being a reassuring, unchanging presence. The grandchild's position in the family shifts overnight: an only child no longer has the full beam of their parents' attention, a younger child is the baby no more. It must be so confusing! They know they're supposed to be happy to have a baby brother or sister, but they can't help feeling a whole mix of disagreeable emotions too, and wishing things were back the way they used to be. I remember some wise childcare guru saying that telling a child they're going to have a sibling is like telling a woman her husband is getting another wife. It's a helpful reminder of the need to see things from your grandchild's point of view. And before the birth it's important that grandparents know what the parents are saying about the new baby so they're on the same page. The same goes for so many other things in the grandchild's life, such as the death of a relative or a pet, the tooth fairy and Father Christmas. It avoids confusion if grandparents and parents can have a discussion about it so that they don't give mixed messages.

Grandparents are often asked to look after the older child when their mum goes into labour, and that's when a trusting bond between you really comes into its own. For the grandparent it's such a privilege to be involved, but it's also an emotional rollercoaster. For weeks before the birth you're on tenterhooks, overnight bag packed and phone clamped to your side until the call finally comes. I'm writing this four days after looking after my grandson and granddaughter, aged four and two, while their baby brother was born. It was a long labour and they kept asking when their mum was coming back, and we wished we knew! They were too excited to eat much and took ages to go to sleep. A video call was a mixed blessing; it cheered up the four-year-old, but made the two-year-old burst into tears. Finally, when their new brother came home we hid upstairs to give the new family time on their own. It was unforgettable.

Grandparents' great strength is that they can be clear-sighted about what the older grandchild is going through in a way that parents often can't see, not only in the early days when they're still in the baby bubble and bleary-eyed from lack of sleep, but also in the months and years ahead. Many grandparents have been through sibling rivalry with their own children and know a bit about how to ease the pain. As well as supporting the parents in the early days by loading the washing machine, they can help by focusing on the older child and not the baby. Their role is to play the same old reassuring games and pander to a grandchild who may well be reverting to behaving like a baby themselves.

It also helps to take the baby off into another room so that the parents can be with the older sibling one-to-one. Maxine, who had three children under four, remembers, 'My mother-in-law came to stay when my youngest baby was born and she became my rock. Her being there just felt so right, and I felt so grateful to her. She wasn't the sort to be pushy or judgemental in any way. She'd look after the children when I went to the loo, she'd help me make food, she'd keep an eye on the toddler and the three-year-old while I fed the baby, she was an extra pair of hands. I think when the extended family works, it works really well. New mothers really need an understanding family who will support them.'

Favourite grandchild

Everyone agrees that it's terrible to have a favourite grandchild, but many grandparents secretly do! In one survey, 42 per cent of grandparents owned up to having one. Even if the grandchildren aren't aware of favouritism, their parents probably are. Grace says, 'Our sons always say we have our favourites. My husband's was Courtney, the little one, and Kaleisha, the eldest, was mine. I think it's partly because I was in the delivery room when she was born, and that's why I'm so close to her, even though she lives so far away now. I try not to show any preference, because what I buy for one I buy for the other, but some children know your soft spot and they work on that. Kaleisha knows how to get round you for anything!'

It's often said that grandparents prefer their daughters' children to their sons' children, and that could simply be because they see more of them. Many grandparents admit favouring the child who shows them the most affection, or who reminds them of their son or daughter at the same age. Sometimes it's about having a similar temperament or interests in common, or seeing them more regularly.

If you feel guilty about having a favourite, it could be that spending special time together without the others will make all the difference. Like many grandparents, Jen is drawn to the grandchild who shows her the most affection. 'I totally fell in love with my grandson from the beginning, and he adores me too. I would say he's my favourite. His younger sister is completely different, and while I'm very fond of her we don't have quite the same rapport. She was born during Covid so I saw a lot less of her in the beginning, which clearly had some effect on our relationship. But I think the main reason I wasn't getting on with her was that she was a bit jealous. That didn't occur to me really. She wasn't showing me affection because she was fed up that I was always with her brother. When I arrive she doesn't rush up to hug me, whereas her brother throws himself at me, and of course that's very nice. Now I've realised I have to be fair, so I make a point of spending more one-to-one time with her and I take them on special outings on their own. And if I buy my grandson five books from the Oxfam Bookshop, I have to buy his sister five books too. But I sometimes forget, and all these things add up. She absolutely notices, she's sharp as anything.'

It's always a mistake to make comparisons between grandchildren, whether they're siblings or cousins. It may be OK in private with your partner, but never in front of the middle generation. It's too easy for a well-meaning remark to be taken the wrong way or sound critical when repeated out of context. Even apparently innocent comparisons of grandchildren can rekindle the flames of sibling rivalry between your adult children. In this context, I find Professor Geoffrey Greif's advice useful. Having researched adult sibling relationships extensively, he believes that parents should try not to discuss an adult child with their siblings. It's a habit that can be hard to break, but it's worth it. It applies to grandchildren too: resist the temptation to talk to your son or daughter about their nieces or nephews. This can be hard to stick to when your daughter-in-law invites a comparison between the cousins, or asks whether your other grandchild is walking/talking/reading yet, but it should be possible to come up with some fairly neutral response. Molly says, 'My mum does a lot of the comparing between cousins that you should never do with children of a similar age. It's fine for me because my daughter is the one who has done everything first! Mum would never say anything to my brother, only to me. I always respond by saying "Children are all different", and she says, "I know, I know, I'm just saying. . ."'

STAYING CLOSE TO GRANDCHILDREN AS THEY GROW

- Be proactive about nurturing the relationship; don't expect that it will just happen.
- Read children's books yourself. Don't just stick to the old classics that you loved with your own kids, but explore contemporary picture books and fiction for older children.
- Keep up with your grandchild's interests by doing your own research into their latest passion.
- Look for books related to a school project.

- Find ways to get involved with their life at school. Most grandchildren are keen for their grandparents to come to shows and nativity plays.
- You could get a job or volunteer at your local primary, reading with children or even becoming a school governor. You'll get first-hand insights into what schools are like now, and how they've changed. Some grandparents are lucky enough to live near their grandchild's school, but helping out in any school would be just as good.
- Don't dismiss computer games: ask your grandchild to show you how to play them.
- Be present when you see your grandchild and give them your full attention; your mobile phone can wait.
- Never talk down to your grandchild, but be careful to be age appropriate.
- There's nothing more rewarding than getting on to a child's wavelength and tapping into their imagination. Five-year-olds really do believe in pixies and mermaids, and that's a wonderful thing.
- When you visit or they come over, prepare things that might interest them, or plan fun stuff to do together. But be flexible: it's also good to follow their lead. That's especially important with toddlers.

WHEN GRANDCHILDREN LIVE FAR AWAY

Circumstances often get in the way of closeness. If grandparents are busy with careers and other commitments, or if relations with the middle generation are fraught, it can be hard to see grandchildren enough. (For more on divorce and estrangement, *see* chapter 10.)

But the biggest barrier is when families live miles apart, whether it's a four-hour drive or a 24-hour flight. Four years ago, Grace's son and his family went to live in Trinidad. She says, 'I was heartbroken when they went, and it shattered my husband more than anything else. About a month before they left they came over one Saturday after church and said they were going to the Caribbean. We said, on holiday? And they said no, we're going because Elliott has a job there. Obviously, the sunshine and the sea and the beautiful sky enticed them. But they found it isolating and lonely. They thought they could manage on their own but they realised their family and grandparents are a great help and support, so they came back earlier this year. My eldest granddaughter is studying abroad, and I really miss her too, but we talk all the time.' It's doubly painful because grandparents often have to put a brave face on how they feel, because they want the best for the family.

Of course, there's a big difference between living oceans apart on different continents and being in different parts of the same country. If you both live in the UK, it should be possible to stay with each other regularly, although it inevitably takes more effort and planning than if the grandchildren are down the road. And that's not to mention the cost of petrol or train fares and accommodation if you don't stay with the family. Gail, whose baby granddaughter is a five-hour drive away, says, 'You have to plan everything in advance; you can't just think you could pop over and see them this weekend. We're fortunate that we're retired, because if we were still working it would be much harder; we would have to set off after work on Friday and leave early on Sunday afternoon. When Orla was first born there wasn't enough room for us to stay, so we rented an apartment nearby, and the advantage of that was that our son and daughter-in-law really did get the idea that we didn't want our visit to make life difficult for them in any way. I spoke to them both to make it clear that we were quite happy to stay in our apartment doing jigsaws or whatever until they messaged us to say it was a good time to pop round, and that they should just say if they were tired and wanted us to leave.'

What saddens many grandparents, like Gail, is that they are not able to respond instantly to help out if the grandchild or parent are ill, or there's some other everyday emergency, although if the family are in the same country they should be able to get there relatively quickly. They also worry about how close their relationship with their grandchild will be as they grow up, and it's especially painful if the other grandparents live nearby and see them often. Children change so much, and so rapidly. It can be particularly tough in the early years, when FaceTiming a distracted toddler can leave you feeling bereft at how far apart you are. Screens help, but they are no substitute for a cuddle.

Gail says, 'It does make me sad that my son and his family live so far away, and I try quite hard not to think about it. You just have to make the best of it and make it work. I know my son and his wife feel it too. They thought they couldn't have children, and my son has said that they would never have moved so far away if they'd known. One thing I really notice is that I can't just drop in to help out or babysit for an hour if Samira has a doctor's appointment or whatever. I really miss being able to make their life easier, in the way my mum used to help me. She had a cot and high chair and toys in her house and my children were absolutely delighted to visit.

'Sometimes it seems to take nearly a day for baby Orla to come to me without crying. I am very aware that she won't be as familiar with us as she would be if we lived nearer. We're babysitting for the first time in a few months, and we'll have to be careful that we've visited soon enough before then so that Orla is used to us again. Otherwise she won't be happy if we turn up and they go out. As she gets older she'll become more familiar with us, as long as we are able to keep visiting. But she won't get to know our house, because there will be far fewer times when she comes to us. And when we visit she'll already be doing the things she could do anyway, although hopefully our visit will be special in itself.'

Distance inevitably has an impact on closeness. Many grandparents who live far from their grandchildren have wonderful relationships with them. But it's heartbreaking if your grandchild bursts into tears when you first arrive because they don't remember you, or won't stop crying because you're not familiar with the trick of soothing them to sleep. You can't share life's everyday concerns and happenings, you can't do a regular school pick-up or get to know your grandchild's friends. It's hard to choose the right present because you think they're still mad about dinosaurs when they moved on to Minecraft months ago.

When families live in different countries there may be an additional barrier if your grandchild doesn't speak the same language. The obvious solution is Duolingo, but it takes time to learn a language. Pam's three-year-old grandson speaks no English, only Chinese. 'It's heartbreaking because we really cannot communicate,' she says. 'We wouldn't know if he was telling us he needed a poo or wanted a drink. It's obvious when he's unhappy, of course, but otherwise we haven't got a clue. And you can't say things to distract him from doing something dangerous. So really two or three days is enough, because our son has to be there as the interpreter. I know I should learn Chinese. My son is teaching him English whenever he sees him, which is as often as he possibly can.'

How to stay close at a distance

Distance doesn't have to rule out closeness. There are so many things that grandparents can do to make sure they are a presence in their grandchildren's lives, although to some extent it's up to the parents too. When his daughters were growing up, Don took them to stay with their grandparents in New York as often as he could afford to, and they were devoted to each other as a result. It helps if the bond is well established before the family leave. Charlotte's two older grandchildren moved to Poland after living with her for eighteen months. She says, 'Even though we are living in different countries there is a relaxed relationship with Alfie, who was three when they left; he always comes up and cuddles me. Whereas Agata, who was just six months, was a typically shy and reluctant toddler when she met us later, and building a bond with her has been much more like the experience my own parents had with my children, where contact was intermittent and they had to work quite hard to build a connection.'

Child psychotherapist Ryan Lowe is reassuring: 'I don't think distance is a problem if there's a good link with the parents, and they help the grandchildren to think about their grandparents. So grandchildren will have a mental picture of their grandparent, even in their absence, because they are in the parents' minds. The parents will have talked about them, and the grandparents will have sent birthday presents. My children's grandparents live in Miami and my children only see them once a year, if that. But they adore them, and always have.'

Technology has transformed long-distance family relationships by giving grandparents a window into their grandchildren's worlds, and vice versa. It makes all those Granny-ish 'Look how much you've grown!' exclamations a thing of the past; these days, children can potter about in the background while their grandparents and parents chat, and join in when they feel like it. Tech keeps you in touch with the ordinariness of daily life, and that's a big help whether you live two hours' drive away or on a different continent. It even allows grandparents to read picture books with their grandchildren and help with homework in a hands-on way, or play online Scrabble. The psychologist Professor Peter Smith has seen its benefits with his own grandchildren in Japan. He says, 'One of the big changes in grandparenting has been the internet, because it's made communication between grandparents and grandchildren so much easier. In the past, physical proximity was a big determinant of grandparent-grandchild interaction. If you lived a long way away, it was obviously difficult to see them, and writing letters and even phone calls aren't the same as FaceTime or Zoom. So to some extent technology has changed that dynamic of grandparent-grandchild interaction.'

However, some parents are strict about screens and, if that's the case, staying in touch offline requires grandparents to be a bit more inventive. One grandmother I know set up a kind of informal book club with her teenage grandson: she reads what he's reading and they compare notes on the phone. Finding a shared interest to follow, whether it's a football team or a TV show, is a great way to spark a dialogue. Letters and cards shouldn't be dismissed just because they seem a bit quaint and take so long to arrive. They're more personal than an email, and exciting because they're unusual, and might even contain a little something. A child who's learning to read will love a letter they can read themselves. Above all they are tangible evidence of a lasting connection, to be treasured. For the same reason, the psychotherapist Karen Woodall recommends sending boxes of good things to grandchildren. You don't have to spend loads of money, just include little tokens of love, like a T-shirt or book or toy you think they would like, with a card saying you're thinking about them.

MAKING THE MOST OF VISITS

When grandchildren are in the same country

One big issue for families who live far apart is they either have to stay with each other or find somewhere close by. If they're in different parts of the country that might be for a long weekend or half term, while if they're in different parts of the world it's likely to be for longer, and less often. Either way, it's really great to have this kind of concentrated time with grandchildren, whether it's for a few days or longer. There's room to relax together, and to tune in to their changing moods and all their likes and dislikes. Grandparents have the advantage of being exciting and special: you can go out for lovely outings and treats, which will create lasting memories simply because they are out of the ordinary.

Yet everyone knows that staying with people can put a strain on relationships, however much they love each other, and that's true whether you're the host or you're staying with them. Each side can find it difficult to fit in with the other's way of doing things, from the time they eat in the evening to the amount of TV they watch and when they go to bed. After a couple of days, tension can mount. How well it works depends on how easy-going and willing to compromise both families are, and how compatible they are domestically. Gail says it helped that her daughter-in-law moved in during lockdown. She says, 'Now that we can stay in their house I'm aware it's an extra pressure on them and that they might feel they need to entertain us, or worry about the baby crying at night. I've always tried to make it very clear that we didn't want our visit to make life difficult for them, and that Samira should carry on doing everything she would normally. After all, if they were able to come and stay with us I would be looking after *them*, but that's not possible until the baby is a bit older and can be in a car seat for longer than two hours. Generally we all get on really well, and I don't feel like a guest; Samira is very happy for me to help myself to drinks and that kind of thing. But every so often she gets tense about something and that can make us feel a bit awkward. At Christmas she went off, leaving a bit of an atmosphere, and then Dan went off, and we were left sitting in their kitchen, not knowing what was going on. I had thought she would feel able to tell us that she was tired and needed to go to bed, but when it came to it I think she just didn't like to. Maybe she could have asked Dan to tell us. We would have been quite happy if she had.'

Most grandparents find there's a difference whether they are in their son's or their daughter's house. Izzie, whose son and daughter both live in the south of England, while she's in Dundee, says, 'We follow their way of doing things whichever house we're staying in, although when they're in my house it's my rules. It makes a difference whether we're staying in my son's house or my daughter's, because it's her house, whereas my son's house feels more like my daughter-in-law's. You have to adapt. My daughter is very strict about meals and manners, with a tablecloth and everyone sitting round the table, whereas in my son's house they mostly have TV dinners. And while my daughter's children never used to be allowed many sweets or chocolates, my son's kids were allowed to eat pretty much anything. I used to tell my daughter I was going to let the kids have ice cream or whatever because seeing us was a special occasion, and that was fine.'

It's a big advantage if grandparents live in a place with loads of fun stuff for kids to do, whether that's by the sea or in the middle of the countryside (although a city full of fabulous shopping opportunities might appeal more to teenagers). Some grandchildren have their own bedroom at their grandparents', and that's such a lovely idea, but if there's not enough space for that, special duvet covers and a selection of familiar toys and books will make them feel just as at home. Many grandparents keep the full kit at their house: cot, high chair, buggy, paddling pool, but if they don't have space it's often possible to borrow from friends.

When grandchildren live overseas

Grandparents whose grandchildren live overseas don't always have the luxury of what you might call proper holidays, because they often blow most of their annual leave and travel budget on visiting the family. They could be forgiven for the odd twinge of envy when their best friends buzz off to Barbados or to see the Northern Lights. Sandra used to cram all her annual holiday into five weeks every January, so that she could fly out to New Zealand to look after two of her grandchildren while her daughter-in-law worked flat out on an annual project. They have lived in New Zealand since they were born; they're now 19 and 21. 'I think having looked after all my grandchildren when they were small helps a lot with our relationship now that they're grown up. My granddaughter came over to travel round Europe last year and we just got on. I knew her and she knew me. It definitely helped that my daughter-in-law trusted something in me when they were little, and she still does, which is very special really. It was up to me to look after them; she didn't interfere. So I got to know Minnie and Cal really well when they were tiny, and that was very nice for me, because New Zealand is such a long way away. When I arrived every year I didn't know the children that well, but I still felt very close to them. I was there when the little one was born, so I knew her really well from a tiny little squidge and I've always felt particularly close to her. It's always been jolly hard leaving them and saying goodbye. But that's life. If you can't arrange it differently you just have to get on with it. I didn't want to go and live in New Zealand.'

Each precious visit crams months of experiences into an intense week or more. Although it seems a waste not to spend every waking moment together, it's sensible to balance it with some time apart, and to be flexible about plans and expectations when long-distance family comes to visit. Be mindful that they will have other people to see, including the other grandparents, and it will just make things tense if you expect them to fit in with all your plans, or to be around all the time. Teenage grandchildren in particular need to see their friends or just do their own stuff.

By the same token, when you're visiting the family it's good to give each other some space. It's often more comfortable for everyone if you can afford to stay in your own place nearby for some of the time, although you miss that delicious 6 a.m. wake-up! Pam says,

'I've always been careful to give my daughter-in-law space. When the grandchildren were younger I would take myself off for a couple of hours while they were at school or nursery. I'd just sit in a coffee bar or go for a walk to get out of her hair, because otherwise I'm sure I would have got on her nerves. My other son loves having all his family together in his house, so it's difficult to stay elsewhere, whereas my husband, who is his stepfather, prefers his own space and sometimes feels at a bit of a loose end. So we end up compromising: we tend to stay with them for a bit but also elsewhere, and then we often rent a villa for us all at the seaside. That way everybody is happy.'

If a young grandchild hasn't seen you for a while, it's best to take the lead from them and give them time to warm to you. Of course you're dying to give them a big hug, but it might be overwhelming; I always think of Maurice Sendak's 'Wild Things' roaring about wanting to eat Max up because they love him so much. The middle generation can offer really useful clues to the best approach. Leanne's mother-in-law lives in Crete, and only gets to see her grandchildren in the UK twice a year. Leanne says, 'It's really tough for her. When she first arrives my three-year-old is like, Who are you? Go away! Lorraine is really excited to see her and full of love, and Alisha is like, this is too intense, and pulls away. It's extra tough because my mum sees the kids all the time, and she's one of Alisha's favourite people.

'So we started giving my mother-in-law a few tips before she arrived. I advised her to play a bit hard to get, because if Alisha feels like someone wants her she'll either ignore them or run away. It really worked, although you could see that it was very hard for my mother-in-law to hold back. She's here this week and I've suggested that she picks Alisha up from nursery tomorrow and they go out on a date together. My sister-in-law wanted to bring her kids too but I had to text her to say sorry, I really want your mum to have a nice time with Alisha and if the other grandchildren are there your mum doesn't get a look in. It's very un-me to do that, so I'm proud of myself.'

STAYING CLOSE WHEN YOU LIVE FAR APART

- Make good use of tech that allows families to see into each other's lives and makes for relaxed communication.
- With older children, you could play Scrabble or chess online.
- Send each grandchild individual packages of goodies with a card saying you're thinking about them.
- Find something in common: follow the same football team, read the same books, watch their favourite TV programme.
- If you've got a pet, send photos and funny stories.
- Keep abreast of children's emotional and physical developmental milestones (*see* Resources for two useful NHS leaflets). For example, it's helpful to know that 10-year-olds are discovering that life is increasingly complicated and that six-year-olds generally prefer to keep school and home life separate. (So that's why the answer to 'What did you do at school today?' is often 'Nothing'!)
- When you visit grandchildren in another country, don't stay with the family all the time, and break up your time together with trips and outings, so you don't get on each other's nerves.
- Don't expect to spend every minute together. Recognise that when they come to visit they may have friends to see and stuff to do.
- When you stay with them, make it clear that you don't mind if they say if they're tired and need to go to bed.
- Tell them there's no need to change their plans, and that you don't need entertaining.
- When you first meet after a long separation, try not to overwhelm little ones with hugs. It can be helpful to discuss the best approach with the parents beforehand.

MOVING NEAR YOUR GRANDCHILDREN

Moving closer to your grandchildren is a tempting option for grandparents who live far away, or just want to cut down the tiring childcare commute from one side of town to the other. But if it involves moving to a new city or even another country, and giving up your friends, neighbours and all the other good stuff about where you live, it requires long and careful consideration of all the minuses as well as the pluses. The most important factor is what your adult child and their partner think: they need to be on board from the start. In their enthusiasm, grandparents naturally make the mistake of assuming that their kids will love the idea just as much as they do, and that it's entirely their own decision. But the painful truth is that the family may not want Granny and Grandpa living round the corner, and even if they do they certainly want to be consulted first. Dr Reenee Singh works with many couples who face this problem: 'Sometimes the grandparents expect to be able to move near the grandchildren, and they don't feel they have to ask permission. To the daughter-in-law it can feel kind of suffocating, too close for comfort.' It's worth remembering that in-law relationships often thrive on a bit of distance.

Grandparents also need to be fair to their other adult children: will moving near one mean you're less available to help their sibling, whether they have children or not? Iwona had long discussions with both her daughters when the idea of her moving closer to the eldest, partly to help with childcare, was first mooted. 'I can't even remember who suggested it first, but it very quickly became a plan. When I was still just thinking about it I asked my younger daughter how she would feel if I moved up north. Her immediate response was "yes, do it!" She liked the idea of being able to visit her sister and I in the same city, whereas before we lived 200 miles apart. I think it's OK as long as she knows that I'm there to help as much as before.'

BUILDING A CLOSE RELATIONSHIP WITH YOUR GRANDCHILD

It's essential to make the decision with your eyes wide open. Families and jobs are unpredictable: your grandchildren's family might well end up moving, and that has to be factored in. There need to be other reasons for moving that are nothing to do with the family. This means researching the new area thoroughly and thinking selfishly about your own needs and interests. There should be plenty of opportunities, through work or volunteering or courses, to forge an independent new direction outside the family. You also need to think about how much you'll miss your friends, how easy it will be to see them, and how likely it is that you'll meet new like-minded people. It's also sensible to look forward to how your own life and the grandchildren's will change over the next ten years, as their needs, and yours, change. No one should rely on their adult children for their social life, and it takes gumption not only to reinvent yourself in a new place, but to make it look effortless, so that no one worries about you being lonely. The last thing anyone wants is to add to the family's burdens.

Ideally, each side supports the other. Iwona helps look after her two grandchildren, while her daughter helps her with DIY and heavy lifting. Iwona left a village in southern England for inner-city Sheffield, where she's literally two corners away from her daughter. When we spoke, nine months after the move, she admitted she was still in the process of shedding her old life and adjusting to her new one. She had thought through all the possible pitfalls, but moving still felt like a huge risk. 'The move was traumatic, massive. I had second thoughts all the time. I had to put everything from my flat in storage because the first house I was buying fell through at the last minute and I had nowhere to live. It was all quite hand to mouth. The day of the move I drove up the M1 in a terrible blizzard thinking, OMG, what am I doing? Because in a lot of ways it didn't make sense. But at the same time, why would I want to be anywhere else but near my grandchildren? Besides, for a long time I'd been a bit fed up with where I lived. The flat was too big and the area had become a magnet for retired people, and that's not who I wanted to be around all the time.

'And while I miss my lovely friends, after my husband died I knew that they always saw his shadow behind me. Here I don't even tell people I'm a widow, and they don't ask. Everything is new, and that's exhausting too. I volunteer at a really cool arts space in town and I seem to know a lot of people already. A lot of them are my daughter's friends, but that's really nice. You meet three different people on the way to the bakery.'

THREE-GENERATION HOUSEHOLDS

More and more grandparents are sharing a house with their adult children and grandchildren. According to the Cambridge Centre for Housing and Planning Research, there were 1.8 million multigenerational households in the UK in 2019. In many families, the primary driver is financial and practical necessity, but there are other benefits for all three generations, not least the security of feeling deeply embedded in an extended family. In a survey for Legal & General in 2019, 8 out of 10 people who had lived in a multigenerational home said it was a positive experience.

During the Covid pandemic it was quite common for new parents to 'bubble' with grandparents, and that opened people's eyes to the mutual advantages of sharing living space. Grandparents and grandchildren can flow in and out of each other's lives in an easy, day-to-day way: no one has to be on best behaviour. Babysitting is on tap: if parents feel like going out, they only have to ask. But free childcare is not a given. Both sides need to preserve their own time and space. Charlotte, whose son moved back into the family home with his wife and 17-month-old baby, says, 'We were always happy to babysit but we made it clear that we weren't there for childcare.

I felt a bit guilty about that, and asking them for rent felt tough as well, but we couldn't afford not to. Initially, it was supposed to be temporary. My son asked if they could move in with us for a few weeks when the lease on their flat ended, and they left 20 months later! We moved a sofa into our bedroom to give us our own space.

'It was lovely, and we don't regret it, but it was chaotic and mad and you can't have a dinner party. After twenty months, day in day out, including night-times, it was a bit of a relief when they left. We didn't get up in the night, but we still woke up. My husband works from home and he's very patient about having toys constantly underfoot, but not that patient! But it was very special, and we'll never have that time again. Having had the grandchildren with us all the time, I feel much closer to Alfie than I ever felt to my own grandparents. It was a real wrench when they moved to Poland, but I felt I'd had a really good go, and that it was the other granny's turn.'

While grandparents have a good idea of what they're letting themselves in for with their adult children, partners can be an unknown quantity. It's much harder to say what you think to a child-in-law, and it tests the nerves if they overload the washing machine or let the toddler unravel loo roll all over the living-room floor. There'll no doubt be times when grandparents drive their son- or daughter-in-law mad too. The secret is to be clear what the boundaries are and respect them. Privacy is a big issue. In Legal & General's survey into multigenerational living, 39 per cent of people complained about the lack of boundaries, while 44 per cent said that they had less privacy. One grandmother who moved into the basement of her son's house was mortified when she overheard her daughter-in-law complaining that she kept dropping in unannounced. Another family I know came up with the ideal solution, to see themselves as 'related neighbours' who respect each other's space by always making a date to meet up, and putting babysitting in the diary rather than taking it for granted. Iwona is careful about this: 'I don't pop in informally. We're quite polite with how we book in with each other. But living round the corner means that I am around them and they are around me, so there's not a huge amount of guard up between us. That's a big change. When I moved in to my own house, I immediately gave my daughter the keys. I've got a bit more garden than them, and they always know that any home I have is their home too. Whereas I wouldn't have the same attitude to their house. So there is still that parent-child thing going on.'

Angela and her husband live on the top floor of a pub they converted some years ago; their son and his family live in a self-contained flat downstairs. It's all pretty fluid: when we met, Angela's 13-year-old granddaughter had recently moved into a bedroom in her grandparents' flat. 'It was a formal arrangement from the very beginning,' Angela explains. 'They pay us rent and they have the same privacy as an unknown tenant. We have boundaries, but they're flexible. We would never walk in to their flat without knocking. We text or phone to arrange visits and make a date to meet up.

'It's always been pretty organic. My husband or I will take the children to school or pick them up if their mum is busy with work; we've done quite a lot of that recently. When the grandchildren were little, they'd come pottering upstairs and make themselves at home. That was always nice. Mai used to dress up in my clothes and they'd go into my office and stick things on the wall and write all over my paper. I never minded, I thought it was fun. We've had a few contretemps with my daughter-in-law about letting the kids use my iPad and raid our cupboard for treats. When they were younger they took more notice of their parents and less of me, but now they don't take very much notice of their parents! By and large, it's been pretty easy. These days we often won't see them for a week or even two. I'm pretty relaxed about that. It just feels that it's a family and we don't have to make a big thing of it.'

HOLIDAYS WITH GRANDCHILDREN

Holidays with the parents

Holidays with grandchildren are very much the vogue, both with and without the middle generation. Holiday companies are keen to promote the idea both at home and abroad. Research for Virgin Holidays in 2019 found that 7 in 10 families had taken multigenerational holidays, while upmarket resorts with spas and kids' clubs have sprung up all over the Med. It's not hard to see why they're so popular, particularly among families who live far from each other. It's a win-win for everyone. Being close up for a week, or even a long weekend, is a great way for grandparents to reconnect with their adult children as well as their grandchildren, while the middle generation gets a break. There's time and space for everyone to have a proper catch-up and create lasting memories.

For many grandparents, a holiday is the perfect way to get the whole family together. I always get a pang when I see a multigenerational gang at the airport check-in desk or greeting each other on the beach with all their gorgeous paraphernalia. My brother's nine grandchildren are scattered in different parts of the UK and Denmark, and their annual holiday in Devon or France has kept all the cousins close over the past 18 years. There are huge advantages for the middle generation: there are other people to amuse their kids, and they get to hang out with their adult siblings, nieces and nephews.

But that's the ideal; unless the adults think carefully about what the grandchildren really need and like, the reality can be far from fun. The psychotherapist Phillip Hodson describes a nightmare holiday in Cornwall when two of his grandchildren were under five. After a taxing 300-mile journey, the little ones both came down with a vomiting bug. He remembers, 'Every single mile of the drive was misery and all the time in the cottage was misery. Ambition ran before reality. Our older grandchildren had loved going to Cornwall so we assumed the younger ones would too. But they were just too young for it. Very young children do not need car adventures lasting multiple hours. Beautiful landscapes are lost on them. Changes in sleeping habits are disastrous. By the end of it, the adults were wondering who to blame for the holiday flop.'

The fundamental rule is that as long as the grandkids are happy, the adults will be too. That's partly luck: it doesn't rain, the grandchildren find friends, they don't get sick. But it's also down to planning, choosing the right child-friendly spot and an age-appropriate holiday that also keeps the adults amused. Phillip Hodson is right: interminable car journeys and long-haul flights with young children can be a nightmare, although I know families who've braved both and had a fabulous time. Hotels aren't always the best choice either, although the pay-off is that the adults get a break from cooking and can focus on the kids. My own ideal is a child-friendly holiday house with plenty of toys and a garden, two minutes' walk from the sea and the pub.

Holidays can also be very revealing. They're a window into what family life is really like and how the parents are getting on. Strict routines like nap times can be irritating if they get in the way of outings, never mind the age it takes to get out of the door with little ones. Stella says, 'My view of my daughter-in-law has been a bit coloured by our holiday, because although she adores their daughter, she just doesn't do as much of the hands-on parenting as I expected her to. I wasn't so aware of it until I was seeing it close up. I think she behaves like that at home too, but I really couldn't say anything to her or my daughter. Maybe it's always one parent who does more?'

Holidays without the parents

I've just heard from a friend who is gearing up to have both her grandsons to stay for four weeks over the summer holidays, so that their mum and dad can get on with their work. It seems like a big ask, but for parents it's often the only solution when school's out. Shipping the kids off to their grandparents is obviously cheaper than activity clubs and it's less hassle to organise than playdates with friends. According to Saga research, without grandparents' help in the holidays a third of parents wouldn't be able to work. Often grandparents go to stay with the family, but if the grandchildren come to theirs, it gives the parents an even bigger break. It's hard work and a big responsibility, but it's a real treat to have extended time with grandchildren on their own, especially if you don't see them often. Meanwhile it's exciting for them to be in an environment that is both different and reassuringly familiar. It helps to find out what's going on in your local area that your grandchild will enjoy, book a few activities, and fill the freezer.

Going away with grandchildren is even more exciting. In 1985, the grandparenting guru Arthur Kornhaber set up his first 'grandparent camp' in the Adirondack Mountains, where grandparents could spend a week bonding with a grandchild, canoeing, doing crafts, telling stories and sitting round a campfire, or none of the above if they just wanted to hang out together. It was originally designed for grandparents who live far from their grandchildren and want to find a way to really connect with them, but it could suit anyone. The idea has been taken up by companies in other parts of the US, although I haven't yet heard of anything similar in the UK. Above all, it's about doing things together; it's the total antithesis of parking the grandchildren in a hotel kids' club.

It might sound a bit forced, and we Brits tend to side with grumpy teenager Wednesday in *Addams Family Values* about the American camp concept. But Arthur Kornhaber is a wise man, and the ingredients of his camp idea provide good inspiration for any DIY holiday with grandchildren, with or without their parents. The key is to plan ahead and think carefully about how your grandchild would like to spend their days, and what you would enjoy doing together. Make lists of activities with your grandchild as well as asking their parents for ideas. Finally, have strategies in place in case they get homesick.

Some grandparents regularly take one grandchild away at a time. One intrepid grandfather I know took his seven-year-old grandson to Venice last year, and they had a lovely long weekend together, surviving on ice cream, pizza and a giant bag of bite-size ham sarnies from home. Such exclusive one-to-one time is guaranteed to maintain a close relationship with an individual grandchild, particularly if they have siblings, and creates unforgettable memories. The only problem is that you have to do the same for all of them!

I also take inspiration from another American grandparent, Cynthia Hogg, who is an enthusiastic advocate of what she calls 'Skip-generation travel', and blogs about her experiences on her website. Skipgentravelguru.com is full of ideas, most of which she's tried and tested herself, and tips on making long journeys bearable. There are even suggestions for volunteering breaks with older grandchildren, working on projects that have meaning for both grandchild and grandparent.

3

Your Grandchild's Parents: Your Adult Child

No relationship with a grandchild exists in isolation. It depends a great deal on how well you get on with their parents: your son or daughter and their partner. Research consistently concludes that the quality of the grandparents' relationship with the middle generation has a profound impact on their relationship with their grandchildren. Certainly, when the children are young, parents dictate when and where you see your grandchild and what you do together. They inevitably influence what your grandchildren think of you, even when they get older and more independent. Don's parents lived outside New York, but despite growing up in the UK, his three daughters had a close relationship with them. He explains, 'I got on better with my parents than my brothers and sister did, and that affected the way our children felt about their grandparents. It also affected the way my parents got on with their grandchildren. The importance of that cannot be overestimated. My daughters knew their grandparents better than their cousins did, even though we lived so much further away. Because I liked my parents I would take my daughters over there at every opportunity, and as they got older they'd stay with them on their own. So despite the distance there was an incredible intensity to the devotion, on both sides. I think the underlying level of devotion is probably more important than actual contact.'

Your relationship with your son or daughter changes for ever when they cross over into the otherworld of parenthood. You are both parents now, and sharing such a momentous experience creates a new mutual understanding. Molly says, 'It's like a conspiracy of women and men who have experienced this mind-blowing event. It makes you closer, because you've both been through this massive physical experience. You don't need to describe it to other people who have been through it.' Overnight, you see each other in a totally different light. Most of the grandparents I spoke to said they felt a lot closer to their adult children, and that one of the unexpected joys was getting to know each other in a whole new way.

It's common for adult children to gain a new respect for their parents when they see what good grandparents they are, and when they experience for themselves the anxieties, dilemmas and compromises that parenting involves. This can be a bridge into a new, more adult and equal relationship. Relationships that weren't that great in the past often improve if both sides can build on this new respect and move forward on a different footing. At the same time, many grandparents feel deep satisfaction and pride when they see what a good parent their son or daughter is. Gabriella says, 'My daughter has always been quite critical of me as a mum, and now I think she suddenly gets me in a way she never has done before. Through being a grandmother I feel like I've been given a second chance to show her who I am.'

Adult children love how much grandparents love their child and never get bored of hearing about the latest sign of genius. And they love you because you give them a break, and save them a fortune in childcare fees. The child is a new shared passion, and not just the child itself, but everything that surrounds them. A grandparent's antennae are out for a grandchild's current obsessions, whether it's a book about the Elizabeth Line or a pint-sized Henry Hoover. This new closeness is a nice surprise after the empty-nest phase when you might have drifted apart a bit. Iwona says, 'My relationship with my daughter definitely changed. It was in a weird place before. My husband died the year before she had her first baby and for a long time I felt that, although I was relating to her as an adult woman, she was still relating to me like my child. It was uncomfortable, and we had a bit of a rub-along. I felt there was room in our relationship for a different kind of vibe between us, and that's happened with the kids.'

THE FIRST WEEKS AND MONTHS

In the early days, both generations are feeling their way in uncharted territory. New mothers and fathers are shell-shocked, sleep-deprived and sensitive. New mothers need their mums in a way they haven't for years. In many cultures, it's common practice for grandmothers to move in with the new family for several weeks after the birth, to take care not just of the baby, but of their daughter too. This new vulnerability takes many new mothers by surprise and turns the relationship on its head. Molly, whose daughter is now four, remembers, 'I was very fragile for the first twelve weeks. I felt like I needed my mum a lot more than I had, so it sort of flipped our relationship back again. The smallest thing could tip me over the edge emotionally because I was just so full to the brim already and sleep deprivation just makes everything so close to the surface. I think my mum found it hard to see me so upset. I always got really sad when she was going home, and we would both be crying as she said goodbye, which sounds so silly now. But she and I don't pretend we're OK when we're not OK, and that is really crucial, especially in those vulnerable moments.'

Grandparents are vulnerable in their own way too, as they get their heads round a new role in which they have less influence and control, and try to work out where they fit in with their adult child's new family. So it's nice to feel needed. Stella, whose daughter and her wife had their first child two years ago, says, 'Throughout pregnancy and early babyhood my main concern was Lauren, not the baby. I don't know if that's a mother-daughter thing. And suddenly she was quite clingy, she was like, I really want my mum so much. To be honest, I felt quite gratified to be needed by her.'

Sons need support too

It's sometimes forgotten that sons also need rest and time to process the birth, which can be as awesome and traumatic for the new father as it is for his partner, although not as physically painful. The transition to fatherhood, combined with sleep deprivation and the weighty responsibility for a new life, is massive. At a time when attention is naturally focused on the new mother's needs, new dads need to know that someone is there for them and understands what they're going through. They continue to need support when the blissful bubble of paternity leave ends, usually after just a few weeks, and hopefully that comes not only from their own parents, but from their in-laws too. Ideally, both sets of grandparents support both new parents, not just their own adult child, through the ups and downs of parenthood.

Some new fathers even experience a form of postnatal depression, and they seem to be prone not just with their first baby but with subsequent children. Fortunately, awareness is growing. The transition fathers go through is explored in a play I saw at London's Bush Theatre called *The Cord*, by Bijan Sheibani. In it a new dad is pulled back from breaking point by his mum as she navigates her own transition to becoming a grandmother. Midwife Freya Mahal says, 'Men can be as prone to postnatal depression as women. Sufferers often hide it from the people close to them. At a recent baby massage class for fathers I asked if anything had surprised them about becoming a dad.

One new father said, "No one asks how I am! They all ask how mum and baby are. I'm losing my sh*t and no one realises!" So grandparents can help by looking out for signs that new fathers are struggling, such as low mood, or not looking after themselves, or intrusive thoughts. They can facilitate a decent rest, and if the new dad still doesn't feel better, suggest they talk to the health visitor or GP.'

NEW COMPLICATIONS AND TENSIONS

The power balance shifts

There's no doubt that grandchildren bring families closer. But things get more complicated when your children become parents, and some friction is par for the course. There is a shift in the balance of power as the dynamics between you evolve. While that's just as it should be, it can be disconcerting. Issues that could be brushed aside in the past loom larger. New tensions develop simply because you're often thrown together more and the inevitable differences in parenting ideas come to the fore. Even happily harmonious relationships between the generations can get tense when grandchildren arrive. At the back of grandparents' minds lurks the worry that if they upset the middle generation, it could affect how much they see the grandchildren. Midwife Freya Mahal says, 'Sadly, I've seen relationships break down or become the source of much stress and strain. New mothers tell me stories about having lots of pressure from their mothers and in-laws to go back to work, or not to go back to work, to breastfeed or to bottle-feed. Those sorts of issues are very often the ones that can cause tension, or even a rift. But I've also seen relationships between new parents and grandparents grow and deepen as a new mutual respect has developed.'

It's totally understandable that adult children want to bring up their children the way they think best. They don't usually want advice from the older generation, and if they do they ask for it.

For their part, grandparents often know they shouldn't interfere but can't resist offering suggestions. It's tough not to, because grandparents have learned so much, not least from their mistakes, and long to pass it on. Iwona, who looks after her granddaughter one day a week, says, 'There are times when I still find myself thinking, I wouldn't do it like that. I might have come close to saying something a couple of times, but when I realised what I was doing, and felt my daughter's reaction, I very quickly backed off and I managed to keep it in my head. I've also learned to be careful about asking a question, because even that can have hidden criticism in it. And to be honest I think they're much better parents than I ever was.'

Both sides are highly sensitive to criticism or rejection. It's almost inevitable that someone will put their foot in it, even though they know each other's moods inside out and have been reading each other's body language for years. Grandparents often talk about treading on eggshells with their adult children as well as their children-in-law: they feel anxious about saying the wrong thing, but can't always predict what might be annoying. They get hurt too: it's not uncommon for grandparents to come away from a visit feeling a bit bruised. They can't put their finger on why they're upset by a casual question about how long they let the baby sleep. One grandmother remembers her daughter exploding into a rant about how controlling she had always been, when all she'd done was offer to make dinner. Tessa puts the adult child's point of view: 'All the history between you means your scenarios aren't neutral. You've got 34 years' worth of gripes going into it. I find it much harder with my mum than I do with my mother-in-law. With Marcus's mum there isn't the history. I can take it from his family because I can detach myself. But I can't take it from my mum – it just drives me insane. I strap myself in when she comes to visit!

'When my daughter was about six months old we went on holiday, just the three of us. The first night I couldn't get her to sleep. Her cries were echoing round this hotel complex and I was so stressed and really upset. My mum proceeded to tell me what she used to do when I was a baby. I said, "I don't care! Do you not think I would be doing that right now if I thought it worked?" My mum didn't get that upset . . . well, not massively. She's quite good at just riding with it. But she also knows I don't want to hear it, and it's not going to change anything, so she's better off not saying anything.'

Conflicting expectations

The root cause of most disagreements is a difference in expectations. Grandparents might expect to be able to see their grandchild whenever they like; adult children might think grandparents haven't got anything better to do than babysit. Grandparents can make all kinds of assumptions about everything from their grandchild's upbringing to schools and religion, even about the baby's name. They're then often hurt and surprised when their children have very different ideas.

It may seem minor, but names matter a lot to people, often more than they think, and these days that's true of surnames as well as first names. Just think about the upset when Prince Harry gave his daughter the late Queen's private childhood nickname, Lilibet. Grandparents often find it hard to bite their tongue when possible names for an unborn baby are being discussed. Some people are dead-set on family traditions. A new father recently complained on Instagram that his mother had told him he had no business breaking with the hallowed family custom of naming the eldest child after his grandfather; a bitter row ensued. Lisa now looks back at a disagreement about her granddaughter's name as an important lesson: 'My daughter Mira and her partner took ages to name the baby, weeks and weeks. In the end we were told her middle name was Tiger Lily, and we just thought that was so ridiculous. My husband told Mira how we felt, saying she'll be laughed at and mocked at school. Of course it was very silly and old-fashioned of us to think like that, and she and her partner were understandably very cross and hurt. Our younger daughter was angry with us too. It caused a bit of hurt for a while, but we learned a lesson. It made us realise we had no right to interfere in that way, and looking back I feel quite ashamed that we thought we could. Now I don't think I have a say in things, unless they ask for advice. You have to stand back.'

Money

Money is a classic cause of tension and resentment, because it's so knotted up with guilt, control, independence and letting go. That's even more the case now, with the often-yawning wealth gap between baby-boomer grandparents, who are generally seen as living in financial clover, and their adult children, who are often struggling to make ends meet. In many families, grandparents are happy to help out financially if they can afford to, by buying the grandchildren clothes, contributing to the deposit on a house, helping out with nursery or school fees, or extras like music lessons. It's not necessarily that they feel guilty or want to make up for the unfairness; it's just what families do. But research at Birmingham University into intergenerational financial giving found that help often comes with a negotiation about how the money is used. Even if it's unintentional, there may be strings attached: grandparents might feel they have some control over where the family lives, or which school the grandchild goes to. 'I want to be generous, and give my money to the family before I die,' one grandfather said. 'But I don't want to use money in the way my parents did, as a means of controlling.'

Wise grandparents with more than one child and more than one grandchild do their best to be scrupulously fair about gifts and money. Even if the grandchild doesn't notice, their parents will. It's simply not on to dole out money for nursery fees to one set of grandchildren and not another, or to pay for your granddaughter's driving lessons but not her cousin's. If one of your adult children needs more financial help, because they earn less than their siblings or need help to fund fertility treatment or whatever, it's important to have an honest conversation with their siblings, listen to their point of view, and make it clear that you will balance things out at some point in the future, either when their need arises, or in your will. It's also crucial to factor in adult children who don't have children, and to talk to them. They might understandably be put out if grandparents spend much more on their grandchildren than on them.

'Do you want your sandwich cut up in triangles or squares?'

Differences in parenting ideas are one of the biggest causes of friction. Grandparents think they know best and are itching to pass on their hard-earned experience to their sons and daughters. Meanwhile, new parents can have some wacky ideas and sometimes go on as if they're the only people who've ever had a baby. Current notions about 'gentle parenting' baffle some grandparents: 'Don't you *ever* say no?' an exasperated grandmother recently asked her daughter. Grandparents have seen so many parenting fashions come and go, from Penelope Leach to Tiger Mothers, that we can't help raising an eyebrow. But while sometimes the two generations really are poles apart, often the differences are just in the superficial details; they basically agree about the fundamentals, although that's sometimes hard to remember. Gentle parenting, for example, advocates empathy, and that's something both generations would surely agree on.

One really noticeable change is that parents today are even more child-centred than we were. To many grandparents, this feels like a step too far. Toddlers are bombarded with endless choices that drive a lot of grandparents mad: 'Do you want your sandwich cut up in squares or triangles? Do you want to go to the park or playgroup?' I think it's partly because our adult kids think more proactively about their children's mental health and emotional development than we ever did, and that's surely a good thing. They are more mindful of the possible consequences of adult behaviour towards their children, and more careful about what they say to them. They may well have had therapy themselves, and even if they haven't, therapeutic ideas are part of common discourse now. This has had a significant impact on parenting, while the children's book market is flooded with titles like *Ruby's Worry* or *I Am Stronger Than Anxiety*.

Grandparents have to remember that parents know their child best and what feels right to them, and that's what really matters. So unless they ask for advice, it's best to keep quiet. And even if they do ask, don't expect them to follow it! Parents today are already bombarded by conflicting bossiness and unrealistic expectations from social media, podcasts and all the rest. They just need to work things out for themselves. As a consultant family psychotherapist at the Child and Family Practice in London, Dr Reenee Singh helps grandparents and parents to work through their differences, and see each other's point of view. She says, 'There's almost a sense of entitlement that comes with being a grandparent. The problem with a lot of adult families I work with is that the grandparents try to impose their ideas about how the grandchildren should be brought up, and I have to coach them not to say these things, even if they think them. It's about being respectful of the young parents' space and their own ways of bringing up the child. It's about negotiating that in a very sensitive way, especially if there is a cultural difference, or indeed any kind of difference. Of course grandparents still have views, but it's not helpful to make them known unless you can do it in a very tactful way.' (More about disagreements when grandparents do childcare in chapter 5.)

Above all, it's good to be curious about new parenting ideas and keep an open mind. It's clearly a mistake to dismiss everything as social media flim-flam. There have been significant changes since our own children were young, and that's as much to do with scientific research as fashions on social media. Grandparents need to get on board with these changes, and get their heads round the underlying philosophy. A first step is to check out one of the grandparenting courses that have sprung up in the past few years, run by medical professionals who know their onions.

The best advice I've heard about dealing with parenting disagreements comes from Geoffrey Greif, Professor at the University of Maryland School of Social Work. He believes grandparents are wrong to automatically assume their views on child-rearing are right, and instead should 'be open and curious about how the next generation is thinking about parenting'. The most obvious way is to ask your kids, and listen carefully to what they say without jumping in with what *you* think or what you used to do. A neutral question, like 'What's the current thinking on this now?' is a pretty safe bet.

I've also found it really helpful to talk to other young mums and dads, like my friend Becca, who runs the online Noisy Book Club for parents of young children. This makes the whole discussion less personal than with your own kids, which can make both sides feel defensive. Another way is to read the childcare books the parents recommend, because it's easier to talk objectively about ideas in a book, or on a podcast, that might otherwise create friction. Rosa asks her daughter to send her podcasts if she's heard a good one. 'I'm really interested, because it helps me understand how she's parenting,' she says. 'It allows us to have a neutral conversation, and that can be very helpful, because neither of us feels like we're being criticised. Some podcasts talk about stuff that I wish I'd known with my children, while I think others create unrealistic expectations.'

Support or interference?

When it comes to treading the fine line between support and interference, the big challenge for grandparents is that they have to balance two often conflicting roles: they are parents as well as grandparents. Old parenting habits, like unsolicited advice and coming up with solutions, are hard to shake off, and they usually don't go down well with adult children. Ada, who lives near her daughter's family in Buenos Aires, still finds herself slipping back into parent mode, even though her daughter is in her forties and has two daughters of her own. 'Even now if she calls me up and tells me about a problem I instantly feel I have to solve it for her. I know, because I have learned, that that is not what she wants from me. What she wants is for me to listen and to be there. She will solve the problem eventually, because she always does. It's my fault. It's something that I have to control in myself, otherwise I end up getting irritated too, and saying I'd rather not know. When her first baby was born I remember saying, it's better to do this or that. She would listen but she did things her way. She would look up things online and get advice from her friend in Spain. At first I felt hurt, and then I realised that she has her own way of doing things and that's the way it's got to be. It's her experience, she's got to go through it, she can't live on my experience.'

Often, the most helpful thing is simply to listen without interrupting or trying to work out how to make things better. Dee Holmes, a family counsellor for Relate, says, 'It's really important to recognise when someone's asking for advice or when they're just telling you something. If your son or daughter rings up saying they've had a terrible night, it's best to resist talking about your own experience and what worked for you. It's more helpful to ask directly whether they want advice, or just want to tell you about it.'

> ## WHAT GRANDPARENTS COMPLAIN ABOUT
>
> - Treading on eggshells.
> - Feeling frustrated that they can't say what they think.
> - Parents who pay more attention to parenting advice on Instagram than to grandparents.
> - Feeling taken for granted.
> - Adult children who think their parents have got nothing better to do than look after their children.
> - Having less control over how often they see their grandchildren than they'd expected.
> - Patronising instructions.

> ## WHAT THE MIDDLE GENERATION COMPLAIN ABOUT
>
> - Grandparents who say what they think through the grandchild, as in 'Aren't we a bit old for the buggy?'
> - Unsolicited advice.
> - Grandparents who won't accept that ideas about parenting have moved on.
> - Not following parents' rules about naps, snacks, screens and so on.
> - Grandparents who expect to be entertained by their grandchildren, rather than helping out.

- Demanding grandparents who need waiting on hand and foot when they visit.
- Grandparents not offering to babysit enough.
- Grandparents who assume they can drop in whenever they feel like it.
- Grandparents who leave the house in more of a mess than they found it.

SUPPORTING THE NEW FAMILY

A grandchild sets the relationship between his or her parents in stone. Even if they separate in the future, they'll stay connected to each other, and to you, through their child. Your adult child's partner is part of your family now, whether you like it or not, and ideally grandparents have welcomed them into the fold long before babies were a twinkle in the eye. The new family the parents are creating together is separate from, but at the same time closely connected to, both of the families they themselves grew up in. And from now on an adult child's first loyalty is no longer to their parents but to their partner and children. Ouch! This gradual shift starts when the couple first become an item, but it's cemented when a baby arrives, and that can be painful at times. According to Professor Geoffrey Greif, an expert on in-law relationships, 'The hardest thing when couples get married is, how do they stay a part of their family of origin yet also form a new family that has a protective barrier around it that neither grandparent can break through?' It helps if grandparents can recognise what a delicate, and sometimes impossible, balancing act this can be for the middle generation, even more so when there are step-parents and step-grandparents in the mix. There are bound to be times when adult children feel torn.

Giving the family space

As well as love and support, the new family needs space to establish themselves as a new unit, and work out their new *modus operandi*. Grandparents need to stand back and accept that family time is separate and precious, and respect their need for time on their own. This can make them feel a bit left out. Bill, who is a single grandfather, says, 'Aaron did keep me away a bit. He's always been very self-sufficient, and he and his partner are very self-sufficient too; they don't really need anyone else. They're not unfriendly, it's just that they're emotionally complete. I'd sometimes message to say, I'm in the area, can I drop in? And he'd say, "well actually at the weekend would be better". I don't feel there's an issue, or that he's depriving me of seeing my granddaughter or anything. But obviously it would be lovely just to be able to drop in – that sort of relationship is nice with anybody. I didn't feel hurt. It was just like oh yeah Aaron, he's in control. In a sense he doesn't need me there so that's OK, that's good, in terms of them. But in terms of me? Well . . . I can live with it. I can understand it, and it's perfectly fine.'

It's always helpful to see things from the adult child's point of view. With babies and young children, it's often not convenient to have friends and family dropping in unannounced. The house is probably in chaos and parents are desperate to catch up on their sleep. So it's always best to check first, give plenty of warning, and respect boundaries. And keep in mind that there are usually other grandparents and even step-grandparents for them to make time for too. One new mum told me she has five weekends out of every eight booked up with visiting her daughters' grandparents and step-grandparents. That doesn't leave much time for the new family to hang out on their own or spend time with their friends. However, if grandparents feel less welcome than the other set of grandparents, it's horribly jealous-making: *see* chapter 8 for help and advice.

Some grandparents also miss spending time alone with their adult child, which inevitably becomes rarer and more precious when they have children. It probably affects paternal grandparents the most because, on the whole, sons don't go in for long phone chats and are less likely to suggest one-to-one meetings than daughters or daughters-in-law. So paternal grandparents often end up hearing about their son from his partner. Some grandmothers, like Rosa, often feel excluded from conversations with adult kids because they're busy with the grandchildren. 'When we go over to my daughter's, it always seems to happen that my partner has quite long talks with her, but I miss out because I'm playing with the grandchildren. That's the default position, and it feels very gendered. It's so frustrating because I overhear these juicy snippets of conversation and I'm dying to join in. I have talked to my partner about it, and asked him if he could play with the children so I can get a chance to talk to our daughter. But when you're in the moment it's hard to put into practice.'

When grandparents disapprove of anything to do with the way their grandchildren are being brought up, whether it's ruthless sleep training or endless after-school activities, they can tend to blame their child-in-law, not their adult child. It's hard to accept that your own child would voluntarily choose to do things so differently from the way they were brought up. Of course, the painful truth is that they do! It's important to see the couple as a team who have hopefully discussed whatever it is. It's rarely a good idea to have a quiet word with your child, and it's absolutely *verboten* to dis your son- or daughter-in-law because whatever you say is bound to get back to them. Grandmother Lisa says, 'I've learned that I have to take into account my daughter's relationship with her partner. That had never occurred to me before. So for example, one of the things that drives me mad is putting my granddaughter to bed. They've never had set bedtimes, and you have to lie next to her until she goes to sleep. In the end I said to Mira, my daughter, I think she's a bit too old for this, just let her cry for a bit. I think Mira would have done it but her partner couldn't bear to let her cry. I realised I couldn't push it because it would have been interfering in their relationship. So I just shut up and bit my tongue. You have to take into account the relationship between the parents, and you have to be quite sensitive about that.'

However, there will be occasions when your adult child openly disagrees with their partner, and that's really awkward. Grandparents are torn. They naturally tend to side with their own adult child, and they may well have strong views on the matter, but they want to keep the peace and don't want to alienate their child's partner. It's awkward enough if your child takes you aside to sound off or to get your backing. But it's particularly difficult if your child-in-law asks directly for your opinion on whatever the disagreement is about, whether it's the choice of school or dummies, and tries to get you on side. It's best to stay as neutral as possible while offering your own adult child moral support, because the last thing you want is to be used as ammunition in the dispute, as in 'Your dad agrees with me'. The wisest course is to acknowledge that it's a difficult decision without committing yourself either way.

Supporting your adult child's relationship with their partner

Negotiating dilemmas like these is part of the pivotal role grandparents play in supporting their adult child's marriage, which in turn supports the grandchildren. Research suggests that good relationships with parents/grandparents are linked to marital harmony. Many grandparents, like Stella, take this very seriously, not least because they worry about the future. She says, 'Lauren gets quite fed up with her wife sometimes; I've had a couple of chats with her about it recently, and it's quite hard to know what to say. You can't go "that's outrageous, how dare she!" So I worry about them a bit. My view as a grandparent is that being gay parents, it would be more difficult if they were ever to break up. So I desperately need them to be fine, and I do what

I can, mainly by not rocking the boat, and making things OK for my daughter-in-law as well as my daughter.'

Even simple things can make the world of difference to a couple, whether it's babysitting on regular date nights, or looking after the child overnight or for a weekend, so that they get time to be partners as well as parents. With a young baby, midwife Freya Mahal suggests babysitting with the parents at home, so they don't have to go out. This takes the pressure off a new mum who might not feel ready to leave her baby, and it allows couples to have uninterrupted time together on their own, eating a takeaway, or just having a much-needed rest.

However, the right kind of support is not always quite what you think. In the early days, Rosa put her hand up for anything she could do to help her daughter and her partner, who both have demanding jobs. But after a while she came to the conclusion that it would actually be more helpful to do less: 'When we finally decided to step back, it was almost as if they grew up as a couple. I felt that they had been relying on us too much, rather than working out strategies themselves. I'm talking about obvious things, like there was total chaos with laundry. My partner and I used to clear up and sort stuff out, which meant my daughter and her partner didn't have to take responsibility for it themselves. Looking back, I feel that without realising it we were colluding with a situation that wasn't healthy, but that none of us could stop. I couldn't step back and let them struggle, but that meant that they didn't have to work out how to manage things themselves. It needed things to get really uncomfortable to force us to make that transition. It's an interesting outcome: they seem better as a family now.'

It's equally important to make it clear that you still see your adult child and their partner as individuals and not just as conduits to your grandchildren. It never occurred to me how much this mattered until Emma Barnett asked me a pointed question on *Woman's Hour*, about how adult children can seem to be not quite as important to their parents when grandchildren are born, because there's another focus. I'm not sure I totally agree, but it made me see that adult children could get a bit miffed if their parents only have eyes for their grandchildren. Meanwhile, grandparents can be forgiven for feeling that their kids are only interested in them as babysitters! Of course grandchildren are a big talking point, particularly since they're usually in the room when you get together. But that's not enough. Both grandparents, and adult children too, need to be curious about the whole person, all the other things that make each other tick and the broader landscapes of their lives.

HOW TO BE HELPFUL WITHOUT INTERFERING

- Support both parents, not just your own adult child.
- Be imaginative about what would help the parents most. Make suggestions, but don't be offended if they have other ideas. You might think offering to cook is helpful, when what they really want is the washing done, or the child taken out so they can have a break.
- The ways in which you supported one adult child when their children came along might not work for their sibling. Individual needs are different.
- Check before plunging into a deep clean or picking up the baby as soon as they cry.
- When you visit, bring healthy, ready-made food you can all eat on the hoof: sandwiches, soup, yogurts, salads, fruit, cheese, plus treats like cake and chocolate. One mother-in-law offered to bring lunch and she turned up with ingredients, which no one had time to cook. Big mistake. Your role is to help, not create more work.

- If you don't live too far, ask whether it's helpful to stay the night or not. Molly, who is very close to her mum, says, 'With hindsight I really appreciated Mum not staying when she came to help because I didn't have to host her.'
- With a new baby, offer to babysit with the parents at home, so they can have uninterrupted time to themselves without feeling pressured to go out if they don't feel ready.
- With older children, look after the child for a night or weekend so the parents can have much-needed time on their own as a couple.
- Affirmation is key: let them know they're doing a great job.
- Do they want advice or just want to get something off their chest? Resist the urge to come up with a solution. What's often needed is someone who will just listen, acknowledge how they're feeling and give them a hug.

THE PAST SHAPES THE PRESENT

The relationship between grandparents and adult children is influenced by two things: how you got on before the grandchildren arrived, and how you get on with their partner (more on this in chapter 4). Tessa says, 'Being an only child adds to the intensity of my relationship with my mum. I feel a lot of responsibility not to break the silent terms of what we've agreed as our family dynamic. I always felt that I had to be present in her life and not make her feel like she was abandoned, and since my daughter was born I feel even more responsible in terms of giving her valuable relationships. I'm conscious that I have a lot of power to make her happy. I want to do that as much as I can, even though there are times when it has me pulling my hair out.'

The past shapes the present. If your relationship is basically solid, it acts as a kind of ballast if things get difficult or tense. It's reassuring to remember that you've weathered arguments in the past and come out the other side. When Sonia's husband, Mo, had a row with their daughter's partner, she feared it might shatter their close connection and threaten their relationship with their two grandsons. 'I was terrified that my daughter might stop us seeing the kids. It was the worst argument we've had since she was grown up,' she remembers. 'I was quite surprised at how furious she was with us. She went straight into a number about how when she was little we made her do this and that, which was just so not true! I could just see the five-year-old in her; it wasn't based on any real experience. Although it was a frightening and very uncomfortable few weeks, underneath it all I felt that we were too close to our daughter for her to stop us seeing the boys. There would have had to be more tension in my relationship with her for that. In the end I suggested we met without the kids to talk, and the men apologised.'

At the same time, the presence of a grandchild makes both adult children and grandparents look back at their joint history through fresh eyes. Many grandparents say grandchildren have made them wish they'd done things differently. It can make adult children reflect on their own upbringing, often in quite a critical way, and question the decisions their parents made. Angela says, 'My son often says to me, "When we were young you had no boundaries. You always want to please everybody." I say, "Didn't I? I think I had a few. I used to make you go to bed and things." But it's true. Being strict doesn't come easy to me. My son is much tougher with his children about things like manners and how they talk to people.

'And over the past few years he's quite often said that I sent him away to boarding school too young. He said, "Now I have a nine-year-old daughter myself I think it's so wrong to send a nine-year-old away. I feel what she would feel." We've talked about it at some length. I said I'm really very sorry, if I could go back and change things I would. In the end I sent him an email saying we missed you every day, it was a crazy thing to do, but it seemed like the best thing for you at the time. That was good. It feels like it's dealt with now, which is a real relief. Because he used to be quite sharp with me.'

The issue might be something that seems fairly trivial, like not being allowed to learn the guitar. Or it could be major, like the parents' break-up, or giving a younger sister preferential treatment. An adult child who feels badly let down by their mother or father in childhood may still feel resentful as an adult, and that can come out in unconscious ways. They might even want to protect their own child from being similarly let down by their grandparents, and seek to create a distance between them. It hurts if an adult child declares their intention not to make the same mistakes with their own children.

However painful it is, grandparents need to listen with an open mind, and try to understand why incidents they thought were minor continue to trigger strong emotion. Adult children need to feel heard, and not to have their feelings brushed aside. A crucial part of that is acknowledging that your version of the past isn't the only valid one. Dee Holmes, a family counsellor for Relate, says, 'When adult children have children it can go one of two ways. It can make the adult child see how hard parenting is, and understand why their parents didn't always get it right. But on the other hand, having children of their own can make adult children reflect quite critically on their upbringing. They think, "Why didn't my parents do better? Why didn't they do this for me, or why did they do X, Y and Z when it's obvious you should do the opposite?" Or they look at what their parents are like as grandparents and feel a bit jealous that they weren't like that when they were children themselves.

'Grown-up children have their own narrative of what their childhood was like, and the grandparent has their narrative. It's really important to be able to acknowledge what your adult child is feeling and not dismiss it. As the parent it could be very easy to just say, don't be silly, you didn't really want to learn the guitar, or you have no idea what it was like living with your father. Whereas it's actually about trying to get to the place of acknowledging it and being able to say, "I can see and totally understand why you feel like that, and if I'd realised the implications I might have made a different decision". It's really important to acknowledge that the other person has a different narrative, and that you can see why they feel that pain. It's difficult to get past that if somebody doesn't feel heard.'

HOW TO GET ON WITH YOUR ADULT CHILD AND THEIR PARTNER

- Be careful not to treat them merely as conduits to your grandchild: be interested in their whole lives.
- Think about where you usually meet: in their home or yours or somewhere neutral? Think about what feels easier and more relaxed, and why.
- Negotiate with both parents about arrangements, and when it's appropriate, text them together. It shows that you're thinking of them as a couple.
- Give the family space. Remember that they have a lot to cram into their weekends: seeing friends, other grandparents and family, as well as just being on their own.
- Try to avoid doing things that could make you feel resentful, and don't let resentment build up. Think twice before cancelling your own plans to babysit at short notice, and don't commit to more babysitting than works for you.
- Be curious about their parenting ideas. Never assume you know best. Listen to the childcare podcasts and read the books that they recommend.

- This advice from Professor Geoffrey Greif may seem extreme, but I've tried it over the past year and it makes a lot of sense: try to avoid discussing an adult child with their sibling. When you're with them, it's good to be fully present and focused on them, and that's less likely to happen if you're talking about their brothers and sisters. It also applies to grandchildren: don't compare notes about one of your adult children's kids with another.

4

Your Grandchild's Parents: Your Daughter-in-Law or Son-in-Law

The moment your grandchild is born, the relationship with your son- or daughter-in-law changes for ever. Before, if you felt a bit lukewarm about them, or thought your adult child was making a terrible mistake, you could get away with keeping your distance and praying that they would have a change of heart. Now there's much more at stake. They hold the happiness and well-being of both your grandchild and your adult child in their hands. From now on, your happiness depends on them too.

It's a reversal of roles. In the past, they were the ones who wanted your approval and tried to fit in with your family's weird ways. Now it's up to you to stay in *their* good books. They have huge influence on your evolving relationship with your adult child as well as with your grandchildren. As a paternal grandmother, I'm haunted by research that found that sons are more likely to be detached from their families if their parents don't get along well with their wives.

By contrast, daughters still tend to remain close to their parents even when there is conflict with their husbands.

There are times when most grandparents find the relationship with their son- or daughter-in-law challenging, and vice versa. It's pretty obvious why: you don't choose your adult child's partner, yet you're thrown together. They're family, but you can't rely on unconditional love to see you through the prickly times. Whether you get on or not is largely luck. You might have very different ideas about bringing up kids, totally different interests, different personalities, a different sense of humour, and come from completely different backgrounds. Douglas, who has mixed feelings about his four sons-in-law, says, 'If someone is a difficult person, they don't stop being difficult when they marry your daughter. I don't feel that sons-in-law are sons. They're more like friends – or not, as the case may be. How we get on depends entirely on personality and circumstances.'

Becoming a parent changes people, and how you feel about them. A laid-back son-in-law starts to get irritating if he lets your daughter do all the work, and gives in to the kids while she has to hold the line. An impressively organised daughter-in-law can seem obsessive and a bit bossy as a mother. It's up to grandparents to cut new parents some slack as they find their way. The other issue is that while you know your adult child inside out, you can only second-guess what might irritate your child-in-law. There is a formality that isn't there with your own child. It's easy to misinterpret body language. Sometimes it's tricky to tell whether your son-in-law is genuinely pleased to see you or smiling through gritted teeth. One grandmother says, 'It's hard to work out whether my son-in-law wants me there or not, and how I fit in when I visit.' If there is a falling-out, it could take a long time to undo the damage. That's especially true if you live far apart and only see each other occasionally.

YOUR GRANDCHILD'S PARENTS: YOUR DAUGHTER-IN-LAW OR SON-IN-LAW

Simply acknowledging that in-law relationships require sensitive handling is half the battle. But it's important not to get hung up on the negatives and forget how enriching they can be too, warts and all. Everyone has so much to gain from strong relationships with the extended family. According to Professor Geoffrey Greif, who is an expert on in-law relationships, a good way to nurture a closer bond with your child is by building a stronger relationship with your child-in-law.

Yet the general assumption that in-laws are inevitably problematic gets in the way. These relationships are plagued by misleading stereotypes that have little to do with real life. The journalist Angela Neustatter says, 'There is an aura around the idea of mothers-in-law, that they are a threat, and that even if they're not saying anything disapproving they are there watching and being critical. I don't want that to be the case, although I am probably a reasonably formidable mother-in-law!'

It's true that some in-laws are impossible: we've all heard about possessive daughters-in-law and opinionated fathers-in-law who expect to be waited on hand and foot. But each in-law relationship is individual, and is shaped by a whole range of issues, from what you have in common to family context, cultural background and personal experience. Professor Greif says, 'We learn about in-laws in general by watching our parents interact with their parents-in-law. It's not just a random thing. If after every family gathering everybody is complaining about each other's in-laws/parents/grandparents, that is going to send a message. Any observer of their own family is going to see how the older generations and the middle generations are run.' Expectations of how in-laws should behave vary widely, not only between individual families but between different cultures and classes. In Western society, sons tend to be drawn in to their wives' families. It's the opposite in many cultures, where paternal grandparents are either number one, or the difference just isn't such a big deal.

Even within the same family, there can be surprising differences in the way in-laws get on. Kate had two husbands: the first, who she divorced, was not that friendly to her parents, while the second loved them dearly. Clearly, it's not just about personality and background. It helps if you get on well with your adult child; this naturally gives parents a head start with a son- or daughter-in-law. And of course your child-in-law has a huge influence on how your adult child behaves towards *you*. Partners shape each other's tastes, opinions, politics, religious beliefs and views on bringing up kids in ways that may not chime with your own. Rita has had a difficult relationship with her son's wife for over 20 years. She says, 'My daughter-in-law causes a lot of problems with my son. He usually comes over on his own, and when he does he's always on the phone to her saying he'll be back in a minute. I don't know what I did wrong, although I think it goes right back to when my granddaughter was a baby, and she's 23 now! I've tried really hard with her but nothing seems to make things better.'

Whether your son- or daughter-in-law gets on well with their own parents, or keeps their distance, it's bound to have an impact. If a daughter-in-law is close to her mother, for example, it might feel like there's not much room for her mother-in-law. But if her own parents don't give her the support she needs, or she doesn't get on with them, like Stella's daughter-in-law Megan, she may turn to her mother-in-law. 'Even now that they've got a child, Megan doesn't want to see her parents. So we are her family, and that's quite a responsibility. She competes with my younger daughter's boyfriend a bit; she needles him about being a posh boy and things like that. She's lovely and really good company, but there's quite a bit of pressure in being her only family: I'm always trying to be what Megan needs me to be. That's my role in the relationship, to make things OK for her, even though instinctively I'm so much more involved with my daughter.'

MAKING THINGS WORK WITH YOUR SON- OR DAUGHTER-IN-LAW

Living with mixed feelings

Most in-law relationships ebb and flow between warmth and appreciation, silent irritation and defensiveness. There are bound to be times when sons- and daughters-in-law feel the grandparents are interfering or disapproving, while the parents-in-law feel they've been put in their place. Sonia says, 'I'm aware that if I tidied up, my son-in-law would take it as an implicit criticism. But I find it so frustrating when I sort the washing out and it's still in the same piles when I go back the next week.' Both sides need to be able to sit with a convoluted mix-up of feelings and not get too thrown by the inevitable minor chord. You can both live with occasional irritation if there's a solid grounding of mutual goodwill. What matters most is the overall feeling you have for each other. That's why it's so important that grandparents spend time getting to know their child's partner, and make them feel they belong, before they have children. The honeymoon period following a new birth, when both sides are high on warm feelings, and differences in parenting styles have yet to emerge, is another unmissable opportunity to cement a connection with a son- or daughter-in-law you don't know well, or to reboot a relationship if there's been tension in the past.

The touchstone of any good relationship is that you can both be yourselves; you don't have to pretend everything's great when you're struggling, and neither of you has to put on a front or tidy up too much. People naturally feel most at ease with their own families, but in-laws can be relaxed with each other too. Many grandparents have told me that things got easier when grandchildren came on the scene, and the feeling is often mutual. Iwona, who moved into her daughter's attic for three months while she was looking for a place to live, says, 'There's more of a connection with my son-in-law now because of the grandchildren. It's become less formal, I suppose, whereas before we were more on our best behaviour. It's become more everyday without being every day.'

You don't have to be best friends

While honesty and feeling that you can be yourself are the ideal in any relationship, it's not always desirable or even possible for in-laws. Sometimes it's better to accept your differences, lower expectations and aim for a relationship that's not perfect but good enough. You don't have to be best friends, just get on OK. Professor Greif says, 'What we found in our research is that people who have direct communication with their in-laws tend to value their relationship more than people who don't. But you don't have to have direct communication to make things work. A mature view of an in-law relationship is, I get this guy, I understand him and I'm going to make this work for my wife or my daughter's sake. I'm not going to confront him, I don't want to stir the pot. He's not going to change my views on abortion or Trump, and I'm not going to change his views.'

This works for Leanne, whose mother-in-law visits every six months or so. 'My mother-in-law doesn't show emotion. She shows her love by doing things and giving things, and I found that really hard at first. I had postnatal depression with my first baby and when she used to ask how I was and I'd say "I feel awful, I'm really struggling", she couldn't cope; she didn't know what to say. It was really hard because I was knackered and not good at saying what I needed and it felt like there was this brick wall. But when I got better I realised it wasn't personal, and that I didn't need to say how I really felt; it was OK just to say I was fine. That's the level she gets to emotionally, so that's the level I am with her. I really try not to let my personal feelings get in the way; the kids' relationship with her should be separate.'

Dealing with tension with sons- and daughters-in-law

The prime suspect in most disagreements is resentment. It eats into otherwise loving relationships. There's so much potential for both generations to feel resentful about all kinds of things. Grandparents feel taken for granted if they're treated like childminders who don't get invited to the fun stuff, while the middle generation resents silent criticism, unsolicited advice and being forced to cater for in-laws who are supposed to be helping out. Vanessa May, Professor of Sociology at the University of Manchester, says, 'Resentment is really difficult to express in relationships, and my sense is that in some families there are unexpressed reservoirs of resentment. There are things that people don't say or talk about for fear of rocking the boat. But while people might not necessarily express their resentment within the relationship, I think they're quite good at expressing it outside it. People generally complain about their families quite a lot! So there are avenues for talking about it, and therefore I don't think it's a completely hopeless situation.'

The best way for both sides to prevent resentment building up is to be clear about your own needs and boundaries, and how flexible you're prepared to be, while paying attention to the other person's needs too. They may not be aware that they're causing resentment, so it's important to communicate clearly and kindly, and not to try to second-guess what they want. If you're in doubt, just ask them. It's always hard to say no to anything to do with grandchildren, so if you're a people-pleaser take a pause and think about how your own plans will be affected, as well as the family's needs. Everyone has their own parameters. Some grandparents are perfectly happy to babysit while their son-in-law goes out with his mates or their daughter-in-law gets her nails done, but others are reluctant to give up their precious time unless the parents have a worthy reason, such as work. However, it's important to remember that parents who look after their children full-time need a break too.

Relationships improve naturally

As time goes by and children can spend more time away from their parents, in-law relationships often improve of their own accord, simply because you're not thrown together so much. When you visit you can take the grandkids out, or they can come and stay on their own. Research confirms that in-law relationships generally improve with time. Professor Greif suggests that as people mature they become more skilled at handling delicate relationships and choosing their battles. It sounds counter-intuitive, but as people's faults emerge they can let down their guard and feel more relaxed with each other. You get the measure of what presses their buttons and what makes them laugh, and they get the measure of you.

Meanwhile, as new mothers and fathers become more experienced as parents they become more confident about saying what they mean without sounding patronising or bossy. They tend to lighten up about routines and rules. Don says, 'My son-in-law can be a bit too tough. He's instigated a no-screens policy and he's banned anything that contains sugar. I know you have to be careful, but if everyone else is eating ice cream it becomes cruel to deny it to the child. He's beginning to lighten up a little bit now, and of course it may turn out that he's handled it all perfectly.'

Communication improves as in-laws get to know each other and they become easier to read. Hilary says, 'I've always liked my daughter-in-law and found her interesting. But in the beginning I didn't quite know what her sensitivities were, so I was always tiptoeing around a bit. At one point I was getting quite stressed out about contributing to their bills when they were both on benefits and I didn't want the electricity to get cut off. She said, "I really hated hearing that you were stressed about it. I don't want you to feel resentful." I have to remember that she takes these things to heart. I'm learning. Now I have kind of got the measure of her and we've got better at working out together how to live around these things.

She's better at expressing herself if she doesn't like something, and it's much better to know how she feels.'

MOTHERS-IN-LAW AND DAUGHTERS-IN-LAW

What makes the relationship special

Becoming a mother-in-law is daunting. While 'grandmother' sounds cosy, 'mother-in-law' is quite the opposite. Relationships with daughters-in-law change dramatically when grandchildren arrive. They can get closer and more affectionate, but they can also get even more complicated and challenging. Indeed, some research, along with the endless chat on internet forums, suggests that things actually get worse. Danielle says, 'I used to get on really well with my son's girlfriend before she had the baby, but now I find her a bit patronising and a bit obsessive about things like nap times and food. And she seems to be changing my son into a different person.'

I make no apology for including the voices of daughters-in-law here, because I think there's a lot to be learned from listening to their point of view. Steph remembers, 'My husband's mother was very bossy and questioned everything I did, which made me feel even more useless. She was very much, "I've had three children, I know what I'm doing". Gallingly, the baby would always settle for her and never for me. She'd smile smugly and say, "Well, I do have a knack." I was completely out of my depth; I really didn't have a clue. Looking back, I think she relished my insecurity, and felt she was in competition with me and with my mother. In the end we had an enormous row and she stomped off.'

We all shudder when we hear of daughters-in-law who get in the way of grandparents seeing their grandchildren. I know one grandmother who had to apply for a contact order, and a daughter-in-law who banned her mother-in-law from the house. But I've also spoken to mothers-in-law who got on so well with their daughters-in-law, like Grace and Sarah, that they asked them to assist at the birth. While mother- and daughter-in-law relationships are usually painted as extremes, the reality for most women is somewhere in between. Angela says, 'My daughter-in-law can be very moody as well as very loving. And sometimes I'm quite frightened of her if she's in a moody state. She's quite forthright, she always says what she thinks. I just have to step back and accept it, because that's her stuff and she has to be able to say what she means. I say OK, fair enough, they're your kids, I won't do that. I am aware of my need to be someone who she is glad is in the life of her children. She knows I adore the kids and that I will always be there to help if necessary.'

Some women feel more relaxed with their mother-in-law than with their own mother, perhaps because there's more emotional distance and less history. A quarter of the daughters-in-law in Professor Geoffrey Greif's research said their relationship with their mother-in-law improved with the birth of their first child, while only 10 per cent thought it had got worse. (Even fewer sons-in-law, just 2 per cent, thought it had got worse.) What's slightly unnerving is that the same research found that mothers-in-law tend to have a rosier view of the relationship than their daughters-in-law. That gave me pause for thought. When I asked Professor Greif why that might be, he just shrugged and said, 'Wishful thinking!'

'My daughter-in-law has won the battle!'

Most grandmothers and daughters-in-law want to get on with each other and make an effort to make the relationship work, even if things get tense at times. Hopefully, they both have the same goal: for grandparents and grandchildren to have a good connection. The first step is to acknowledge that this is a universally tricky relationship. Everyone comes up against friction at some stage, and it's best not to

YOUR GRANDCHILD'S PARENTS: YOUR DAUGHTER-IN-LAW OR SON-IN-LAW

take every discordant note too personally, because sometimes that's just the way it is.

Handing the baton of family life on to your daughter-in-law, and accepting that they know your son better than you, is painful. Perhaps an element of competitiveness between women is inevitable. 'My daughter-in-law has won the battle!' one mother-in-law declared. It seems to be true whether your daughter-in-law is married to your son or to your daughter. Stella, whose daughter Lauren is married to Megan, says, 'I think potentially you can be closer to a daughter-in-law who is married to your daughter than you can to a son-in-law, although I get on really well with my younger daughter's boyfriend too. But I also think you're more competitive with your daughter's wife. I remember when Lauren and Megan first got together it was like, there's another important woman in her life, so in a way you've got a slight jostling.'

There's another reason behind the tension. Mothering, like grandmothering, is a highly emotional business. Despite all the theorising, being a mother is less head and more heart: it's physical, ingrained, instinctive. Just think about how a baby instantly relaxes in its mother's or grandmother's arms. Daughter-in-law Tessa says, 'You think you're being reasonable, but actually it's all emotion. It's very difficult for mothers-in-law *not* to tread on your toes. Silent criticism is a big thing with grandmothers. With my husband's stepmother you can feel it radiating off her. She's never worked, so she's always defined herself by being a mother. She is the queen of unsolicited advice. She is a very judgemental person and can't help herself interfering. It means I don't ever bring up any problems because I know she will have an opinion.'

My sense is that mothering is central to women's identities in a way that, although things are changing, fathering isn't to the way men feel about themselves. So it's no wonder grandmothers and mothers feel protective and defensive about their own way of doing things.

Anything that's perceived as criticism hits a nerve. Disapproval and irritation are expressed not just verbally, but through pursed lips and loaded questions, like 'Are you taking him out without his hat?' Daughter-in-law Leanne says, 'The thing that really drives me mad is that my mother-in-law is always talking through my daughter, as in "We're a bit big for the buggy now, aren't we?" I find myself doing the same thing with my husband sometimes, and it's so uncool! It's so passive-aggressive. I can see my mother-in-law is working really hard at not saying anything disapproving, but I can also tell she's thinking, "Why don't you just put the baby in a cot like you're supposed to?" She never gives an opinion, it comes out more as a question, or she'll talk about some other young mother who's doing something she does approve of.'

If the grandparents' mantra is 'Don't interfere', then it probably applies even more to paternal grandmothers than it does to maternal grandmothers. Most mothers-in-law quickly discover that they can't get away with offering advice in the way that mothers can, so they tend to bottle things up and can end up feeling frustrated and a bit superfluous. However, there may be times when they feel so compelled to speak out for their grandchild's sake that it's worth the risk of causing upset. The problem is that if grandparents say anything even remotely critical about, say, a grandchild's behaviour, it can take a very long time to repair the damage with a daughter-in-law. It feels much safer to keep quiet. As Professor May says, 'The boundary that surrounds the nuclear family of parents and children is very strong when it comes to talking about the children's upbringing. Unsolicited advice can be taken as overstepping the boundaries.'

Yet in other contexts, speaking your mind and being honest about how you feel are considered virtues. Biting your lip goes against the grain to this generation of feminist grandmothers. Jane felt she had no choice but to raise her concerns when she was worried about her older granddaughter, but it created a rift with her daughter-in-law.

She remembers, 'I had no problem with my daughter-in-law until my second granddaughter was born, but since then it's been quite a struggle, and I'm sure it's not been easy for her either. We have different approaches to bringing up children. At one point I felt I had to say something about my older granddaughter that was really worrying me. My daughter-in-law was upset by what I said, but she is not the kind of person who argues. The real problem is that since then she's become ultra-sensitive, so now even when I say something that I hope is OK it's very hard for her to take it on board. I see it as my fault and not hers.'

Blurred boundaries

Boundaries that were clearly defined when it was just your son and his partner get blurred when grandchildren arrive. Some grandparents feel entitled to drop round in a way that was unthinkable before, and however well-intentioned, it can feel intrusive. I heard of one mother-in-law who insisted on popping in at a time when her daughter-in-law had told her she had other visitors, and that's clearly not on. Daughters-in-law are more vulnerable than sons if they're the ones who are at home with young children, and they're more likely to feel invaded by a mother-in-law than their own family. Most of us aspire to a rose-tinted ideal of extended families popping in and out of each other's houses, but it often works better when lines are clearly drawn from the word go about visiting and respecting the daughter-in-law's space. That might sound a bit heavy-handed, but in fact all that's required is sensitivity.

However, it can be hard for mothers-in-law to accept boundaries without feeling hurt or taking offence, particularly if they expected to see the grandchildren whenever they wanted to. It's painful if a grandmother offers to help and her daughter-in-law says her mum's already got it covered. And it can be a surprise to discover that you have to ask permission to visit. Hilary says, 'When my daughter-in-law was pregnant I thought I was going to have to rearrange my whole life to be on call. But as it turns out I have to ask to see my grandson for a couple of hours. It's like a negotiation. When I ring to ask if I can come round, my daughter-in-law will say, "I don't need it right now" or "we're just going to have a sleep. . ." She might suggest another day, and that's fine by me. In some ways, it's a bit of a relief to feel that I'm not required as much as I'd expected to be.'

Daughters-in-law can often feel ambivalent. They want their child to have a warm relationship with their grandparents, even if they find them a bit trying. And there are times when new mothers need all the help they can get, but don't like to ask, and certainly don't want their mother-in-law to think they can't cope. Many new mothers feel they have to make an effort to tidy up and look presentable with their in-laws, while they can be as messy as they like with their own parents, and that makes a big difference to how they feel about the in-laws visiting, particularly in the early weeks. Dr Reenee Singh says, 'It's such a dilemma for the young mother, who desperately needs someone around but really wants a person she feels completely comfortable with. What I pick up from many of my clients is that they have to entertain the grandparents who are not their own family, however close they might be.' Ambivalent feelings can then lead to mixed messages and confusing body language. It's understandable if grandmothers get the wrong idea about how to be most helpful. Many daughters-in-law I've spoken to are thrilled if anyone offers to tidy up or do the laundry, but to others it feels intrusive or judgemental. I heard of one mother-in-law who took her own bed linen when she went to stay; she was only trying to help, but it came across as critical.

It's always best to think how you would feel in your daughter-in-law's position, and check what would be most helpful before embarking on a deep clean. Reflecting back to your relationship with your mother-in-law when you were a young mother is also illuminating. At one stage, Hilary's daughter-in-law got so upset that she moved out of the flat they shared. She remembers, 'One day, when Aminah was out, my son asked me to help him tidy up. I ventured into their bedroom, which had absolutely everything everywhere. What really got me was this pile of dirty baby clothes in the corner. So I thought, great, I can help by putting a few loads of washing on. And then I went slightly overboard and I tidied up the room at the same time. When my daughter-in-law got back she was absolutely mortified, but she didn't tell me immediately. She packed her bags and went to her mum's with the baby. A few days later her mother rang me to say how upset she was.

'I prostrated myself and texted Aminah and said I'm so sorry, I really overstepped, will you forgive me? Fortunately, she did. She moved back and it was fine and I learned my lesson. If I'd thought about it, of course I should have asked her first, but I just did what I wanted to do and I saw it as me helping. I now see that I was answering my own need rather than thinking about what was best for her. It must have looked very judgemental. I'm really careful now about that kind of thing.'

Your son's role

The great thing about daughters-in-law is that they introduce a welcome new dimension to relationships with sons. They chat about different stuff and open up a wider range of interests. An empathetic daughter-in-law will encourage a son who doesn't give much away to open up emotionally, and she'll make sure her husband's crew are included in family occasions. Suddenly, your birthday is being remembered! Hilary and her son have always had a challenging relationship, but marriage has changed things for the better. 'I've learned a few lessons from Aminah about how to handle Joe,' she says. 'She doesn't get on his case about things, which is what I tend to do. And she doesn't take umbrage as quickly. I see him differently now, just because she sees him differently. I have another perspective on him; I can see him in the round a lot more, and that's important.'

Your son also plays a key role in how well you and your daughter-in-law get on. There will inevitably be situations when he feels torn between his love for the woman he lives with and his love for the woman who brought him up. It helps if grandmothers can appreciate what an unenviable position this can be. It's quite common for sons to leave the two women in their lives to work things out between themselves and hope they won't have to get involved. But it doesn't have to be that way, according to Deborah Merrill, Professor of Sociology at Clark University in Massachusetts: 'I think part of the problem up until now has been that sons weren't playing a role, they weren't saying anything to their mothers or their wives. In fact, sons can play a role, for example in telling their wives that sons need time with their mothers. There is a lot of room to work this out at an individual level. I don't think problems are a given.'

It can also help both the grandmother and her daughter-in-law if a son can establish boundaries without upsetting his own mother: this obviously requires sensitivity and a clear understanding of what the particular situation requires. Daughter-in-law Leanne says, 'My partner is very good at putting in boundaries, both with my own parents and with his mother. I had postnatal depression when we visited his family for the first time with the baby, and he put in a lot of boundaries: he'd say we're going to see you on these family days, but apart from that don't ask and don't just turn up. It caused a lot of tension between us afterwards, because he felt bad about doing it, and I felt guilty about being ill. But it was helpful that he'd done that so early on, because he can set boundaries when his mother comes over now.'

It also helps if sons are more proactive about communicating with their mothers and fathers. The general feeling is that men can be a bit lax about responding to messages from their parents, sending them family photos and arranging to meet up. As a result, the frustrated mother-in-law has little choice but to communicate through her daughter-in-law, who in turn feels guilty and resentful because she's already got enough on her plate. Clearly, when it comes to practical arrangements it makes sense to text the person who is organising the kids that day, but there are other instances where irritation could be avoided if sons communicated more readily and grandparents were less reluctant to bother them. A group chat with both parents usually works well. Angela has got into the habit of texting her son and his partner together. 'It shows that you're thinking of them as a couple, there's an inclusiveness about it,' she says.

Sometimes a daughter-in-law feels particularly vulnerable, perhaps after a traumatic birth or because her own parents live far away. If that's the case, her parents-in-law have to be super patient and understanding, because often the best way their son can help is by creating a kind of exclusive bubble around the family. It's up to him to help his parents understand what's going on so that they don't feel shut out and find it hard to empathise. Dr Reenee Singh explains, 'There are some situations where I coach sons to talk to their parents independently of their spouse if she is feeling overwhelmed. They might say, I know you're doing this out of good intentions but is it OK if you don't come round this weekend, or if we don't go for such a long holiday together? or whatever the flash points are. Negotiating the distance and closeness is something I encourage both sides to do. In extreme situations the son may have to draw a boundary around his family and state his loyalties quite clearly. Although that can be a really powerful intervention I have reservations about it, because the nuclear family is a Western idea, and there is so much to be gained from having grandparents around, and close relationships with the extended family.'

FATHERS-IN-LAW

Although it's mothers-in-law who suffer most from negative stereotyping, fathers-in-law also have a formidable reputation: think Robert De Niro in *Meet the Parents*. Grandfathers traditionally get irked by sons-in-law who don't pull their weight when it comes to bringing home the bacon or doing their bit around the house and now, increasingly, with the children. 'My son-in-law gives in to things because he doesn't want grief, whereas my daughter holds the line,' says Mo. I still remember my dad fuming silently at his son-in-law curling up with a book; there was clearly a lot more at stake than surface irritation. But it's not just about male rivalry; grandfathers' relationships with their daughters-in-law can be difficult too. One man couldn't even bring himself to look pleased when his son announced that they were expecting his first grandchild. Another said his daughter-in-law had ruined his son's life. Many men feel bad if they're embarrassed by breastfeeding, but they know they couldn't possibly say anything.

Men aren't plagued by the stereotypes that beset mothers-in-law, perhaps because the relationship with their children-in-law tends to be cooler and less complicated. Fathers-in-law are more likely to keep their distance emotionally. They don't seem to worry so much about saying the wrong thing, and they are generally less inclined to take things personally or read too much into a casual remark. Hilary says, 'My husband is much less involved in the emotional side of things than I am. He's free from worrying about our daughter-in-law's sensitivities because he's not involved emotionally with her. Women with women are a lot more emotional.'

There may be other upsides to less emotional intensity. Geoffrey Greif found that with some fathers-in-law, advice giving is not seen as interference or meddling by their sons-in-law, but regarded as a natural aspect of their relationship. That's quite different from the way a mother-in-law's advice is often perceived by the middle generation. Professor Greif suggests that this could be because of the closer connection that often exists with mothers-in-law, which makes it more likely that they will spark a negative reaction, a feeling that they're interfering when they involve themselves in parenting or organising family events. A slightly more distant father-in-law might not generate the same negative response.

However, it follows that as fathers- and sons-in-law become more hands-on in family life, there's potential not only for the connection between them to become friendlier and closer, but also for more tension and conflict. Professor Greif's research found that grandfathers now are more invested in the way their grandchildren are brought up than in the past, and that's even true of men who aren't fully engaged with their grandchildren. He believes that this greater investment could lead to more disagreement with the middle generation, and create 'a new arena not only for intergenerational connection but also for intergenerational strain'.

This increased tension between two very involved 'new' men was played out in a recent disagreement between a hands-on grandfather, who looks after his two grandsons one day a week, and his son-in-law, who does the lion's share of the childcare. Mo recalls, 'I arrived one morning to take the boys to a music workshop. They were both still in their pyjamas, they hadn't had breakfast, and there was no milk in the fridge. That was annoying enough, because I'd taken a day off work and set off early to get there on time. The kids started saying they didn't want to go, but I managed to persuade them that it would be fun and got them dressed. But when their dad came downstairs he gave in and said it's OK, you can stay at home if you want to. By doing that he totally undermined my authority, and set me up for a really challenging day with them. I just said, I can't deal with this, and I walked out. I was very wary of my son-in-law after that, and I still am. I felt he didn't take me seriously. I didn't see the boys for six weeks, which felt like a very long time. In the end we had a conversation about what happened and we both apologised. My wife totally backed me up but she did say we were both being a bit blokey in not communicating properly.'

But blokey communication isn't all bad, according to Professor Greif. He says that by conspiring *not* to talk about difficult stuff, whether that's feelings or politics, men manage to keep the relationship on an even keel. They recognise that it's not just about them, but that their relationship has repercussions for many other members of the family. This approach clearly works for Paul, who describes himself as a traditional father, and has three married daughters and four grandchildren. 'Our sons-in-law all have different personalities but we all get on. We all love a laugh and a joke and a drink. Reece, who's the youngest, doesn't have the same interests as us. He loves football, whereas none of us do. We've got nothing in common but you always find that bit of common ground where you can talk. It's nice to have some men in the house, although we don't only talk about male things. What really matters is that I know they love my daughters, they'll protect my daughters and my grandchildren, and they're respectful to my wife and my parents. I've told each of them to treat my daughter like she is the most precious thing on this planet.'

HOW TO GET ON WITH YOUR SON- OR DAUGHTER-IN-LAW

- Take the long view. When you get irritated or upset, try to put it in perspective by thinking of the good things in your relationship.
- Make them feel part of the family. Be careful about in-jokes or things that might make them feel like an outsider.

YOUR GRANDCHILD'S PARENTS: YOUR DAUGHTER-IN-LAW OR SON-IN-LAW

- Don't express indirect criticism through your grandchild.
- Don't take things too personally. Remember, this is by its nature a universally tricky relationship.
- Deal with reality. Don't waste precious time wishing your child had married someone else.
- Aim for a relationship that's good enough rather than perfect.
- If you're upset by a comment or a text, take a pause before responding. Remember that texts often sound unintentionally brusque. Acknowledging a message with a neutral emoji buys time to think carefully about replying in a way that doesn't sound tetchy, needy or passive-aggressive.
- Talk to a friend you can trust to be sympathetic and sensible and who won't gossip.
- Put yourself in their shoes. It's helpful to think about how you got on with your parents-in-law and what was irritating and endearing.
- Don't discuss grievances with your son or daughter, or anyone else in the family, apart from your partner.

5

Childcare and Babysitting

These days, it's not unusual to catch the eye of a fellow grandparent at the school gates or pushing a buggy round the park. This is the biggest change for grandparents: the new expectation that they will provide some childcare so that their adult children can go out to work. It's also a new source of tension in many families. Around one in four working families rely on grandparents to look after the kids, and the estimated nine-million-strong grandparent army saves parents thousands of pounds in childcare fees. What's more, many families couldn't function without grandparents' help in the school holidays. 'Grandparents are saints,' says Emily, having just shipped her two kids off to her mum's for half term.

Grandparents are the obvious option for parents who are stuck between a rock and a hard place: they can't afford childcare, yet they can't afford not to work. A full-time nursery place takes about 65 per cent of the average parent's weekly take-home pay, yet escalating rents and mortgages mean that both parents have to work. Today, an average house costs around nine times average earnings, more than double what it was in the 1980s, when it was more like four times average income. Professor Vanessa May says, 'Both generations are under a lot of pressure, because in many families both parents have to work to make ends meet, but because of the cost of formal childcare in the UK they then end up being reliant on grandparents to provide at least some informal childcare.'

There's so much chat in the media about grandparents feeling put upon and exploited, but the truth is much more nuanced. Some grandparents resent what they see as unwelcome pressure. They feel they've brought up their children and don't want to do it again. Meanwhile, some adult children feel upset and disappointed if grandparents say no. The family therapist Judith Lask says, 'There's often quite a lot of family conflict now around expectations of grandparents to be part of regular childcare. Increasingly, grandparents are more likely to be working or have other commitments. I know a lot of grandparents who feel in a really difficult dilemma because they're being expected to look after their grandchildren, but they feel they've moved on. They are very happy to be a grandparent but they don't want to stay in the parent role – they'd rather have the special treats and the weekends.'

Other grandparents feel torn. They welcome the opportunity to be closely involved in their grandchildren's lives, and want to support kids who are struggling financially. But they've got their own lives. Grace, who has looked after all her seven grandchildren at different times, sums up the ambivalence so many grandparents feel: 'My sons were happy knowing that they didn't have to pay out so much for childcare. But it's hard on us when adult children expect that grandparents should just be there at their beck and call, because we have our life to live. But you have to do it. And I got a lot of pleasure out of looking after my grandchildren; they were like my heaven, and it helps us to keep young. I think grandparents are very important; they take the burden off parents and they give stability to the children.'

Grandchildcare may be free, but it still comes at a cost. Many grandparents work themselves or have elderly parents or younger children who need them too. As the state pension age rises all over the world, many grandparents can't afford to retire. The trade union Usdaw claims that 1.9 million grandparents have reduced their hours of work, given up a job, or taken time off work to care for a grandchild. Whether they work or not, grandparents have other stuff to do: they take courses, travel, campaign, have demanding volunteering roles. They also need time for their friends and interests, whether that's gardening, cycling or playing the guitar. Above all, they want to live life to the max, and that may or may not include childcare. A regular commitment doesn't rule those things out, but it certainly imposes limits.

There's a lot to be said for the extended family being involved in bringing up kids; it takes a village to raise a child and all that. However, childcare is a job, a set-in-stone commitment. It brings formality into family relationships, and that can create resentment and irritation on both sides. Both generations feel awkward about saying what they really think, because it's too up close and personal; there's so much at stake. Too often, grandparents complain privately about feeling they're being taken advantage of in a way that a nursery or a childminder wouldn't tolerate. They put in the hours, and yet their views and feelings are dismissed. Sonia says, 'It can so easily tip into being taken for granted because there's an assumption that there is no cost to you because you haven't got children, and therefore it can't be difficult for you.'

Adult children have mixed feelings too

The child's parents are equally ambivalent, although their feelings are often ignored in media discussions about grandparents and childcare. It's understandable if they have reservations about being dependent on their parents and inviting them to play such a key role in their child's upbringing. They naturally find it hard to express their needs and concerns to a grandparent, especially to a mother- or father-in-law, as directly as they could to a professional carer. And it's infuriating if grandparents won't do things their way because they think they know best. Professor Vanessa May, co-author of research on the paradoxes of grandparenting, says, 'Some adult children are not necessarily that happy to have to rely on grandparents, because it can create these ties of dependency and mutual obligation that they might prefer not to have. They might want to feel that they are more independent or autonomous. It might also open up the opportunity for grandparents to know more about what's happening in the family with the grandchildren, but also then offer them more opportunities to interfere.'

So it's not surprising that a study comparing childcare in Finland – where public provision of childcare is relatively affordable – with the UK and the Netherlands found that when there was an affordable alternative, parents who worked non-standard hours preferred professional care because the boundaries are more clear-cut, it's more straightforward to negotiate, more dependable and doesn't come with additional emotional costs.

While governments are finally beginning to acknowledge the indispensable contribution grandparents make to the economy, that's not backed up with practical and financial measures to support them. The powers that be are happy to exploit the goodwill of grandparents, and there have been various attempts by politicians, like US vice-president J. D. Vance, to place some responsibility for childcare on grandparents. Meanwhile, governments continue to ignore the looming childcare crisis created by the rising retirement age across the world, which inevitably reduces the number of grandparents who are available to do childcare.

There are some exceptions, like Sweden, where parental leave can be transferred to grandparents in some circumstances. In the UK, occasional glimmers of hope have fizzled out: in 2000, a government commission even looked into paying grandparents for childcare, and in 2023 the idea was again discussed in parliament, while grandparents' leave pops up on the agenda from time to time. Specified Adult Childcare credits, which count as a National Insurance contribution towards the state pension, were introduced in 2011, but only for grandparents under the state pension age whose adult child is eligible for child benefit.

More promising initiatives come from outside government. The trade union Usdaw is campaigning for better support for grandparents who have to balance paid work with caring for grandchildren. In 2021, Saga blazed a trail by introducing a week's paid leave for grandparents on its staff. In the US, a few companies, including Booking.com, offer 'grandternity' leave, which allows grandparents to take time off work to support children and grandchildren.

It's OK to say no

Some adult children feel really let down when grandparents don't want to commit to formal childcare. If their friends' parents do it, they automatically assume their parents will too. At the London Intercultural Couples Centre, director Dr Reenee Singh sees many clients who are unhappy that their parents are not doing more. 'I've heard it so many times: adult children say, "We're so busy and overwhelmed with our children and where are the grandparents? They're not offering enough." I'm seeing one family where the adult daughter is really unhappy because her parents don't help out, whereas her husband's parents do. She can't understand how her parents can be so busy. But this maternal grandmother is quite clear. She's done enough with her kids and she doesn't want to be tied down to one day a week or whatever. Whereas a lot of grandmothers would jump at the chance. It's different in every family.'

No one should feel obliged to do childcare; there are so many other ways to help the family and have a role in grandchildren's lives. One forthright grandmother said no to two days a week, saying

'Why should I give up work so that my daughter-in-law can earn the money to go away on spa breaks?' But many grandparents feel bad about saying no. The sense that the kids' needs come first is deeply ingrained, particularly in grandmothers. Charlotte reluctantly refused her son's request to look after his two-year-old when he and his girlfriend were living with her because she was getting her own business off the ground. She says, 'I felt very guilty because my son and his girlfriend weren't very well off, and I'm aware that from the outside my work doesn't look like a proper job because I'm in the house a lot. But my daughter-in-law was earning a lot more than me and I was concerned that I would start to feel resentful. They sent Alfie to a childminder instead. I think that was better for him, rather than just trudging around with Granny all day. I have to admit that I find playing with toddlers really boring, adorable as they are. I don't think they ever held it against me.'

Grandparents feel they need a good reason for saying no, and having their own work to do is the cast-iron excuse. One grandmother, who already looks after the kids one day a week, says that if she didn't keep working part-time her whole week could be taken up with childcare. 'Work is the only excuse that my kids respect,' she says. 'It's not good enough to say you're doing a yoga class.' In my experience, it's much more about justifying things to myself than to my adult children. I hate saying no because I love it and I want to help. It's not my adult children who are putting on the pressure, it's me. Rosa, who is freelance, agrees. 'If I'm really busy with work I don't agonise because then it is non-negotiable. I can say no or I don't offer in the first place. But when work is quieter and I have a choice I get conflicted, and I feel I should go and help or take the kids out. I don't think my daughter would be thinking "Mum's off doing something nice when she could be looking after the children", but I would be thinking it about myself.'

Once a regular commitment is established, it can be hard for either side to get out of it. Grandparents who have got used to looking after a grandchild once or twice a week often feel bereft if the arrangement comes to an end, and adult children naturally agonise about breaking the news gently. But some grandparents, like Rosa, are relieved. She recently gave up one day a week's childcare in favour of a more ad hoc arrangement, largely because she kept getting sick, which is one of the hazards of regular contact with little ones. She adds, 'Sometimes I tipped over into feeling resentful if we'd been doing too much, or if we had been looking after the girls on days that suited their parents but didn't suit me and my partner. It's like, why are we having to work on a Saturday when we're the ones doing them a favour? I often get myself in a pickle about how to pull back without causing offence.

'When I stopped looking after the girls I felt light and spacious, there was a sense of the whole thing lifting. So much of it was about getting them into their car seats and making sure the older one got to nursery on time. I would much rather have fun time with them. Yet when I look back on photos of when we were looking after them I'm just so glad that I had that time with them, because it was really special. It was challenging and exhausting and frustrating and it often meant we had to work at weekends and make compromises. We didn't want to do it and at the same time we loved it.'

Not being asked to do childcare

The other side of the coin is that many grandparents would love to look after their grandchild and feel deeply disappointed when they're not asked. From my own experience, I think it's best to make it clear that you're happy to do some childcare rather than waiting to be asked, because a lot of second-guessing goes on between grandparents and adult children, who often make assumptions or don't like to ask. If the parents reject the offer, it might be because they have other plans, or they've asked the other grandparents first, and that can be painful. Or it could be that their ideas about bringing up children are out of sync with the grandparents', and that's painful too. 'Childcare is more likely to happen when the daughter-in-law [or the daughter] believes the grandparents have a similar parenting philosophy,' says Professor Geoffrey Greif.

Fortunately, there are so many other ways to be involved with the grandchildren, such as informal babysitting or setting up a regular date to help out by taking a child to a swimming lesson, for example. One of the best ways grandparents can support the family is to be on call as back-up, because family life is full of emergencies, both minor and major. If a child is too ill to go to nursery or the childminder, for example, grandparents can step in. Knowing there's someone reliable who is always ready to step up in a crisis is an absolute boon for parents.

What's in it for grandparents?

Grandparents take on childcare for all sorts of reasons. It's almost a tradition in some families: their mother looked after their kids and their grandmother did the same. But most grandparents do it because they love it and it's a unique opportunity to build a close relationship. One-to-one time with a grandchild is quite different from the child's parents being in the room. A regular slot in the week or in the school holidays automatically keeps you in tune with the child's latest obsessions, preferences and quirky ways. You're the one who comforts them when they're upset, who chivvies them into their coats, who knows what makes them giggle. You get to know each other's moods and tantrums and build up a close and lasting bond.

Ken and Anita looked after their two young grandchildren five days a week, twelve hours a day for four years, leaving home at six every morning to beat the traffic. They were willing to take on such a huge commitment because they had already had a few years of enjoying retirement to the max, and were ready for something new and rewarding. Ken says, 'I'm not sure who suggested it first.

When our daughter's maternity leave was coming to an end when her baby was a year old, we had a sort of round-table discussion with her and our son-in-law and we all thought it would be good if we could do it. We joined in and learned the routines and it turned out to be a lovely experience for us. Then when our grandson was born two years later, we carried on. We really enjoyed the close contact and caring for the children in the way a mother would. We've been very close to both of them ever since, even though they moved to Holland four years ago, and I think that's because we looked after them since they were babies.'

The great thing about childcare is that it's an automatic date in the diary; you don't have to make an arrangement or wait for an invitation. Wise grandparents acknowledge the new realities of family weekends, which are crammed full of seeing friends, kids' parties, swimming lessons, visiting the other grandparents. A regular weekday commitment doesn't cut into family time, and leaves grandparents free too.

It's also a second chance to have time to focus on children without the distractions of work and bringing up a family. That has particular meaning for grandmothers who were in the vanguard of working mothers, as Anita was. 'Looking after our grandchildren was like a second chance, with the added bonus that you can give them back,' she says. 'We had the time that you never have when you're a parent. We both worked full-time through our daughter's infancy: I had a very short maternity leave and Ken didn't get any time off, because paternity leave didn't exist in the 1980s. So this was a very good experience for us because we felt we filled in a blank in our own life experience. It also gave us a sense of purpose. And I think you're more relaxed as a grandparent.' Many grandfathers particularly regret not having had more time with their own children. So while grandchildcare is traditionally seen as women's work, and research confirms that women tend to do more, grandfathers are now stepping up. Around 14 per cent of grandfathers in the UK provide 10 or more hours of childcare a week.

Regular childcare brings grandparents closer to their adult children and their partners, and that's lovely, although it can also create friction. Professor Greif's research showed that childcare generally improved relationships between grandmothers and daughters-in-law, presumably because they're grateful, and hopefully because it leads to more shared thinking about parenting. It certainly makes you more involved with their everyday lives and helps you to understand their ideas. The brief chats when they get back from work might seem superficial, but they're good grounding for a closer bond. Gary, who looks after his grandsons one day a week, says, 'My son and I share something massive that we didn't before: he knows what it's like to be a parent, and how fulfilling it is as well as what a struggle it can be, bringing up these two amazing kiddies who can charm you in a way no one else can. Even if it's fleeting – I catch him for about five minutes before he rushes off to work – I can still pick up a sense of what's going on for him. I get to see him without his outdoor face on.'

Many grandparents see it as their responsibility to support their adult children; it's just what families do. They also think they'll do a better job than paid childcare. In many areas, good nurseries and childminders have horrendous waiting lists, especially for under-twos. For parents it's a no-brainer to leave their child in the care of someone who loves them as much as they do and offers one-to-one care. When they first go back to work, it's far less upsetting to leave a baby at home with a familiar grandparent than with new faces in a strange environment. Some grandparents, like Ada, who lives in Buenos Aires, worry about young babies going to daycare. 'When my daughter told me she was thinking of sending her baby to a nursery, my immediate reaction was "Oh no!" I didn't like the idea of the baby leaving home when she was just a few months old, in fact

I thought it was awful. So for a time I thought that I would organise my life so that I could look after the baby full-time, although it wouldn't have been easy. I like my freedom, but I definitely would have done it. I told my daughter that I had reservations about the nursery but she didn't pay much attention to me! When I offered to look after Julieta she said don't you worry I will look for a very good nursery. I'll solve it.'

Finally, looking after a grandchild gives you a massive sense of achievement. Yesterday my husband was reminiscing about how he used to feel after a day's solo childcare: 'I could hardly believe I could do it,' he said. 'It's different now, because I know I can.' And being with young kids is good for you. As Grace says, 'Our years are lengthened by it.' It can bring huge benefits for grandparents' health and well-being, both in the moment and in the long term, and that has a lot to do with having the best reason to get up in the morning. That's particularly important in retirement. What could give a more potent sense of purpose than nurturing the next generation and helping your adult children? It's good for your brain too. Recent research found that childcare is associated with a reduced risk of dementia, and has benefits for mental health, while an earlier study of older grandmothers in Australia found that up to a day's grandchildcare a week had a positive effect on cognitive function.

Looking after more than one grandchild

Childcare arrangements are bound to be affected when younger siblings come along, and when there are different sets of grandchildren. Many grandparents don't feel quite as enthusiastic about looking after two or more children, especially if they have to do it on their own. Rosa confesses, 'Sometimes I think, thank goodness I've only got one set of grandchildren, because at the moment my grandmotherliness is contained in one day a week. I'm not sure I'd want to do more childcare. But when my younger daughter has kids she'll expect me to do the same for her as I do for her sister.' However, parents can be slow to understand why. I remember feeling a bit taken aback when my father-in-law, who looked after my baby son one day a week, withdrew the offer as soon as his younger brother was born. Now I totally get why!

It can be a logistical nightmare when there are different sets of grandchildren. Dividing your time equally is nigh-on impossible, because each family has different needs. I spoke to one grandmother whose daughter is a full-time mum with three kids and needs a regular break to get on with stuff, while her daughter-in-law has to work full-time, can't afford childcare, and her own mum isn't close enough to help. Gabriella, who is 69 and has one grandson, says, 'It will be more complicated when my younger daughter has her baby in a few months' time because I will want to offer both my daughters equal help. But they live far apart, and then there's my energy levels and my work. I'd like to be hands-on with them both but I think I've got to balance it with everything else.' Circumstances often make it impossible to give equal amounts of time, but it's still possible to be fair. If one family lives far away while the other is round the corner, for example, you can't do equal childcare, but you can be available to step in when extra help is required, and concentrate your help in the school holidays. Grandparents provide on average sixteen days of childcare during the summer alone, saving parents nearly £1,000 for each child, according to Saga.

However fair you try to be, there's always likely to be some sibling rivalry, and in some families it's more extreme than others. Grace has three sons, and has looked after all her seven grandchildren, although it was often quite a stretch given that they live on opposite sides of the city. 'Sometimes I'd have to ask Lloyd to pick his kids up that day because I had to go down to Elliott's,' she remembers. 'He didn't like that, but I said I have to share myself. From both of them I'd get, "You're more with Elliott" or "You're more with Lloyd". So there was a bit of rivalry. They think it's favouritism, but it isn't. You can't just drop one because his kids are older. I say, when your needs are there I will always help if I'm able to. I would never say it's become a burden or it's too much for me.'

> ### WHAT TO CONSIDER BEFORE COMMITTING TO CHILDCARE
>
> - Think realistically about how much time you want to give up. It's easy to offer too much, because we all think we can achieve more in a week than we can, and end up feeling overwhelmed and/or resentful.
> - Don't forget to build recovery time into your diary. You're not being wet if you need it, however young and energetic you feel, because the responsibility of looking after someone else's child can be draining.
> - What will a regular commitment stop you doing? Will there be an impact on your social life? A lot of grandparents prefer not to arrange evenings out after a day's childcare, and that means that they have less time to see friends, go to classes and so on.
> - How will it affect holiday plans? Will your dates always have to coincide with the parents', or will they be able to find alternative childcare when you go away?
> - Be realistic about how many grandchildren you can manage to look after, especially if you're on your own. No one likes admitting their limitations, but you should never feel bad about saying you don't feel comfortable about looking after all the cousins *and* the new baby *and* the dog.
> - You will almost certainly get asked to do evening babysitting and emergency back-up on top of your regular days. Think about this when negotiating how much time to commit.

- Childcare is a big commitment; it's best seen as a job. Working parents need to know that you will show up without fail. But they also need a back-up if you can't make it because you're ill or there is some other emergency.
- It suits some grandparents to commit to a few months at a time rather than an indefinite period, although for many families that's too uncertain.
- Grandparents are doing their children a favour, so they should have some say in the timings that suit them, and where the grandchild is looked after. But ultimately it needs to work for both sides and it has to be a negotiation.
- Will you look after the child at yours or theirs? What's the journey like? Will you need to stay the night? Factor in journey times and cost (for more on this, *see* p. 136).
- Don't allow childcare to be an excuse to ignore your own ambitions. It's tempting if you're retired to just go along with adult children's demands, but this is your time, and it's vital to think about how you really want to spend it.

WHAT GRANDPARENTS COMPLAIN ABOUT

Having to follow parents' rules and routines

Grandparents often say how much easier it would be if they could do things their way. Some complain about overly strict routines, while others moan about kids who do what they like and graze constantly rather than eating meals at the table. The crunch comes when children misbehave, and grandparents aren't sure how the parents would want them to deal with it. It's a generalisation, but parents tend to reason with a child, while grandparents are more inclined to tell them off. To work well, grandchildcare relies on parents and grandparents being on the same page, so that children get consistent messages. When you're looking after someone else's child you have to do things their way, even if it's frustrating and makes you roll your eyes. But there's usually some leeway if both sides agree on the fundamentals. Iwona, who looks after her granddaughter one day a week, says, 'I've always done things the way the parents want, but with a "me" spin on it. They're very happy for me to have slightly different rules because they are mindful that my relationship with Evie is very different from theirs. I think it works because I respect their principles and I don't deviate from important things that could have a knock-on effect, like giving her sugar. I think they're much better parents than I ever was. Parents now think so much through.'

A grandparenting course can help people understand their adult children's ideas about parenting. They cover changes in babycare and child-rearing over the past 30 years, and the relevant research. Sarah Johnson, a breastfeeding counsellor and doula, set up online Grantenatal workshops when she became a grandmother herself. She explains, 'So many grandparents think everything has stood still since they had their own children. At the same time there's so much information available to new parents on Google and social media. It's overwhelming to know what's right. So we cover all the basics: safe sleep, how to support a breastfeeding mother, baby-led weaning, how to put a baby down in his cot.'

Parents who get home late

For parents, one of the best things about grandchildcare is flexibility. Unlike childminders or nannies, grandparents rarely insist on a strict clocking-off time. It's a gift if parents have the kind of jobs where they often have to work late at short notice. Most grandparents don't mind staying on if the parents check that it's OK. But if the parent goes out for a drink after work without texting, it's annoying. I recently heard of a son-in-law who got home two hours late with no warning text and didn't apologise, even when his furious mother-in-law asked if there'd been a problem.

If it happens too often, patience wears thin. The assumption that grandparents don't have anything better to do is galling. It's unfair on the grandchildren too. They naturally get upset if they've been told that Mum or Dad will be home in time to read them a story, while the grandparent loses credibility. One solution is to get dates in the diary that mean you have to leave at a certain time. It's a gentle reminder that while grandparents are flexible, there are limits.

Being asked to do more at short notice

Grandparents also get fed up when they're asked to do an extra day, often at short notice. Grace says, 'It's always at the last minute! It's like, you're there so you can do it. They never see that you're tired or that you might want to do something else. When we brought the boys up we never had weekends off, we didn't expect to. My mother and my mother-in-law were both in Grenada. But these expect to because the grandparents are around. It's hard, but still, you have to do it.' Grandparents feel ambivalent: they want to help, but can't help feeling a bit resentful if it means changing their own plans. It's a lot to do with context. Most people don't mind stepping up at the last minute if there's a good reason, such as if their grandchild is too sick to go to nursery, or the parents need to finish a job. They're not so happy if the couple are off to Paris for the weekend. Lisa wants to support her daughter while she gets her new business off the ground, but sometimes it gets too much. 'There are some weeks when things get a bit chaotic and we end up doing two or three days rather than the one day we're committed to. I sometimes have to cancel my own arrangements, which is a pain, but I don't mind. But three days is too much and there have been times when I have thought, I can't really take this. I wasn't getting any of my own work done, and although my hours are flexible I still have deadlines. I never feel exploited because Mira is very sensitive to that, and they're both very appreciative. I think I would be able to say if it really got too much. But at the same time I'm glad she feels she can ask for help and that I'll say no if I can't – not that I ever have said no!'

Parents who work from home and keep checking up

Many parents now work from home at least part of the week, and that's been a real boon for families. But it can be a mixed blessing for carers. It's reassuring, especially in the first weeks and months, to know that one of the parents is around. But it can also make things a bit harder, because young children naturally want to see their mum or dad if they know they're upstairs. It can disrupt the flow if the parents keep popping down for a coffee or to check how things are going, especially if the child cries when they go back to their workroom. Helen says, 'My son-in-law often works from home when I'm looking after his two-year-old. At first I found it quite reassuring. He mostly keeps out of the way but sometimes he steps in if she's taking a while to settle for a nap, or if she's upset about something. That feels quite undermining.'

It's particularly difficult when the parent first goes back to work and the child is getting used to being without his mum or dad. If your grandchild knows his mum is at home, he'll inevitably take longer to get used to the idea that you're in charge. However, having been the mum who works upstairs myself, I know how hard it is not to interfere. The obvious answer is for grandparents to take the grandchild out, but that's not always what child or grandparent want. Another solution is to discuss how the parents want to play things. Do they want to be interrupted if the child wants to see them? Do they want to have lunch together? Could they keep a kettle in their workroom so they don't have to use the kitchen? You can then agree a joint strategy that works for everyone.

Mess

Grandparents often complain about washing-up in the sink from the night before and having to rummage through piles of clothes to find what they need. Sonia remembers that when she looked after her two grandsons, 'The house was always such a mess that we couldn't find clean clothes or nappies. It felt a bit disrespectful when we were doing something to support the family, and it meant that something that should be fun was hard work. What made it worse was the feeling that they felt they could behave like that with us because we're easy-going, whereas the other grandparents are more demanding. In the end, we felt we really needed to say something.'

Another grandmother was used to managing her anxiety by being super-tidy and highly organised, but that wasn't possible when she looked after her six-year-old grandson. She found the chaos her daughter-in-law happily inhabited incredibly stressful, but didn't like to say anything because she didn't want to sound critical. Kids need to be free to explore and make a mess, and no one wants to nag about it. But they also quite like tidy-up time. If they come to yours, you can contain the chaos by spreading a big sheet on the floor and covering the sofa with an old blanket.

Catching children's bugs

One hazard of spending so much time with grandchildren is that they pass on endless bugs to grandparents, who take much longer to shake them off. To some extent that's unavoidable because the immune system naturally weakens as people get older.

But it's possible to give it a boost by doing all the things we know we're supposed to do: eating well and maintaining a healthy weight, drinking plenty of water, nurturing good sleep habits and taking regular exercise. These things will in turn help keep energy levels up, and that's what anyone looking after children really needs. A daily supplement of vitamin D is recommended in autumn and winter, and it's important to keep jabs up to date. Other hazards of childcare include bad backs and painful twinges from carrying a baby or toddler around. Regular yoga or Pilates can help, and physios can work wonders.

There needs to be a plan in place for back-up if you're ill; it's not your responsibility to provide cover. It goes without saying that if you develop any ongoing health issues that require hospital appointments and tests, you need to keep your children in the loop from the word go, so that they've got ample time to make alternative arrangements. This may mean being more open with your kids about health issues than you would choose to be if you weren't looking after the grandchildren.

WHAT ADULT CHILDREN COMPLAIN ABOUT

Grandparents who don't do what they're asked

Grandparents often make the mistake of thinking that providing free childcare gives them carte blanche to do things their way. Freya Mahal, who runs online courses for grandparents, says, 'One mother I spoke to ended up sending her children to nursery because her mum refused to follow anything that she was saying about when the children ate and slept. It wasn't even a very strict routine. I think the grandmother felt that she had the upper hand because she was offering free childcare, so she could do what she wanted.'

Some things matter more than others. One grandfather got the sack because he kept ignoring his daughter-in-law's instructions about naps, which meant the toddler was still wide awake at 10 p.m. Another grandmother shocked her son, a paediatrician, by insisting on tucking the baby in with a blanket. Leanne says, 'My mother-in law can't follow instructions at all. The first time she looked after the baby I said, all you have to do is put her down in her pram, put the cover on, don't talk to her and she'll fall asleep. If you talk to her she won't go to sleep and then she'll lose it. The first time it happened I could hear the baby screaming from all the way down the street. It happened every single time. I don't know if it was a case of, "I've brought up three children, you don't need to tell me what to do", but basically she hadn't done any of the things I asked her to and everything went completely tits up.'

Grandparents who interfere

Childcare means that grandparents can't help having an influence on the way the kids behave, whether it's table manners or how much TV they watch, and that can seem like interference. Some grandparents try their best not to, but others seize the opportunity with relish. Steph's formidable mother-in-law used to come down to stay and look after the baby (who's now a teenager) for two or three days a week. She's the only grandparent I've heard of who was paid for childcare. Steph remembers, 'My mother-in-law used to say, "I wouldn't do it like that" and then tell me how to do it. There was a complete lack of understanding between us about bringing up children. She'd say, "I don't know why you find it difficult." It was because I was working and I hadn't slept! She made me feel really inadequate and if I'm honest I was jealous of her. She'd talk about "me and the other mothers" as if she was my baby's mum! And she had all the fun bit, while I would be going to work absolutely shattered after endless sleepless nights.

'Then one evening Alfie had a temperature when I came home from work. She pointed to some adult medicine and said, "I gave him some of this." When I questioned her she started backtracking; she wasn't clear about what she had given him. We had an enormous row and she stomped off. She thought I was being completely unreasonable, and our arrangement came to an end after that.'

Having to criticise their parents and tell them what to do

It's just as hard for adult children to tell their parents what to do – and what not to do – as it is for their parents to hear it. Some adult children feel awkward about asking their parents to do things a certain way; such a complete role reversal is bound to feel uncomfortable. It's even worse if they don't like something that the grandparents already do with their child, and have to work out how to tell them without causing offence. Ellie wrestles with this with her own parents. 'The biggest thing I'm trying to work out is how do I criticise my parents for something they've said or done with the kids without being like, you did the same thing to me? I feel rude telling my parents what to do, but I need to get things done. My dad's supposed to be helping me with a project at the moment, but what often happens when I'm working from home is that my parents arrive a bit late and then they make lunch and the time is ticking while the kids are asleep and I'm desperate to get on. I know I should say we need to work when the children are sleeping, but I find it hard being that directive with my parents. I'm working on being firm.'

Interestingly, many people find they get less tangled up in knots with their parents-in-law, simply because they don't have the same baggage. They can't press each other's buttons in the same way, and both sides are able to be more straightforward. That's not always the case, of course: every family is different, and relationships between in-laws are notoriously challenging (*see* chapter 4 for more on this).

Grandparents who park the child in front of the telly

Some grandparents use their childcare time to do the supermarket shop or get on with their admin. That's fine, up to a point. But it's not acceptable to leave the kids in front of the TV while Grandma gets on with her work calls or plays Scrabble on the phone. Ben's dad used to look after his three-year-old granddaughter one afternoon a week until Ben's wife stepped in. Ben explains, 'My wife isn't keen on my dad looking after Lottie because it's always on his terms. I can see he's hurt, and he wants to look after her more, but the problem is that he imposes his views on how they spend their time together; basically he just does what *he* wants to do rather than following her lead. He either expects her to amuse herself while he listens to a podcast or tries to teach her games that are way over her head. It's especially difficult because my parents are divorced, and my mum looks after our daughter one day a week, sometimes more, so that's painful for Dad too. The difference is that when Mum looks after Lottie she gets down on the floor and plays with her.'

Unreliability

Perhaps because they're not paid, some grandparents think it's OK to take the odd day off, or even to go on holiday. That's totally useless for working parents. Childcare has to be 100 per cent guaranteed and holidays need to be agreed well in advance; routine doctor's and dentist's appointments should be arranged on other days. Will says, 'My mother-in-law is always asking if she can help but she's not much use. If she looks after the boys for a morning she needs a lie-down. And she doesn't take the commitment seriously. There was a time when she looked after them one day a week, but then she would suddenly announce she was going travelling with about a week's notice. I've stopped asking her and if she offers I make an excuse.'

Feeling guilty

More adult children than you might think worry about taking advantage of grandparents. They feel concerned that they wouldn't say no, even if they had other plans or it was getting too much. Mira says, 'I always feel guilty. My parents have been amazing. They step in whenever there have been problems, like when my daughter got chucked out of her childminder's for being "too hard work". My mum gets really tired in the afternoon, and I interpret that as she's annoyed, and that I'm asking too much of her. I always worry that I'm taking advantage, whereas my partner has more faith that my parents will say no if they don't want to do it. And I feel guilty that I'm not being a good daughter, that I'm not giving them enough, because they're seeing a lot of Lara but I'm not really seeing them.'

MAKING CHILDCARE WORK FOR YOU AND THE FAMILY

- Suggest a trial run
  Before the parent goes back to work, it's really helpful to look after the child on your own for a day or two with them close at hand, to iron out any teething troubles and get the child used to being with just you.
- Practise with the buggy
  Make sure you know where everything is and how everything works work well in advance, from the high chair to the white-noise machine. I'm sorry if this is teaching granny to suck eggs, but it's a good idea to practise unfolding the buggy, fastening the straps and getting it in and out of the house (tricky if there are steps) and on and off the bus or train. Some buggies are heavy and some doorways are a tight squeeze.
- Find out about the rules
  Have a discussion with the parents about what children are and are not allowed to do. Grandparents need to know:
  - What the rules are, because children always try to persuade you that their parents let them watch Sonic or eat bananas before teatime. It's undermining if parents get home and say it's fine when you've been desperately holding the line.
  - Which rules are set in stone and which are flexible, depending on the circumstances.

- How to deal with naughty behaviour. What do you say to a child who hits a sibling or another child in the park, or refuses to share?

Special grandparents' rules also need to be discussed, and your own expectations: that children must hold hands when crossing the road, for example.

- Take your own sandwiches

Parents who are rushing off to work don't have time to think about grandparents' needs. Take plenty of energy-boosting snacks as well as lunch, and don't arrive desperate for a coffee, because you need to get stuck in straight away.

- Pace yourself

The number one thing grandparents agree on, whether they're 49 or 79, is that looking after grandchildren is exhausting. Even if you feel energised when you're with them, it catches up the next day, so it helps if you can take that into account when you plan your week. It's not just about age. Looking after other people's children is more tiring than looking after your own. It's partly the responsibility, but it's also that with little ones you're on constant alert to pre-empt them missing their mum, and have to work hard to anticipate what might upset them, and how to make things better when they're sad. Rosa says, 'When I'm looking after the girls I feel quite calm in the moment but afterwards I feel like I've been shredded. I follow a neuroscientist on Instagram who says that grandparents and parents expend huge amounts of energy with young children on regulating their systems. So that when the child is upset the grandparent remains calm, but afterwards they feel totally drained. That makes a lot of sense to me.'

COMMON CHALLENGES TO THINK ABOUT

Anxiety

Everyone expects grandparents to know what they're doing, but they still get anxious. If you're not with your grandchild every day, you can't be totally up to speed with what they can and can't do. You're terrified of leaving a toddler even for two minutes to go to the loo. You don't know if they're fine at the top of the climbing frame (and what would you do if they got stuck or refuse to come down?), or whether they'll stop at the kerb on their trike. Gabriella says, 'When my sister used to pick her grandchildren up from school on their scooters she said it was a nightmare because she couldn't run fast enough to keep up with them, and she just had to trust that they were going to stop at the roads. She thought they should walk with her and she got quite angry with her daughter, who insisted they came home on their scooters.'

The first grandparent I met who came clean about her anxiety was a former police officer I interviewed for my book on retirement, *Not Fade Away*. When she looked after her grandson, she was plagued by intrusive thoughts: What if I fall over? What if the baby has an accident? She never told her daughter how she felt. I admit that when my eldest grandchildren were little, I was haunted by similar fears about choking and accidents in a way I hadn't been with my own children. I think it's because mothers have the confidence of a direct physical connection with their own child, almost like a second sense, whereas a grandparent is that little bit removed. Looking back, I can see that a first-aid course for babies and children would have sorted me out: there are some good ones designed especially for grandparents (details in the Resources section, *see* p. 239).

'How can you be bored and delighted at the same time?'

Looking after grandchildren is bound to get boring at times, just because little ones want to do the same thing over and over again, so

CHILDCARE AND BABYSITTING

there's no need to beat yourself up for not loving every single minute. My favourite description of looking after a grandchild comes from a grandfather in Francis Spufford's novel *Light Perpetual*, who talks about the strange combination of love, boredom and joy as you count the hours before bedtime. Staying at home all day can be more tiring than getting out and doing stuff. It helps to be prepared with a rough schedule for how you'll spend the day, based around the child's routines. Even a simple list of possible activities gives you a head start, and it's a big help if you're tired or preoccupied with work. When I manage to get it together to take stuff with me it usually pays off, and if no one's interested I try not to sulk. This week it was plastic needles, thread and binca canvas with holes to make it easier for little fingers to sew, while last week it was ready-to-roll pastry for cheese straws, and next time I'll take some bulbs and pots. A wise friend says you need conviction and enthusiasm to get kids interested in outings and craft projects, and she's so right. Sometimes kids need a bit of persuasion, but it usually pays off. Going with the flow and doing what they want may be easiest, but everyone's usually happier with a bit of structure.

If grandchildren get grumpy

Don't take it personally if a young child misses their mum or dad, although it's tough if a baby won't stop crying. It obviously helps to have some strategies from the parents that can usually be relied on to cheer the child up. When you're in sole charge with slightly older children, you can't always be the indulgent grandparent. There are times when you have to lay down the law and risk a grumpy response or even a tantrum. If a child is doing something that could be dangerous, like dragging a chair over to the cooker to stir the porridge, or running straight for the kerb, you have to step in, preferably with a calm explanation. I'm still haunted by an occasion when I couldn't stop myself shouting at my three-year-old grandson when he touched something sharp after I'd told him not to. He was inconsolable, I felt terrible, and it took a while to make up.

Another grandson gets fed up if I forget his banana when I pick him up from nursery, and I reckon being a bit tetchy is par for the course at the end of the day. In fact, I think it's a privilege to be one of the people he feels he can be himself with, and anyway, the next time I pick him up he'll be whizzing down the road singing 'Stop Right Now'. That's the beauty of having an everyday relationship with a child. You get the bad moods and sulks as well as the deep conversations and giggles: you get to know the whole person.

Your place or theirs?

It's important to discuss whether you'll look after the child at their house or yours. Often, the decision is made for you: if you live an hour away or have to take an older child to school, it makes sense to be at theirs. Both sides often have strong views. Some parents feel their child will settle more easily in their own home, and want them to make local friends. Journey time is also an important factor. At the beginning and end of the working day, it's much less stressful for parents if the grandparent comes to theirs rather than having to get the child dressed and ferry them across town at rush hour.

But many grandparents prefer to look after grandchildren at theirs, because they know where everything is and they know the area. They figure that since they're giving up their time, they should be able to do things on their terms, and that seems fair enough. But both sides have to be prepared to compromise. One woman I know looks after her grandson two days a week at hers, and one day at her daughter's. It's not easy, because they live on opposite sides of town, but they've made it work.

When the parents get home from work

If you are based in your grandchild's house, it's important to remember that you're invading your adult child's and their partner's territory, albeit in the nicest possible way. Bear that in mind when the parents walk through the door at the end of the working day. They'll be tired and still in work mode, so it's best to back off and don't expect to give them an immediate debrief. They need time to greet the kids and hear all their news, or get changed and take a moment to decompress before switching back into the zone of family life.

Take care of your own needs too

Childcare can be stressful as well as energising and fulfilling. My blood pressure rose after my lot came along, so my GP advised me to get back into swimming regularly, and meditation has helped too. When you're busy, your own needs tend to get put on the back burner, but it's vital to take time out to recharge the batteries. Experts advise building in a recovery day after looking after the kids, if possible. It's equally important to nurture yourself in other ways too, by spending time with friends and making space for the things that give you joy and make you feel fulfilled (apart from the grandchildren, that is). Running around after little ones feels like quite enough exercise, but you need to do your own thing to stay strong, clear-headed and flexible too, whether that's running, swimming or a dance class. Rosa says, 'For my partner and me it's about finding a balance between supporting ourselves and giving ourselves what we need, and supporting my daughter and her partner and giving them what they need. Last winter, Rob and I had weeks of getting ill after looking after the children. It got to the point this winter when my daughter said she thought we should stop. That was tough because I felt like I really wanted to support them.'

6

Grandfathers

Why do grandfathers need a separate chapter? After all, men's voices are heard throughout this book. But both in the media and academic research, they are either ignored or lumped together with grandmothers. Yet their experiences and feelings are not the same. 'Grand*parent* has become synonymous with grand*mother*', says Professor Anna Tarrant of the Centre for Innovation in Fatherhood and Family Research at the University of Lincoln. 'The culture around the grandmother as the caregiver, or the main caregiver, places men on the periphery. Being a grandfather is something men invest in and really want to do but there is no social script.' It is telling that many of the grandfathers Professor Tarrant interviewed for her research were taken aback that anyone was interested in what they had to say. I had the same experience with this book. She remembers, 'Many of the men were so pleased to be asked about being a grandad, because they said people just didn't ask them about it. It was really striking that they were so happy to have that space to talk about it and be recognised in that way. Their wives were surprised too!'

Yet grandfathers have always been significant and much-loved figures in people's lives. Like many boys of his generation, the late Scottish poet and novelist John Burnside was named after his maternal grandfather, a coal miner who remained a strong influence 50-odd years after his death. When he became a grandfather himself,

John Burnside wrote a moving tribute to him in *The Tablet*: 'He could be severe, authoritarian and immovably stubborn . . . Yet the grandfather I remember best was someone else altogether, a kindly, smiling man who spoke to me quietly about the things he valued in life.'

Research consistently shows that the involvement of grandfathers has a positive impact on their grandchildren's well-being, development and behaviour. They're an increasingly important part of the grandchildcare army that makes it possible for many parents to go out to work. These days, it's not uncommon to see a grandad doing the school run or pushing a toddler on the swings. A study of grandchildcare across Europe found that 42 per cent of grandfathers gave regular or occasional help looking after grandchildren, compared to 44 per cent of grandmothers. While it's true that many of these grandfathers are caring alongside grandmothers, and may not have sole charge, it's still an impressive contribution.

In traditional societies, grandfathers were revered as figures of authority and guardians of cultural values; in many cultures, they still are. But these days there are so many other kinds of grandfather too. At one extreme they're active, engaged, hands-on, while at the other they remain resolutely hands-off. These old-school grandads are content to be a passive presence on the sidelines, applauding achievements and doling out treats. They avoid nappy changing and are happy to let grandmothers get on with the business of caring.

But a new breed of grandfather has emerged over the past few decades. The traditional patriarch is giving way to a softer, more caring and approachable kind of man. Men who were 'new' dads when their own kids were growing up in the 1980s and 1990s have morphed into 'new' grandfathers. 'There has been an element of change around involved fatherhood which is impacting on involved grandfatherhood,' says Professor Tarrant. 'The cultural shift towards dads' engagement has embedded more in the last few decades.

At the same time our ideas on masculinity have changed as well.' Men who were hands-on with their own children want to do the same with their grandchildren. Ken, who looked after his two young grandchildren five days a week with his wife, says, 'When we were bringing up our daughter in the 1980s Anita and I wanted to do things differently from our parents' generation, who had distinct gender roles. Being a "New Man" was the phrase in those days. I was concerned to do my share of the cooking and the less pleasant stuff. It was the same when my wife and I looked after the grandchildren. We both did everything, including changing the babies' nappies, and I was happy to do my share.'

ARE GRANDFATHERS REALLY SECOND BEST?

'The grandchildren prefer their grandma'

Grandfathers who want to take on a more active caring role don't always find it easy, because they're often made to feel second best. Images of the perfect grandparent are still associated primarily with women. When people ask about how much childcare I do, they often assume that my husband isn't much help, while in fact he does more than I do. As a result, men tend to underestimate themselves. You often hear grandfathers say things like 'My wife's the expert', or 'If the twins were asked who they'd rather spend time with I'm sure they'd choose my wife'. Rosa says, 'When the girls were babies Rob found it much harder to get them to sleep, whereas I suppose because of my voice and my smell I could get them to sleep on me very easily, and that distressed him. I think the main problem is that he doesn't value what he is to them, and how important he is. But I think there is less difference in our grandparenting than there was in our parenting.' Men often hold back because their wives and daughters don't expect them to want to step up, and don't give them space to do it. Or they lack confidence if they weren't hands-on as dads when their own children were young.

Yet grandfathers have their own special qualities to bring to the table that may be different to grandmothers', but have equal value. And that's true whether they're traditional or 'new' or somewhere in between. That's the conclusion of Professor Ann Buchanan's groundbreaking research at Oxford University. The book she co-edited on grandfathers opens, 'This volume suggests that grandfathers have an important impact on grandchildren that is different and independent from that provided by grandmothers. This role is almost totally unrecognised.'

Men don't have to be 'new' grandfathers to be good ones. They just have to show up and be themselves. Old-school grandfathers don't necessarily have to change to offer something special. While babysitting and childcare are obvious ways to nurture a deeper connection, grandfathers provide other kinds of care. They listen and offer advice. They take kids to football. They are a calm refuge when things are stormy with parents. They support the whole family by doing DIY and taking the car to the garage. Professor Tarrant believes that this is just as much a form of care as the day-to-day nurturing that is traditionally women's domain. She says, 'Men do these things because they're good for their families, good for their children and their relationships with their grandchildren as well. So it's about reframing how we think about those contributions.'

Having an involved grandfather is good for kids, and being an involved grandfather is good for men. Grandfathers who are disengaged from their grandchildren have been found to have more depressive symptoms and fewer positive emotions than men with higher levels of involvement. The new purpose and meaning that grandchildren bring becomes even more important in retirement. Even grandfathers who were totally wedded to their jobs see grandchildren as their most important legacy. Professor Tarrant says,

'The transition from work to a domestic sphere is a huge challenge for retired grandfathers, who are grappling with their identity and trying to redefine their place in the world as ageing men, and often struggle more with the change than women.'

At a time when they might be winding down, the experience of being a grandfather stretches men in all kinds of new ways. They keep learning, both from their grandchildren and their adult children, particularly their sons. Bill says, 'You have to be flexible to be a grandparent – that's the quality you really need at a time of life when people are supposed to become less flexible. I think women are better at that, just because they've often had more flexible lives. Whereas a lot of men, like me, have worked at the same job throughout their lives.'

How grandfathers have changed

Being a grandfather offers a second chance to be nurturing in a way many men couldn't be with their own children, either because they were working full-time, or because they, and their families, saw it as women's work. It might even be that men are more enthusiastic about being a grandparent than grandmothers, who have done it all before and often feel a sense of *déjà vu* at juggling yet another set of conflicting demands and interests. Hundreds of grandfathers in the long-running Grandparent Study, initiated by Arthur Kornhaber in the US, said that being a grandfather gave them an opportunity to spend time with children that they didn't have with their own kids, and they really relished it. This is reflected in Professor Tarrant's work. She says, 'Several grandfathers said, "This is a chance for me to do things differently, because I've got more time. I can invest more in raising the grandchildren, and in the fun side of things." They really enjoyed the time with their grandchildren, and the way they think and made them question their own values and assumptions.'

Yet the dramatic change in men's roles within the family since today's grandfathers were grandsons themselves can leave them feeling a bit lost. Most men want to do things differently, to feel closer and more connected to their children and grandchildren. But it's a big break with the past and there are few role models. Don says, 'As parents, my generation wanted a more relaxed relationship with our children and that aim has carried on to the way we grandparent. I wonder if my generation can be more relaxed about grandparenting because we had open rebellion against our parents? In many ways my father was very old-fashioned. At the end of the day he wanted respect and consideration: when he wanted the grandchildren to quieten down, he wanted them to quieten down, and if they didn't he got angry. But when he was on his own with one grandchild he could have a very relaxed, modern relationship, based on humour and a deep, deep love. My daughters all adored him.'

The way men feel about being grandfathers, and how they behave with their grandchildren, is bound to be influenced by their experience with their own grandfathers. In many cases, that doesn't give them much to go on. My friend Sam is the first in his family for a few generations to live long enough to become a grandfather: neither his own father nor his grandfather were alive when their grandchildren were born. Many men only have faded photographs to boost vague recollections of grandfathers who they saw rarely or who died before they got to know them. Or they remember grandfathers who were distant and slightly forbidding: not at all like the kind of grandfather they want to be themselves. Bill says, 'My father's father died before I was born and my mother's father seemed very old; obviously all grandparents seem old, but he seemed extremely old. And he was very deaf, which adds another layer. He lived up north so we saw him about once a year. He died when I was about six.'

Luckier men had more time to get to know their grandfathers. They often have fond memories and are proud of their achievements and what they went through. They remember twinkly characters with tool sheds like treasure troves, who taught them how to mend things. But what they don't want to emulate is the emotional distance between them. The psychotherapist Phillip Hodson says, 'Grandfathers now tend to be more nurturing, and that's much more rewarding. That's partly because of the change in values from the idea that children should be seen and not heard to the child-centred philosophies of today. Although I adored my grandfather, he was very reserved. His first wife had died when he was in his early twenties, but he never talked about it. We just did stuff together; he used to give me rides on the crossbar of his bicycle down to the river where we used to go fishing and punting.'

What's interesting is that men who see their grandfathers as good role models often reject their own fathers' influence. Almost half of the grandfathers surveyed by the Australian psychologist Susan Moore said they had learned from their fathers how *not* to act as grandfathers, while two-thirds reported that they behaved differently from their own fathers as grandfathers. They were less authoritarian, more involved and interested, looked after their grandchildren more and spent more time with them generally. Niall, who was born in the 1950s, says, 'As parents we were really different from our parents. My dad would have liked to have been seen as a person who played around with his grandchildren in the way that I do, but I'm not sure he really knew how to do it. I think there was a slight element of what are grandads for?'

Don's role model is his grandmother rather than his grandfather or his father. He remembers how, as a rebellious teenager growing up in the suburbs of 1960s New York, his grandmother always calmed things down with his father after one of their frequent rows. 'One instance really sticks in my memory. I was about 13, reading the Beat Poets and wanting to grow my hair long, but my father insisted I got a haircut. I went, but I just had a little trim.

He was furious, and asked what I had spent the money on. My grandmother intervened in a way that was very sympathetic to both sides, and I was grateful to her for that. She explained side a and side b to the other. That is something I've tried to do in my family too.'

Grandfathers learn from their sons

In a surprising reversal of roles, grandfathers today are taking cues from their sons' greater involvement as parents. The current generation of fathers play a big part in babies' and children's daily care in a way that was unheard of when I was growing up in the 1960s. In 2000, one in 1,000 fathers were the primary caregiver of nine-month-old babies in England; now it's 1 in 14, according to the 'Children of the 2020s' survey, commissioned by the Department for Education. There were already signs that big change was underway when my own children were growing up in the 1980s and 1990s, when 'house husbands' were beginning to be a thing. Even so, paternity leave was not introduced in the UK until 2003, and back then a bloke pushing a buggy was a rare sight. These days, no one would give it a second thought. In her research, Professor Tarrant found that sons were a big influence on their dads. 'The grandfathers in the study observed changes in parenting and saw their sons being hands-on. They were keen to spend time learning and investing time in the care of their grandchildren in new ways. They'd say things like "My son was doing all this nappy changing, and I'd never even thought about it before, so I started doing it myself". But there is often an element of asking for permission from the daughter or daughter-in-law, which a grandmother might not feel she had to do.'

In turn, Professor Tarrant found that sons had a positive impact on their fathers' willingness to speak more openly about their emotions. In this respect, attitudes in general have changed dramatically. Two world wars took their toll on our fathers' and grandfathers' emotional openness. But over the last 20-odd years, with men's mental health high on the agenda, it feels like there's been progress, although there's still a long way to go. She says, 'The grandfathers in the study would say "My dad didn't talk about anything, but I feel like I'm actually OK to talk a bit more about things now, because my son says *everything*". It's that middle ground between not disclosing too much, because I'm still a man, but it's become more acceptable to talk. So again, it's that looking down and saying, my son's doing it that way, and actually, I can do it that way too.'

Yet even 'new' grandfathers like Don, who looks after his grandchildren one or two days a week, don't see the role as central to their sense of themselves in the way that many grandmothers do. He says, 'Being a grandfather and a father is not a fundamental part of the way I identify myself. It's one important part of my identity, but it's not central. It's the standard guy thing, identifying through work rather than family. The emotional investment in parenthood and grandparenthood is just not that big a deal for me. I don't go around thinking, isn't it great to have these grandchildren, even though it is great! Being a grandparent means much more to my wife than it does to me. I'm not saying it doesn't mean a lot to me; it does. Maybe I'm emotionally shallow, but it doesn't awaken in me the feelings it awakens in her.'

Why grandfathers lack confidence

When it comes to grandparenting, grandmothers still represent the gold standard, and that seems so unfair. Grandfathers have been dubbed 'the forgotten men' in the family, because they are generally either ignored in research or compared with grandmothers, rather than being studied in their own right. 'The maternal and expressive nature of grandparenting is presumed to make grandfather a peripheral role', Professor Marc Baranowski concluded. This leads to a general impression that grandfathers fall short in some way, which can't be right. Men feel this as much as anyone else. Mira, whose parents look after her two children at least one day a week, says, 'Dad's always like, "Mum's the one they love, she's the expert". He has no confidence. So although I've always felt totally happy about leaving Lara with him, there was a time when I didn't want to ask him because I knew he'd get worried. But he's getting better. Recently he suggested that maybe he could stay for a couple of hours after Mum went home. We tried it and it worked. That's given him more confidence about looking after Lara by himself.'

Part of the issue could be that grandfathers usually work as a team with their wives or partners, while grandmothers tend to spend more one-to-one time with grandchildren. That automatically puts men in a supportive role; they're the B Team. There are clearly advantages: grandfathers can opt out if they'd rather do something else, their commitment is more flexible. But the disadvantage is that they don't get so many opportunities to grow in confidence, because there's nothing like time alone with a grandchild to make you feel you're up to the task.

Some grandfathers just need a bit of practice and a chance to prove that they're perfectly capable, to themselves as much as to anyone else. But what often happens is that as soon as the baby cries or the toddler kicks off, the grandmother steps in, and of course they calm down more readily in the arms of a confident grandmother than a slightly nervous grandfather. I've been guilty of doing this myself, rather than giving my husband the space to try things his own way.

Men who were hands-on fathers with their own children clearly have a head start. At the other extreme are traditional grandfathers who can't be relied on to babysit. I've met quite a few grandfathers who are perfectly happy with the role of handing out treats from the sidelines but certainly don't want to get their hands dirty.

Molly's father-in-law is a classic example. From time to time he comes down to stay to help with DIY. She says, 'He can't cook for himself so he needs everything doing for him. I find this so bizarre and it's quite difficult, because I have to look after him as well as Maud. They have a lovely relationship, but I couldn't leave them alone together for very long. He could babysit, but I wouldn't feel that comfortable because if Maud was having anything other than a great time I think he'd find it really difficult.'

It's partly that men often say they think babies are boring and find it easier to connect to older children. Perhaps that could also be due to a lack of confidence. Earlier in this chapter, Rosa described how her partner felt sad that he couldn't soothe his baby granddaughter in the way she did. The birth of a grandchild appears to affect men and women in different ways. Research by Australian psychologists Doreen Rosenthal and Susan Moore found that grandfathers tended to be less effusive than grandmothers when describing their feelings. They may have been full of love, but it was rarely mentioned; they were more likely to say it made them feel old. This is echoed by what Don remembers about his granddaughter's birth: 'There is a physical thing with grandmothers. Studies have found that women holding babies experience a rise in oxytocin [sometimes called the "love hormone"]. When we made our first visit to the brand-new baby, my wife really wanted to hold her and she was the happiest person on earth. That doesn't mean anything to me. I hardly held Lara at all when she was a baby. My attachment and devotion begin when they start looking around and responding and laughing at my jokes! But even if I was less central to the grandchildren at the beginning, as time went on and they became more fun and funny and interesting to interact with, my devotion to them grew tremendously. Now they're the light of my life, especially the older one. So while I didn't have the instant bond that my wife felt, I've made up for it since!'

Why single grandfathers miss out

There are too many stories of single grandfathers who don't see enough of their grandchildren. Research confirms that being part of a couple makes grandparents of both sexes more likely to be involved with their grandchildren, particularly grandfathers. Single grandfathers, whether they're divorced or widowed, often drift away from their grandchildren, perhaps because they're used to the woman in their life remembering birthdays and organising family gatherings, so it may not occur to them to do what's needed. The same thing often happens if their son or daughter gets divorced. Paternal grandfathers are particularly vulnerable, while maternal grandparents tend to sustain stronger ties.

Meanwhile, some interesting Finnish research found that divorced grandfathers are less likely to see their grandchildren, particularly if they remarry. It seems that men who find new partners tend to devote their energies to them, often at the expense of grandchildren, so everyone misses out. Tessa's father lives on the west coast of Scotland with his second wife. 'I know that if I don't make an effort to go up there to visit him he's not going to see Isla,' Tessa says. 'It's not like he Zooms or anything. When they do see each other I try and make it an easy reunion. But because he doesn't see her very often, and he's got this big beard and big hair, she doesn't really know who he is.

'Before she was born he had clearly been speaking to some lovely lady in his village who was like, you must go over for the birth. So just after my due date he did this Goliath journey and stayed in a hotel near us. The problem was that I had him calling me every day to see if I'd gone into labour. That was very irritating! If it had been my mum I could have told her to stop calling, but I don't have that kind of relationship with my dad. I also couldn't bring myself to say, why don't you wait to come down when the baby is a couple of weeks old? Because actually it was such a lovely gesture. It showed that he really cared, and that it was a big deal to him. I didn't want to get in the way of that.'

GRANDFATHERS' STRENGTHS

As men get more involved and gender roles continue to blur, the similarities between grandmothers and grandfathers are growing. But grandfathers don't have to be like grandmothers. In fact, it would be a shame to lose sight of the unique strengths and skills that make grandfathers special, and that set them apart. It's not a competition; their different skills and experiences complement each other. My husband enjoys stuff I find boring, like Lego, or nerve-racking, like taking buggies on escalators, while he freaks out when I make a big mess with water or paints or cake mix. If I can't do childcare he steps up, and vice versa. Professor Tarrant says, 'In our research, being "a fixer", mending bikes and so on, were identities that several of the grandads talked about. They'd say, my wife does the domestic things like crafts and baking, and I fix things, and I've taught the grandchildren how to ride a bicycle. It felt quite traditional in terms of gender. But this is still a form of care for the family. It's just different to what women do. It's about providing that whole picture of support.'

Other research has come up with impressive lists of grandfathers' strengths: they play a significant role as listeners and confidants, they pass on skills, hobbies and inspire new interests; they can offer moral and spiritual guidance, reinforce family values and model loving relationships; they can offer positive male role models. Of course, grandmothers can offer most of these things too, but perhaps in a different way. Teenage boys in one study were more likely to nominate their maternal grandfather as the grandparent they got on with best. Grandfathers can help their grandchildren get on in the world, whether it's by giving them driving practice or organising work experience. They tell family stories that connect grandchildren with their roots. This has particular meaning in intercultural families, or in families who have moved away from their homeland. My father-in-law spent the last few years of his life writing books about the family's history for his grandchildren, beautifully illustrated with photographs and letters.

Ada, who looks after her two granddaughters in Buenos Aires one day a week with her husband, is conscious that they have different approaches, and that sometimes her husband's calm vibe and easy-going patience is exactly what's required. She says, 'I am more the worrier, while Horacio takes things more easily. He is just a nice person to be around; he laughs a lot with the two little girls. Our youngest granddaughter had trouble separating from her mother when she went to kindergarten. So at the beginning of the school year my daughter said to my husband, why don't you take the girls and see what happens? He did it every morning, and sometimes he would take 25 minutes to persuade Violeta, but finally she would go in. Then one morning, after four or five days of this, suddenly she just walked in with her backpack and said, "Goodbye, Grandpa". The three teachers who were waiting expectantly started shouting, "You're great, Grandpa! Good for you!" He came home laughing; he was so happy about it.'

It's also been suggested that, as men age, they naturally change in ways that make them better suited to being grandparents: they get more laid-back, basically. Gender differences become less marked as men spend more time in the domestic sphere when they retire. They become more reflective as their focus shifts away from the working world and on to the family, and because they have more time they can be more patient. Women, by contrast, are often moving in the opposite direction, and are looking for fresh opportunities outside the family. Niall says, 'I can see that family becomes more important as you get older, in fact it becomes the biggest part of your life.

Having grandchildren and having stuff going on in your life through them is something you're part of, at a time when you're becoming part of less and less all the time. And it's something that you don't lose, unlike jobs and colleagues and friends who start dying on you.'

Age brings a new perspective on what's important in life, while having more free time makes it easier to be in the moment. 'Becoming a grandfather reminds you that life is short,' says the psychotherapist Phillip Hodson. 'You concentrate on the things that matter. One of the luxuries of being a grandfather is that you can be patient, whether that's allowing your baby grandson to pull your glasses down your nose 37 times without getting cross or answering the very direct questions that four- and five-year-olds ask.'

Grandfathers just want to have fun

The grandfathers I spoke to all agreed that one of the many joys of grandchildren was just being able to have fun with no responsibility, perhaps as an antidote to all the years of dutiful fathering and breadwinning. That's great for kids, because it means grandfathers are good at proper playing, and not so bothered about loading the dishwasher or folding the laundry. 'My role is to be an idiot and just try and have a laugh really,' says Niall. 'I've always done it, especially when the girls were little: they thought jumping on me and assaulting me was the funniest thing ever. My wife doesn't do that at all. She's far more useful to them. She can teach them things and cook and do jigsaws and do patient things with them. I quickly lose interest. I can barely do anything patient, although I'll happily build my share of railway tracks.

'I almost used to wind the girls up too much. When my son got home from work you could see him thinking, I've got to put them to bed in half an hour, while I knew I wasn't going to have to put them to bed. I liked to exploit that situation. Partly because it's great not to have responsibility and to be able to have fun with them.'

Care and concern

Fun without responsibility seems like a big departure from the old-style patriarch who upheld the moral high ground. Nevertheless, most grandfathers feel a strong sense of duty towards individual grandchildren and the family as a whole. They still see themselves upholding the family's values and modelling healthy relationships, good manners and considerate behaviour. They're serious about providing stability and continuity, and are keen to pass on their experience to the next generation. Phillip Hodson calls this 'welfare guidance', and my guess is that men can get away with it more than women, who might well be accused of interfering. He explains, 'It's care and concern. It's about handing on what you've learned from living about living. Grandfathers have an opportunity to offer grandchildren something that I regard as essential, which is another view of the world from the narrow spectrum that their parents impose on them. Their parents' view is often defined by their anxieties for their children, and they are stressed and distracted because they have to earn a living. It's not about undermining parents, but suggesting that there is another way to think about something or cope with it or feel about it. I think the reframing ability that grandfathers have is very important and very nurturing in a way.'

Generally speaking, grandfathers, like grandmothers, see their overarching purpose as supporting the family as a whole, and that's as much through indirect support as through spending time with the grandchildren. Grandfathers are great at practical solutions: stumping up cash in a crisis, painting and decorating, helping with admin. I know it sounds gendered, but then many grandparents were brought up in more biased times, and old habits die hard. Although this kind of practical help is easily dismissed, it can be just as valuable as other forms of care. It's just a different way to be involved with the family and keep the emotional connection with grandchildren going, and that's particularly important for grandfathers who are divorced or widowed. Bill, who is single, says, 'My son asked me to build a fence, so I went and stayed with the family for two weeks. It was really nice to be there for that length of time. It made me realise that even if you see your grandchildren quite often you don't really make the same connection with them that you do when you're actually living with them for a week or two. I also realised how little I knew about my granddaughter, because the family moved away when she was nine months. She's two now, and at that age they're changing so much. It was fascinating to see her, although I'm sure that now, many months on, that connection is fading.'

7

Single Grandparents

There have been some pretty formidable single grandmothers on our screens in the last couple of years, from Kate Winslet's *Mare of Easttown* to Sarah Lancashire in *Happy Valley*.

But otherwise, the particular issues that single grandparents face are generally ignored. That's surprising, because grandparenting alone is much more challenging, both emotionally and practically, than as a couple. And these days, so many grandparents are single; the reality is that most of us will end up on our own at some stage, whether it's through the death of a partner or divorce. Grandmothers are statistically more likely to be widowed than grandfathers, because women are generally younger when they become parents and grandparents than men, and on average they live longer.

Of course, many grandparents were single parents for years before they went on to have grandchildren. They're so used to managing on their own with their children that they think nothing of doing the same with grandchildren. They're not envious of their married counterparts; they see positives as well as negatives. Nevertheless, there are things they do miss. Stella, whose daughter and her wife have a two-year-old, says, 'I do wish there was some old git by my side through this, I'm not going to lie. It would be nice to have the grandfather thing going on as well. But I'm in a privileged position in lots of ways, because I feel like such an important person in my granddaughter's life. I was a single mum for so long that being a single grandparent feels very normal. I think it's quite a good thing, it's certainly more nice than bad. I feel the same about being a single parent, that it was terribly difficult, but it's a privilege too. I'm extremely involved in my daughters' lives as they've got older in a way that I probably wouldn't be if I had another relationship, because it's undiluted. Do they appreciate it? I'm not sure.'

It's rather different for grandparents who are recently widowed, divorced or separated. They not only have to deal with their own heartbreak and grief, but also their adult children's, and perhaps their grandchildren's too, if they're old enough to understand what's going on. The left-behind grandparent suddenly faces a very different future than the one they'd always imagined. They don't just miss their partner, they miss grandparenting, and parenting, as a couple. The birth of a grandchild is a massive consolation, but it can also reignite sadness and regret. For single grandparents it's a reminder that dreams of growing older together and sharing the joys of their children's children have been shattered and that the new reality they face is very different. It brings home what people miss about sharing the ups and downs of family life with a soulmate who loves the grandchildren just as much. Molly's father died when she and her brother were teenagers and she now has a four-year-old daughter. Molly says, 'Sometimes Mum gets upset and says that having a grandchild is yet another part of life that she has to accept is not the way she thought it was going to be when my dad was alive. Every happy family experience has also got this tinge of sadness, and that's very much there with Maud as well. I know Maud reminds my mum of my dad. Having Maud makes me miss my dad too. But while it might be nicer or easier if my mum wasn't being a grandparent on her own, it's also wonderful. Almost every day she says how much joy Maud brings her. My mum's amazing the way she always manages to see the positives.'

Perhaps the saddest loss is the shared history of parenting, which is the sea that couples swim in, from the fearful joy of bringing a new baby home to the memories of nightmare holidays, stroppy teenagers and proud moments at school concerts. Single grandparents don't have someone who remembers that Josh pulls exactly the same bad-guy face as his dad did when he was three. That can be painful, even when people have been on their own for years.

PRACTICAL CHALLENGES

Babysitting solo

For single grandparents, the most obvious challenge is that looking after even one grandchild on your own is much more exhausting than sharing the responsibility with a mate. Of course, many married grandparents babysit the kids on their own: it's common for grandmothers to do the lion's share while grandfathers take a back seat, although for me it's the other way round. But there's still someone to come home to at the end of the day, who can cook dinner, share downtime and talk through the day. Iwona, whose husband died a year before their granddaughter was born, says, 'Looking after a toddler on my own is really, really tiring. I know from married friends who look after grandchildren together that it's very different. One of them can cook lunch while the other is playing, then one can have a rest or do something different for a bit. With me, it's just Evie. Which is a lovely thing in itself, but it is full-on for the whole time.' Formal grandchildcare arrangements are less flexible when there's no one to take turns with or to step into the breach if you're ill or if something else comes up. Single grandparents don't have the back-up that couples take for granted.

There are logistical difficulties too. If the family don't live nearby, it's harder to drop everything when the grandchild or parent is sick or there's some other everyday emergency. On holidays with parents and grandchildren, there's no other adult to help out. Stella's daughter is a two-hour train journey away. She says, 'If I had a partner, one of us could dash up to sort stuff out or cook a meal when Lauren or the baby is ill. But that's all on me, and I'd like to be more useful but I'm working full-time. And when we went on holiday it would have made a big difference if there had been another grown-up around. It was lucky that my younger daughter was there, because she helped with the shopping and cooking. She was brilliant but I was thinking, you're not on holiday. And I was thinking, I'm not on holiday either, nice as it was.'

Single grandparents develop strategies that couples don't need to, so that they don't end up doing three things at once with a crying baby in their arms or a toddler throwing a tantrum. They're good at seeing round corners in a way that couples don't need to. They're experts at manoeuvring a heavy buggy down steps and know how to time the heating of a baby's bottle to perfection. Gabriella says, 'As a single grandparent you have the same problems as a single parent. You have no one to call on and you have to get on with things on your own and work out strategies, which are about keeping the child safe. Like putting the baby on a mat in the bathroom when I need to go to the loo, whereas my daughter asks her partner to look after him.'

More than one grandchild

One grandchild is manageable on your own, but when there's more than one under five it gets much harder. To be honest, I've got no idea how single grandparents do it; for some reason it's more of a challenge than looking after your own children. Careful planning is essential to cope with the children's conflicting demands and abilities. You can't leave the toddler having a nap while you take his big brother to the swings. Outings feel a bit more risky: you can't help thinking about what might go wrong. In some ways that's probably a good thing, because it's best to be prepared, but it's daunting too. There's no one to share the responsibility, no one to take charge of the other child if there's an accident or a tantrum or one of them needs a wee *now*. The responsibility feels weightier than it did with your own children. Situations that would be perfectly manageable with another adult can feel totally unmanageable when there's only one. One recently divorced grandfather described taking his three grandchildren under six out for pancakes. When the toddler had a total meltdown and the four-year-old needed a poo, he threw in the towel, paid the bill, and hurried them out of the cafe as quickly as he could, leaving their food untouched.

It makes life a lot easier if it's possible to look after one child at a time, although for many single grandparents who do childcare that's not an option. That's what Denise decided to do after something happened in the park a few months ago that totally unnerved her. When it was time to go home, her two grandsons, who are seven and five, wouldn't come down from a climbing frame that was out of her reach. 'I tried shouting and cajoling but they refused to move and in the end I started walking away. I was beginning to panic but I just had to cool down. I assumed they would follow me, so I walked slowly, but when I went back a few minutes later they were still refusing to move. Usually I'm very easy-going but when I do go I get furious. I swore never to do it again.'

These days, Denise picks the eldest up from school one day a week and takes his younger brother swimming to give her daughter-in-law a break. Both boys take it in turns to stay the night with her on their own. 'Doing things with them one at a time is a luxury; it's the easiest thing. I have trouble looking after both of them; I can't bear the squabbling. Sometimes the five-year-old doesn't want to leave the next day, and refuses to get into the car. Things like that would be much easier if I had a partner, because he's too heavy for me to carry. Other than that, I never think about being a single grandparent because I don't know any different. I just feel that my daughter-in-law needs another one of me, another grandparent who lives nearby, because she's a full-time mum and they can't afford any childcare. So the burden falls on me to help.'

EMOTIONAL CHALLENGES

Perhaps the hardest thing is having no one to share the joys, responsibilities and exasperations of grandparenthood. There's no one who sees things from the same generational vantage point. There's no one to sound off to about irritations with adult children and their curious notions about child-rearing. It's tough having no one who really understands the unique history of complicated family relationships from the inside, in the way a co-parent does, never mind someone who understands you and your insecurities, and why you get triggered by certain things. Iwona, whose husband died three years ago, says, 'Matt was my best friend. I've got some really close friends I'll say a lot to, but not as much as Matt. And when you lose that it is a big deal.' It's too easy to ruminate over concerns about a grandchild's behaviour, or worries that you said the wrong thing to your son-in-law. There's no sounding board, no one to suggest a different way of looking at the situation. Anxieties too easily escalate and it can be hard to keep a sense of perspective. Friends can be a wonderful network of support, but there are limits to how much you can offload, however empathetic they are, especially if they don't have grandchildren themselves. And it's never a good idea to moan about one adult child to their sister or brother.

People who have been on their own since their children were little, like Gabriella, develop their own ways of coping with the emotional challenges of solo grandparenting. 'My daughter had three rounds of IVF, and it was absolute agony for a long time. It really weighs heavy on the mother in you, because you can't do anything. It's always with you, but I'm good at switching off and I can get on with my work.

I put my own feelings to one side. That's something I learned as a single parent. It's probably not good psychologically, but you just get on with the task in hand and wait for the other stuff to bubble up and then you deal with it when it does.'

In an earlier chapter, grandparents talked about feeling left out of their adult children's family bubble. Some single parents feel this more acutely: it's not just 'them and us', but 'them and *me*'. They miss the solidarity of grandparenting alongside someone who is on the same side of the generation gap. Some single grandmothers talk about being the odd one out when the other set of grandparents in the family are a couple, and suspect that they get asked to do less childcare because they're on their own. One American blogger, who moved thousands of miles to live near her beloved grandchildren, writes about the double insecurity of being a single grandparent in a totally new and unfamiliar place. She feels at a disadvantage with married grandparents and unsure how to behave at events like children's parties: should she stay with the kids or talk to the other parents? She writes, 'You can't help but understand deep down inside that the obstacles you faced as a single parent have now just grown exponentially.'

SINGLE GRANDFATHERS

Traditionally, single grandmothers are drawn into the family, or move closer to them, particularly if they're widowed or divorced. The benefits are mutual: grandmothers help with babysitting and the school pick-up, while their adult kids help with the heavy lifting, and that often increases as they get older and the see-saw of care shifts. It's generally rather different for grandfathers. Grandparents, especially grandfathers, are more likely to be involved with their grandchildren if they're part of a couple, and see less of them if they're single, according to Norwegian research into grandparents across Europe. It seems that grandfathers can lose contact with their grandchildren more by accident than design, and that's so sad. Both generations have good intentions: they want to stay in touch, but in practice things slide through a combination of grandfathers who aren't used to being proactive in making family arrangements, and adult children who are busy and preoccupied. Roni says, 'I'm very lucky in that I see even more of my grandchildren since the divorce, whereas my ex-husband will probably see them much less, because he has a high-powered career and a new partner, and it was invariably me who used to organise our visits. My grandchildren are a wonderful support to me, in fact I don't know what I would do without them.'

Grandmothers understand that staying in touch with families is about much more than just picking up the phone. They know what's required to keep the connection alive, while many grandfathers never got into the habit. It may also be that they're less sure about their role and uncertain about taking the initiative. Gabriella's former partner sees his grandchild every four or five months. 'I do think it's a pity that this lovely grandson hasn't got a grandfather on either side,' she says. 'He's got my ex, but he's only been to see him a couple of times since he was born. It's not going to be a real role.'

What's slightly mysterious is that when Gabriella's daughter was first pregnant, she was absolutely sure that she had lost the baby, which would have been a devastating blow after three rounds of IVF. But Gabriella and her ex-partner, who hadn't spoken for months, both felt the same overwhelming conviction that their daughter was pregnant with a boy. They were right! It's an example of how grandchildren can reignite a connection between partners who have been separated for years and create a new bond between them as grandparents. Seeing the child you had together with the grandchild you share is bound to ignite memories of parenting together, good and bad. Knowing that a grandchild shares your DNA, and has the same dark curls as your ex, is powerful stuff. I recently heard the comedian Sara Pascoe talking about what good friends her divorced parents are now they have grandchildren, which she would have said was unfeasible when she was growing up, and there was no communication between them. Her mum even invited Sara's dad and his wife for Christmas. For some couples this new tolerance and warmth feels good, while others aren't up for any kind of rapprochement. And of course, if either partner has married again, it can create tension in their new relationship.

8

Number One Grandparents? Paternal and Maternal Grandparents

The other day, an old friend asked me if it was normal to feel jealous of her grandson's other grandmother. She said, 'It makes me think there's something really bad inside me to feel like this, because she's a perfectly nice woman and I don't usually think of myself as competitive or jealous. But when I go to pick up the baby she intervenes and gets there first, and if he's crying she picks him up before my daughter does. It's so irritating.'

Of course it's normal! Competitive grandparenting is a thing; it's not that different from competitive parenting, except that it's within the family, the prize is the grandchild's affection, and it's generally unspoken. Knowing that there is another set of grandparents who are just as important to your grandchild is pretty mind-boggling. It's so different from being a parent, when the special relationship with your child is shared with only one other person in the same generation, and that's your partner. There are now two random strangers who have an equal biological connection to *your* grandchild and who love them just as much as you do. Yet you might have nothing in common or not even like them very much.

What's weird is that no one talks about this natural rivalry, although most grandparents I've spoken to admit they feel a pang when they hear the other grandma has been spending a lot of time with their grandchild. It's even more shameful if you feel a tiny burst of joy when your grandchild runs straight up to give you a hug and not the other grandma. The only grandparents who don't get what I'm talking about are either saints or have no competition, because the other grandparents aren't around, don't take much interest, or live on the other side of the world.

It often kicks off with what you're going to be called: Grandpa? Nanny? People don't realise how much they mind until someone else bags the name they want. Niall remembers, 'When we went to the maternity ward to meet the new baby, we bumped into Jessie's parents on their way out. We didn't know them very well then, and they turned to us and said, "We're going to be called Grandad and Nana. What are you going to be called?" We were like Oh, OK . . . It was a *fait accompli*. We weren't annoyed, we just worked around it.'

One set of grandparents can't help feeling hurt if they get to spend less time with the kids, or if they are asked to buy the number three present on the child's birthday list while the other grandparent's gift is the top thrill. A grandchild's innocent remark like 'Grandpa's taking us to Disneyland' makes them wince behind the forced smile. There may be a race to be first at the hospital. I've just heard about a paternal grandmother who was asked to delay meeting the new baby for two weeks while the other grandparents were welcomed on day one, which was incredibly painful. Midwife Freya Mahal, who runs online courses for grandparents, says, 'I've seen sad situations where both sets of grandparents were desperate to see the baby first. In one case there was a massive rift, because the children were like, neither of you are, we're going into our own bubble until you grow up.

The new parents stopped talking to their support network for quite some time because of it.'

Family gatherings can be painful, because children naturally gravitate to the grandparent they know best. One grandmother drove away in tears after her grandson's fourth birthday party because he spent most of the time with the other granny. Geoffrey Greif, Professor at the University of Maryland School of Social Work, who has done extensive research into in-law relationships, says, 'There are so many stories where the paternal grandmother visits and the child goes to the maternal grandmother and that makes the paternal grandmother feel all the more left out. Or the two grandfathers are in the room and the grandson wants to play catch with his maternal grandfather – how's that going to make the paternal grandfather feel?' To be fair, the favoured grandparent may not be doing anything to encourage their grandchild; they may even feel concerned about the other grandparent feeling left out. Or they may not be so kind: some grandparents, like Liz, have been hurt by shameless competitiveness and point-scoring. She says, 'The other grandad does everything he can to get our older grandson to play with him, and he looks so pleased with himself when the little one sits on his knee. I just pretend I don't notice. I'm determined not to let him see how much it irritates me.'

The two sets of grandparents are set up to be rivals from the start. It's taken as read that maternal grandparents are number one, leaving paternal grandparents in no doubt where they stand. 'It's just the way it is,' says Sean. 'Daughters tend to gravitate towards their own family. We look after my daughter's little girl one day a week and take her away for weekends in our caravan. Our son's family live about fifteen minutes' drive away but we only see them every couple of months.' It's rather different in cultures where the son's family hold more sway, when it's the mother's side who lose out. Either way, one set of grandparents invariably comes second, and that's hardly a good grounding for family harmony. Daughter-in-law Steph, who has a stormy relationship with her husband's mother, says, 'I think my mother-in-law always felt she was in competition with my mother, as well as with me. But it's not a competition she was ever going to win.'

According to Professor Greif, paternal grandparents sometimes feel that their son is being 'pulled into the vortex of his in-laws': the whole tribe of siblings, aunts and cousins as well as parents, and their way of doing things. It's not just that they see less of their son and his children than they would like, although that's part of it. Paternal grandparents are often uncomfortably conscious of the other family's influence on the way their grandchildren are being brought up, or where they live (near the maternal grandparents), or the schools they go to. They become painfully sensitive to signs that they are seen as less significant: no photos of them on the wall, being left out of birthday gatherings, holidays with the other grandparents and never them. Fran says, 'My son adores his mother-in-law. They've moved nearer to his wife's parents, so they're much further away from me. The other grandma is totally not like me: she's very family-orientated and homely whereas I've always put my career first. It breaks my heart.'

MATERNAL VERSUS PATERNAL GRANDPARENTS

'I understood, but it hurt me'

As a paternal grandparent myself I'm clearly biased, but the idea that one set of grandparents is second best seems pretty outrageous. It's so out of sync with the way things have moved on with the growing involvement of fathers and the increasingly important role that grandparents play. But some things will never change: new mothers will always be drawn to their own mothers, especially in the first weeks after the birth. It's still mostly mums who organise what the kids do at weekends and in the school holidays and they naturally feel less awkward about asking their own parents for a favour with the kids than their in-laws. An entire study devoted to maternal grandparents' advantage by sociologists at Florida State University confirms what we know from experience, that not only are the middle generation of mothers likely to have closer ties to their own parents than to their parents-in-law, but their husbands tend to go along with this bias. It naturally follows that the grandchildren are likely to have unequal relations with their grandparents. Professor Greif agrees: 'From my research and from talking to friends, paternal grandparents don't have the same access because they have to go through the mother. Broadly speaking, the way society is currently arranged women still give more access to children than do fathers.'

It's useful to hear what adult children, who are caught in the middle, think. Molly explains, 'When my mum comes I don't have to host her. She just gets on with things and knows where everything is. It's more of an occasion when my parents-in-law come. I feel I have to host them, and my partner does more of that than me. We see them every couple of months, so Maud isn't as close to them, not at all. That's why I would definitely say my mum is her number one grandmother. I notice the difference with my brother's kids too. There definitely is a big difference in how my mum feels about helping me and giving me advice and how she feels about doing it for my brother, and I think that's to do with being the paternal grandmother. It's about not knowing how my brother's wife will react. My mum would be worried about saying something that would upset her and she would hate to be silently annoying her. Whereas with me she doesn't have to think about that, because we both know, really. We don't ever surprise each other in that way.'

NUMBER ONE GRANDPARENTS? PATERNAL AND MATERNAL GRANDPARENTS

There's no point fighting the mother-daughter bond. The best solution for paternal grandparents is to accept the difference gracefully, while holding on to the knowledge that they are just as important in their grandchildren's lives. You can't be your daughter-in-law's mum, but you can support her in other ways, by doing what you can to make her life easier, making it clear that she doesn't have to make a special effort, and not overstaying your welcome. That doesn't mean it isn't painful to know that the grandchildren see more of the other grandmother because your daughter-in-law feels more comfortable with her. As Ada says, 'I understood, but it hurt me.' She remembers, 'My daughter-in-law always had a preference for her mother – I noticed that from the very beginning, and I could understand it. Our relationship has never been that close, but it was fine. Things changed after her second baby. She had a very difficult pregnancy; there were times when we didn't know whether she or the baby would make it through. As a result she was naturally very possessive of her baby and she couldn't be separated from her. When I offered to look after the children for a couple of hours she would always say no. Of course I understood because she had gone through so much, but it was still painful.'

Paternal grandparents may be at a further disadvantage if their grandchild's birth was difficult or traumatic, or the new mother has postnatal depression. A vulnerable new mother is naturally drawn even more to her own parents, and that may be at the expense of her husband's parents. According to Dr Reenee Singh, a consultant family psychotherapist and director of the London Intercultural Couples Centre, a traumatic birth can sometimes damage relations with the paternal grandparents. It's tough for them, but they need to be patient, and accept that recovery can take a while. She explains, 'There is something around the trauma of birth that often gets projected on to the in-laws, and they get rejected as a result. It's partly because new parents are so vulnerable. Many of my clients suffer from postnatal depression, and they are not in a state of mind to be able to work collaboratively with the paternal grandparents. They only want their own families to be around. It really takes a long time. And many of my clients think part of the birth trauma they experienced is about intercultural differences. They may feel discriminated against by the hospital system, or even by racism in the extended family. They perhaps don't feel their in-laws were supportive enough, or were able to think about racism and take their side. That's when intercultural couple therapy comes into its own, because part of it is unpacking what happened.'

Maternal grandparents can feel second best too

It isn't always paternal grandparents who feel they come second in the pecking order. There are all sorts of circumstances that can make maternal grandparents feel at a disadvantage. How near they live to the family, their age and health, the number of other grandchildren, even their income, can all level the playing field. If the paternal grandparents look after the kids regularly, it might make the maternal grandparents feel sidelined; if the other grandparents are retired, they'll have more time to spend with their grandchildren; if the paternal grandparents are loaded, they'll be able to take the family on fabulous holidays.

But sometimes it's simply that one set of grandparents are more forceful in assuming a superior role. Some grandparents have no qualms about making demands on their adult children, who for their part find it hard to disappoint their parents' expectations about meeting up every Sunday or going on a big family holiday every summer. This leaves the other, easy-going set of grandparents wishing they had it in them to be more demanding, and perhaps resentful that they can be relied on to be accommodating without making a fuss. Claudette, a maternal grandmother, says, 'When the baby was born the other granny insisted that I stayed with her; I wanted to stay in a hotel but my son-in-law said she would be seriously offended. So I decided to just suck it up, but then I had to do everything that she wanted. She was totally in control. It just wasn't what I expected.'

The sense of rivalry seems to get to grandmothers more than to grandfathers, according to Professor Geoffrey Greif. 'The impression from our research is that grandfathers do not have the other grandparents on their radar to the extent that grandmothers do,' he writes. That's perhaps because they get less tangled up emotionally in the whole business of grandparenting and family relationships, or perhaps they just don't admit to it. Professor Greif's conclusions were echoed by the men I interviewed, like Bill. When we met, he was about to give up his bedroom to the other grandmother when she came over from Colombia to stay in the flat Bill shares with his son and daughter-in-law. 'There was never any question about it, it was just Ana's mother is coming to stay here for a few months when the baby's born,' he says. 'It's definitely a cultural thing. She'll have my room, because there aren't that many other options. I'll probably go away for some of the time. It's fine, the maternal grandparent thing doesn't bother me in the slightest. After that, Ana's mother is not going to have much chance to see her granddaughter, because it's not likely that they'll move to Colombia.'

Paternal grandparents are vulnerable

Feeling second best inevitably makes grandparents insecure about their relationship with their grandchild and their place in the family. Paternal grandparents often feel they have to fight their corner, and they sometimes overcompensate by bending over backwards to help, even if it means taking on too much. When the baby is first born, they may feel so desperate to be as close to the child as the other grandparents that they drop everything whenever they're asked to babysit. At this stage, when both sides are working out their new roles, it can certainly feel like a competition. Deep down, it could be that paternal grandparents have an additional ulterior motive that they're not even aware of themselves. They not only want to help their son, but also hope that if, God forbid, the marriage should ever end, their daughter-in-law will still value her relationship with them. They also want to support the parents as a couple. Irene is upfront about this. Her son was in a casual relationship with his American girlfriend when she got pregnant out of the blue. Their baby daughter is now a year old and they're still together, but Irene says, 'I'm terrified that they'll split up and she'll go back to California with the baby, so I've cut down my hours at work to help her out. My friends say she takes advantage of me, but I don't care. I'll do anything to help make her life here good so that she's more likely to stay. And anyway I love looking after my granddaughter.'

Fear of divorce lies at the heart of paternal grandparents' vulnerability, because they know that if it happens they are likely to see less of their grandchildren. Indeed, any kind of marital discord weakens ties between grandchildren and their paternal grandparents, according to the sociologist Maximiliane Szinovacz. This is another good reason for both sets of grandparents to make an effort to get on. It makes a huge difference to grandchildren's well-being if grandparents can stay on reasonable terms despite the divorce, and do everything they can to keep animosity in the family to a minimum. But that is a big ask, and it's only possible if they have already established a good relationship in happier times. (More on this in chapter 10.)

HOW TO AVOID FEELING SECOND BEST

It's not a competition

The intense involvement of maternal grandparents in the early days doesn't last for ever, so it's wise to take the long view. It takes a while for each set of grandparents to settle into their place in the child's life.

NUMBER ONE GRANDPARENTS? PATERNAL AND MATERNAL GRANDPARENTS

As the grandchild grows, and people explore the kind of grandparent they want to be, the balance can even out. When people get to know each other a bit better, and realise that the other grandparent's style is rather different to their own, they can each carve out their own way of doing things. Rivalry may resurface from time to time, but if both sides can be open-hearted, sensitive and focus above all on the grandchild's interests, things have a chance to settle down. If the overall feeling is mutually warm, both sides can cope with the occasional bum note, so it's worth nurturing the sense that you're sharing rather than competing.

It helps that most sons- and daughters-in-law are keen for their children to have a close relationship with *both* grandparents. Even when they're biased towards their own family, they usually make an effort to be fair. Tessa, whose daughters have three sets of grandparents and step-grandparents, says, 'We see them all equally; my partner and I definitely think about that subconsciously. I feel a responsibility to make sure my mum has a good relationship with the girls, and if my partner wasn't around I would feel the same responsibility to his parents. I'm always careful to tell my mum when we're going to see his family so she doesn't feel left out. I'm conscious that she might, even though she's never said anything.'

As fathers become more hands-on with their children's daily care, they're more likely to want to involve their own parents with their kids in the same way that young mothers do, for the same reason that they feel more at ease with them. If a father is looking after the kids and needs some help, he's more likely to ask his own mum or dad. Fathers now tend to be more in tune with why it's good for their children to be close to both sets of grandparents, and take steps to make it happen. This takes some of the burden away from daughters-in-law, which has to be a good thing, and it's a welcome sign that change is underway. Helen says, 'I admit I was a bit jealous of the other grandmother at first, because she and my daughter-in-law are very close, but these days I only get the occasional pang! It makes a big difference that my son is quite sensitive to the whole paternal grandparent thing, although we've never talked about it. When my husband was helping with the older kids last Friday, he made sure he got to hold the new baby: he knows his dad would love a cuddle, whereas his wife might not have thought of it. And then at my granddaughter's party my son came over to me when both the grandchildren were playing with the other grandma – I felt like he didn't want me to feel left out. When we were clearing up at the end there was a lovely moment when the other grandma and I were both holding hands with our granddaughter, and it just felt really warm.'

Have confidence in your grandparenting

So it seems that these days, paternal grandparents have more agency than they think. Young mum Tessa throws down the gauntlet: 'I don't think there is a number one grandparent for my two-year-old, even though my mum is convinced that she's number one just because she's my mum. In fact, as Isla grows up number one will be whoever she sees the most. I don't think she'll feel closer to anyone other than who she has the best relationship with. It's all to play for!'

No pressure then! My husband's parents were inspiring in this respect. There was no way they were going to be second best. They were proactive in making sure their grandchildren loved going to visit them, by thinking creatively about what they would most like to do and planning heavenly afternoons of drawing and exploring the cupboard full of familiar old toys and dressing-up clothes. They organised summer holidays by the sea with cousins and friends with kids the same age, which made it fun rather than dutiful. They didn't wait to be asked; they took charge and did things on their own terms.

Sometimes circumstances conspire to favour paternal grandparents. When Pam's Japanese daughter-in-law was expecting her second baby,

NUMBER ONE GRANDPARENTS? PATERNAL AND MATERNAL GRANDPARENTS

she asked Pam to stay for six weeks in place of her own mother, who had health issues. Their already good relationship became even closer. 'While as a paternal grandmother I definitely feel in a secondary position, those intense few weeks together cemented my relationship, both with my daughter-in-law, and with my grandsons, who are 9 and 14 now. It's very painful having my grandchildren living so far away, but at least we have that grounding. Maternal grandmothers are traditionally much more closely involved in Japan: when a woman gives birth, her mother comes to stay with the family. I did all the cooking and washing and looked after my five-year-old grandson to give Takami time to bond with her new baby. She mostly stayed in her room for the first week or two; she said she wasn't supposed to go out for a certain number of days.'

My wise friend Mandy, whose sons' children are in their twenties, says the secret is to be confident in yourself as a grandparent. Grandparents who feel secure that their own contribution is special don't feel threatened or competitive. Midwife Freya Mahal agrees: 'It's important that grandparents recognise that the other grandparents may have a very different role. And that they don't feel threatened by it or see it as a competition – it's just different.' Each grandparent's contribution is unique, and they complement each other: there's no need to copy or compare. Just think about your own paternal and maternal grandparents, and your parents and parents-in-law; it's their differences that make them special. If one grandparent's thing is to buy the kids clothes, or take them to the zoo, it's easy to find other ways to show your love. One of my favourite children's books has always been *Katie Morag and the Two Grandmothers*. The two grandmothers start out as rivals, and they're chalk and cheese: Granny Island wears dungarees, drives a tractor and sees her granddaughter every day, while Granny Mainland has the glamour of novelty and nail polish. Katie Morag loves their differences, and of course they end up seeing the good in each other too. There's another great picture book about rival grannies by Baroness Floella Benjamin, called simply *My Two Grannies*, illustrated by Margaret Chamberlain.

Building a relationship with the other grandparents

It obviously makes life easier for everyone in the family if both sets of grandparents get on well. Apart from anything else, grandchildren have super-sensitive antennae for negative vibes, and it's confusing if there's tension in the air when the people they love are in the same room, or there's a sharp intake of breath whenever Grandpa's name comes up. It really helps to get to know the other set of grandparents and understand more about what makes them tick. It's much easier to empathise with people you know than vague figures who loom large in your grandchildren's lives but who exist largely in your imagination, where their flaws can so easily get blown out of all proportion. You're less likely to get a pang when your granddaughter says 'Monday was an exciting day because Granny came!' if you're on good terms with Granny. Besides, the other grandparents offer invaluable insights into your child-in-law and what made them who they are. Bill says, 'It's always helpful to spend time with someone's parents, because it helps you to understand them. Having Ana's mum to stay is a reminder of what a big leap my daughter-in-law has had to make culturally in coming here from Colombia, and how resourceful she is.' The odds of the two sets of in-laws getting on well increase if they get on well with their own children.

The big advantage is that the grandparents can work as a team if necessary. That's absolutely invaluable in a crisis, if a grandchild or parent has to go into hospital, for example. Besides, there's nothing like a calamity to make people unite and overcome their differences. But it can also help with more everyday arrangements like the school pick-up, and happy events like the arrival of a new baby. For Hilary, whose daughter-in-law dropped out of uni when she got pregnant, a lasting friendship grew out of shared concern. Her co-grandparents include two biological grandfathers, two grandmothers and two step-grandmothers, and she sees huge benefits in their varied approaches to grandparenting: 'The other grandmother is a very different kind of mother to me. She's quite mother-earthy and home-schooled her kids. She now lives with a woman who is also very maternal and grandmotherly, and it's rather nice that there's another granny on the scene. It also feels like a real bonus to have this bond for life with Aminah's parents. We work as a team. We keep in touch and we've had a lot of Zoom calls over various things. When my daughter-in-law was pregnant, and everyone was quite worried because she was so young, we used to have regular summit meetings about our anxieties. These days, we see the other grandparents every six weeks or so – they're coming to supper next week. I like them both very much. Although we're from very different backgrounds and cultures, they've got similar interests to us, and they're a similar age. Who knows whether our kids will stay together? Even if they part, we'll still have this grandchild in common. There is something quite solid about that.'

Some families are more open-hearted than others when it comes to welcoming new people into their lives. I know many grandparents who have made a big effort to get to know each other and meet up, with or without the grandchildren; they see each other for dinner and go for walks and even stay with each other. Meeting without the grandchildren is a good idea, because there's less comparing notes and more chance to talk about a whole range of things that have nothing to do with the family. However, I've come across many other grandparents who operate perfectly happily without seeing much of each other, not because there's any bad feeling but because they're too busy or live far apart. There are no rules.

What matters most is to avoid tension or standoffishness, not least because it puts adult children in such a tricky position. They are stuck between a natural bias towards their own parents and a desire to be fair to both, and have to juggle the grandparents' different expectations. Leanne, whose mother-in-law visits a couple of times a year, while her parents live nearby, makes a huge effort to be fair. She says, 'I used to feel, I do this for Mum so I should do exactly the same for my mother-in-law. But I've realised that relationships and dynamics are different, so experiences are different. Now I'm just like, Craig's mum's here, what can we do to make sure she and Alisha have a really nice relationship? And just being conscious of the fact that she's not going to experience things that my mum would.'

Grandparents who feel they need to explain to their son or daughter that something's irritated or upset them should be careful not to bitch about the other grandparents or get too emotional. Their adult child may find their parents-in-law difficult too, but no one should jeopardise such an important relationship by trying to get them on side. The golden rule is, never say anything to your adult child that you wouldn't want your child-in-law to hear. Claudette says, 'I think both my daughter and my son-in-law are beginning to realise how I feel, but he is very protective of his mum and worries about her being on her own. The other day my daughter said, "Mum, I need to know how you feel so that I can do something about it." The problem is, I don't really know what I feel, and it makes me feel quite mean.'

HOW TO GET ON WITH THE OTHER GRANDPARENTS

- Don't compare yourself to the other grandparent; focus instead on your own special relationship with your grandchild.
- If the other grandparent buys lots of treats every time they come, don't try to up the ante or copy them.
- Carve your own niche: each grandparent brings something unique to the table.

- Grandparents' qualities complement each other. It's a bonus for grandchildren to have grandparents with different talents and interests.
- Never forget that the more people a grandchild has who love them, the better.
- If you don't see as much of your son's children as you'd like, suggest he brings the kids over to give your daughter-in-law a break. It's unfair to leave all the arranging to her.
- It hurts if your grandchild rushes straight to the other grandparents at family gatherings. But remember that young children often feel overwhelmed if there are a lot of people around, and they can't be expected to be diplomatic.
- If it feels like the maternal grandparents are taking over in the early weeks of the baby's life, take the long view. Paternal grandparents can come into their own later.
- Get to know the other grandparents without the grandchildren. It's a good idea to go for a walk or an outing together, because it gives everyone something to talk about that has nothing to do with the grandchildren. That makes it less tempting to compare notes, and there's more of a chance to get to know each other not just as grandparents.

9

Longing for a Grandchild: Supporting Your Adult Child Through Fertility Treatment

No one can control when they have grandchildren, or whether they will have them at all. It's in the hands of fate and, to some extent, of your adult children. It's so random, and so unfair. Some people, like my mum, have 13 grandchildren, while others, like my best friend, have none. Some people have grandchildren way before they feel ready, while others are left wishing and hoping as the clock ticks relentlessly by.

The time inevitably comes when you long to know whether your child is planning to have kids, and hope they don't leave it too late. 'It hit me a couple of years ago when I held a colleague's baby at work and this overwhelming feeling came over me: I want to be a grandparent,' Maxine remembers. 'Suddenly I wanted a baby in our family, in our lives. I hadn't felt it ever before, and I thought, I'm ready, when is Abby going to do it?' Meanwhile, your friends' lives are being swallowed up by their grandchildren. You can't help wondering if there's a problem, and worrying that a woman's fertility declines rapidly in her thirties. If your daughter is gay, there's added concern about the hurdles that need to be jumped, not least the cost. If your son is gay, having a baby through surrogacy seems even more daunting. If your daughter doesn't have a partner, you wonder if you dare suggest egg freezing. If your son doesn't have a partner, you wish he'd get a move on. Male infertility is often ignored but it contributes to about half of all fertility problems and affects 7 per cent of the male population.

Do they want children?

Some adult children declare their firm intention not to have kids, leaving grandparents-in-waiting to either accept their decision and move on, or hope that they'll change their minds. Other adult children are less clear, and their parents have no idea what their plans are. Some would-be grandparents are totally brazen about asking. One 29-year-old complained that her mother dropped constant hints and bombarded her with articles about declining fertility rates. She said that her mum's nagging was the best contraception in the world! Others are more cautious. They long to know but don't want to cause upset by asking in case their son or daughter is having problems. They naturally feel nervous of broaching such a delicate and personal subject. Gabriella's daughters both told her that they were having difficulty getting pregnant, but she has no idea what's going on for her son. She says, 'I once asked Max about it and he said, it's up to Heidi, his partner. And then I never asked again. I've no idea whether they're trying or they don't want kids. Heidi is probably talking to her mother about it, and not me, and that's completely how it should be. I don't think I ever put pressure on any of my kids to have children, because it's not my business. But when they were hitting their thirties I did say one thing to all of them that I wanted them to hear from me:

"How you live your life is up to you, but think about having children, because it has been the best thing I've ever done in my life."'

The clock is already ticking for those would-be grandparents who waited until their late thirties and forties to have children themselves. In turn, our adult children are also delaying starting a family: the average age of women having a first baby is now 31. Meanwhile, there's a constant stream of friends and colleagues sharing snaps of their latest grandchild. It takes its toll: one grandmother told me that her oldest friend, who has no immediate prospect of grandchildren, is so heartbroken that she no longer speaks to her. Ellen Glazer, a social worker in Massachusetts who specialises in infertility, has written widely about the impact on grandparents and 'grandparents-in-waiting'. She says, 'Many of us who consider ourselves good people can become mean-spirited when someone else's daughter gets pregnant. Negative thoughts set in when holiday cards arrive with the news of yet another grandchild. As we get older and realise we have precious little time with any future grandchildren, anxiety about if and when it will happen increases.'

Parents have so many unspoken expectations about what their future will look like, and even if they're a bit vague, they often involve grandchildren. Some people don't even question that they will be grandparents one day. I've often heard newly retired people wishing and wondering about grandchildren, because they've got time on their hands to help and are keen to find a new purpose that they had assumed would be grandchildren. Suddenly, there's a gaping hole to fill and the future has to be reassessed, for the time being at least. Gabriella remembers, 'A couple of years ago when both my daughters needed IVF, and I thought I might never be a grandmother, I felt very sad. I could see why having grandchildren would be wonderful, the icing on the cake. But I also thought, my life is very good as it is, and having my children in it is lovely. I could see that life is too short to risk putting happiness on something that doesn't exist.'

It's a bitter blow if it turns out that your adult child needs fertility treatment. You can't help thinking about the hard road that lies ahead. Fertility treatment is much more of a norm than it was in the early days in the late 1970s, when Ellen Glazer went through it herself. Success rates have greatly improved, but it's the agonising uncertainty that's so hard for everyone to deal with. Ellen, who works with infertile couples and single people, says, 'You don't know the outcome, you have to keep going almost on blind faith, not knowing where it will lead. Many people say, if I knew I could have a baby three years from now I could cope with it. But they can't know.'

One in seven heterosexual couples has difficulty conceiving. Fertility treatment is no longer exclusively for medical issues that hamper a successful pregnancy, but helps single women and gay couples too. Men and women going through it these days may well know friends who've experienced it themselves. There's a whole network of support and a plethora of information out there. But for would-be grandparents it's perhaps less familiar territory. They face the double whammy of coping not only with their own longing for a grandchild, but also the rollercoaster of emotions that their adult child is going through.

FERTILITY TREATMENT FOR HETEROSEXUAL COUPLES

The elephant in the room

Some adult children are totally upfront with their parents about problems conceiving, and keep them in the loop about treatment. It's a lot to do with what the relationship was like before the crisis of infertility: some adult children confide in their parents, and feel comfortable about relying on them for support, while others are more private and self-sufficient. There's no right or wrong; families are just different when it comes to emotional frankness, although sons generally seem to be more reticent than daughters. If kids keep things to themselves, parents who suspect something's up are in a delicate position. They don't want to put their foot in it, so they wait for their adult child to bring up the subject. Infertility becomes the elephant in the room. Sometimes it might be worth taking the risk of opening up the conversation to normalise it, and make the couple feel less isolated. The key is to ask a simple question rather than dropping hints, to be sensitive to the response and resist the temptation to probe.

Pam suspected her son and his partner had been having problems for some time when the subject finally came up in casual conversation. She says, 'It's difficult to find the balance between being interested and being nosy, and then looking like you don't care if you don't say anything, which would be awful. A few weeks ago my son happened to mention that if he and his girlfriend had a family it would make more sense for him to stay at home with the child. I immediately tuned in to this and I thought, is he mentioning it because he wants me to react? I had been deliberately not reacting because I didn't want to appear too keen. So later I said I was sorry, but that I didn't want to come across too strong. That opened up the conversation. He said they'd always known getting pregnant would be difficult, but that they didn't want to go down the IVF route. So I mentioned some gay friends who were considering adoption, and he said that's what they might do too.'

Sons need support too

My guess is that daughters are more likely to confide in their mothers about fertility issues than sons, in the same way that they're more comfortable discussing the physical side of pregnancy. After all, it's women's bodies that are most affected by assisted conception. But of course men are deeply affected in other ways, and as the supporting partner they need support themselves. Yet parents of sons are often in the dark until there's a positive pregnancy test or the pregnancy is safely past the twelve-week milestone. It's not surprising if they feel a bit left out of the long run-up to the pregnancy, and wish they could have offered more moral support. They can only imagine what their son's been going through.

Parents naturally feel unsure about how best to support the couple through an ordeal they may have no experience of themselves. They are used to being able to help their adult child and feel desperate that there's so little they can do in a situation that is totally beyond their control. It's natural that most people know a lot more about pregnancy than they do about infertility, until it becomes an issue in their family. Both Gabriella's daughters went through three rounds of IVF. She says, 'I had no idea what was involved, or how brutal IVF was: all the injections to put your body into different states, and then taking the eggs out under anaesthetic. Every time you have to hope, and then there's lots of disappointment. It's brilliant that it can be done, but it was absolute agony.'

How to be supportive

There are different ways to be supportive. The most straightforward is to get a good understanding of what's involved and what your child is going through, both physically and emotionally. The Human Fertilisation & Embryology Authority (HFEA) website is a good place to start. Talking to friends can be helpful, but only up to a point, because anecdotes can bring false hope and passing them on to your son or daughter might understandably annoy them. IVF is available on the NHS, but not all couples are eligible, and waiting lists can be long. So, increasingly, parents help to pay for private fertility treatment if they can, which in the case of IVF can cost around £5000 per cycle in the UK: it's been estimated that as many as one in three couples undergoing IVF get financial help from would-be grandparents. That, at least, gives some sense of control.

Ellen Glazer thinks parents should ask their adult child directly what would be most helpful. 'Some daughters want their parents to go to doctors' appointments and hold their hand, while others don't. Make it clear that you're there for them as much or as little as they want, that they can use you as a sounding board and that you'll support whatever decisions they make. But as well as showing that you're interested, and want to know what's going on, they also need permission to have long gaps off. It's important to allow your child to control the communication. If they feel in control, and that it's OK to be silent sometimes, they are more likely to share.'

When adult children are considering alternative options, their parents need to keep an open mind. That's a big ask if would-be grandparents have reservations about a grandchild who doesn't share their DNA. They are less likely to have a knee-jerk reaction if they've done their own research, read about some real-life examples, and understand the implications of what's being considered. Ellen Glazer, who has two grandchildren through surrogacy, admits that accepting surrogacy was not a stretch for her. She says she was familiar and felt comfortable with it before it ever became personal. Still, she offers this advice for other grandparents whose children may be considering surrogacy, egg or sperm donation, or embryo donation. 'If your child is hesitantly considering a "plan B", he or she will be very sensitive to your reaction. It will mean a lot to them to know they have your support and that you will love and cherish a grandchild regardless of how the child comes into the family.'

Dealing with your own emotions

Perhaps the biggest challenge for parents is dealing with their own feelings so that they don't make things harder for their adult child.

They have to wrestle with all kinds of difficult emotions: helplessness, anger and resentment at the unfairness of it all, and sadness for their child as well as for themselves. It's particularly tough if they have no other grandchildren. They may even blame themselves, if they too struggled with infertility, or think they may have given their daughter the wrong message about pursuing her career. Then there are the highs and lows during treatment: the ecstatic text at 4 a.m. to say the pregnancy test is positive, followed by panic and despair a week later if the blue line fades. At times like this, parents have to contain their own emotion in order to communicate calm and positivity when underneath they're overwhelmed by disappointment and uncertainty. They know that some families go through years of treatment before they have a baby, while others finally have to give up and find a way of moving on and adapt to a very different future than the one they'd long dreamed of.

Gabriella says, 'My eldest daughter, Ruby, involved me all the way through, but she didn't want me to tell anyone else. She was completely private about it. My younger daughter was the opposite: she wanted people to know she was going through IVF, but that's just how she is, she doesn't like secrets. I think Ruby felt a real sense of failure about not being able to get pregnant, which really upset me. She withdrew at times when she was too sad to talk about it. Which is quite right; I'm not her friend, I'm her mum. I told her I was always available, but I also said I understand if you want to go quiet too. I got very good at wording texts and I knew when she didn't want to talk. I'd come up with ideas about nice days out and things to lift the spirits.

'It was like a heaviness in my heart all the time, and all the way through IVF, because you knew there was something your child wanted so much. It's with you 24/7. I'm not really a believer but I was making all these deals with God, like I don't mind not getting that job if Ruby gets pregnant, really childish stuff. But

I felt I had to deal with fate as well as the family. I lived it in parallel, not through her. Because she's my daughter I felt that I carried her emotions as well as mine about wanting her to have a baby. So we were very enmeshed, and we saw each other much more than in the past.'

Treading on eggshells

The last thing that people who are having any kind of medical treatment need is to be constantly asked how things are going. It's yet another fine balance between showing you care and not being intrusive. One daughter got so fed up with her mum's enquiries, however well-intentioned, that she kept her pregnancy a secret for twelve weeks. This can be frustrating and puzzling for parents, especially if they thought they had been given permission to be involved. It doesn't help that the hormonal upheaval of IVF, combined with the vulnerability of infertility, inevitably makes people painfully sensitive and moody. The smallest trigger can make someone switch, and both parents and partners often feel they're treading on eggshells. Gabriella remembers, 'I knew when not to ask. You wait for them to give you news, you don't ring up and ask, because they'll tell you when they're ready. My younger daughter said her emotions were just everywhere; at times she felt quite mad. It must be a nightmare for their partners too. I can't remember either of my daughters being snappy with me, presumably because they were taking it out on the person closest to them.'

Ellen Glazer believes that the best way to avoid the eggshell feeling is to be upfront. 'Walking on eggshells is just the worst feeling. I think you can say something like, "I'm inevitably going to put my foot in it sometimes, because this is such a tender subject, and if I do, please tell me and I'll do my best. I don't want you to be hurt by anything I say, but I would rather our communication was open."'

FERTILITY TREATMENT FOR SAME-SEX COUPLES AND SINGLETONS

Different options

If your child is single or gay, it's natural to worry that you might not have grandchildren at all, or assume that there will be hurdles in the way. Yet the number of same-sex couple families is growing. In 2021 nearly a quarter of lesbian couples and six-and-a-half per cent of gay male couples had children. The number of lesbian couples having fertility treatment in the UK increased by 154 per cent between 2008 and 2018, while one in five adoptions in England in 2023 were by LGBTQ+ parents.

But there are still obstacles. The biggest is cost. Fertility treatment is not available for LGBTQ+ couples on the NHS in most health authorities in the UK, with a handful of exceptions. A single cycle of IUI (intrauterine insemination), the most common treatment for single and gay women, costs around £1000. Since it generally has a third of the success rates for IVF, many women need more than one cycle. A cycle of IVF is more expensive: it costs around £5000. Meanwhile, surrogacy can cost anything between £10,000 and £80,000, depending on the treatment.

Egg freezing is also expensive. Many would-be grandparents wonder whether they should suggest it to daughters before their biological clock starts ticking too loudly. It's growing in popularity for single women who haven't met the right partner yet, and want to put their fertility on hold so that they have a better chance of conceiving when they're older. However, experts advise that egg freezing is not a guarantee of a future pregnancy. They point out that although success rates have risen slightly, the data is still very limited. The procedure is similar to IVF: drugs are taken to promote egg production and then the eggs are collected under anaesthetic. Again, it's not usually available on the NHS and the whole process costs between £7000 and £8000. Success rates decline for women who are over 35 when their eggs are frozen, so there's always that slight panic about leaving it too late. Ellen Glazer thinks parents should bite the bullet: 'Parents could bring the subject up by saying to their daughter, if you wanted to freeze eggs, I could help financially. They could also say that they think it's worth at least visiting the issue and finding out what's involved, because they don't want them to look back with regret. Regret is the most painful of feelings.'

The biological connection with a grandchild

In many cases, including surrogacy, one parent will have a biological connection to the baby, and so will the grandparent, while the other will not. Generally speaking, for gay men it's the partner whose sperm is used. For gay women it's often the partner who gives birth, unless one woman transfers her eggs, or the couple use donated eggs or embryos. Grandparents understandably worry about how they'll respond to a grandchild they have no genetic connection with. After all, one of the first things anyone says about a new baby is 'Who does he look like?' Both the grandparents I spoke to admitted that it's important to them. Natalie says, 'It does matter to me that my granddaughter is my daughter's child. She looks a bit like my daughter Zoe, and she is not going to look like her other mother. If they have another baby they're talking about transferring Jade's eggs into Zoe, because Jade doesn't want to get pregnant and give birth herself.'

Stella agrees. 'With my granddaughter my main feeling was familiarity. Twenty-five years after I'd held either of my babies I picked her up and it was like yesterday. She just felt like one of mine. I suppose I think of her being more my daughter's child than my daughter-in-law's. My lesbian friend who's got two children says the biological thing is bigger, definitely. Having said that, her son's grandparents, her parents-in-law, who were quite prickly when she and her partner first got together, absolutely doted on her son, their grandson. So that's how little biology mattered to them. They were completely like any other grandparents, obsessed, doting, showering with love. And they didn't change when three years later they had a biological grandchild as well.'

I don't want to make too big a deal about the biological connection but equally I don't think it should be brushed under the carpet. It's clearly important for grandparents to understand how the non-biological parent might feel. The comedian Jen Brister's memoir, *The Other Mother*, is full of helpful insights. I also came across a really good article by the novelist Beth Lewis, written five years after her wife gave birth to their daughter. She describes suffering from imposter syndrome for the first year, and said she felt more like an over-enthusiastic aunt than a 'real' mum. It's this kind of insecurity that perhaps makes non-biological mothers try a bit too hard in the early days in a way that new fathers don't feel the need to. Natalie says, 'Jade is brilliant. The only trouble is that she wants to cuddle the baby constantly and picks her up all the time, whereas a man might not do that so much.' Beth Lewis said she felt a lot better when she found out that attention and affection are just as important as DNA in triggering the bonding hormone oxytocin.

Known donor or sperm bank?

Some single women and lesbian couples conceive with a sperm donor they know, who may want to be involved as a father. If they do, it brings another set of grandparents into the mix. People come to different arrangements. Some men want minimal involvement, while others want to see the child as much as one day a week, every other weekend and every other Christmas. This could have an impact on time with grandparents in a way that an anonymous donation through a sperm bank would not. Would-be grandparents often have their own strong views about this, and they may or may not get involved in discussions. I can't help wondering if grandparents who contribute financially to fertility treatment feel they have more of a say. Natalie says, 'Originally Jade and Zoe wanted to use a friend's sperm, but I thought a known donor was a very bad idea and I said so. It's opening Pandora's Box because you never know how involved the donor will want to be, and it's always possible that men might change their mind about that. I talked to Zoe about it, but not with Jade, because she's quite private about it. They went through all the pros and cons, and listened to a lot of podcasts, and they came round eventually.' Stella took a rather different view: 'Lauren and I talked about whether she wanted a known father on the scene, which from talking to my friend I think is preferable, although she found it quite hard because the fathers have a claim. Lauren was absolutely sure she didn't want that so they used a sperm bank. They know the anonymous donor's age, work, education and rough appearance, which was vaguely matched to Megan's colouring, but that's all. When Shannon is 18, she'll be able to contact him – that's part of the deal.'

High-profile gay parents, like Tom Daley and the crime writer Val McDermid, have done a lot to dispel prejudice about same-sex families. But while I was writing this chapter I happened to hear a Radio 4 documentary about lesbian mothers that recalled how different attitudes were, even as recently as the 1990s when my dear friend Reen had a baby on her own. When national treasure Sandi Toksvig came out in 1994, she had to take her three children into hiding, and remembers outraged articles about the impact on her kids and on society in general. Her relationship with her partner didn't survive the strain of such negative media attention. In the 1970s and 1980s, widespread discrimination led to dozens of lesbians losing custody of their children when they got divorced after they came out. Judges reasoned that children might be embarrassed or confused by having lesbian mothers, and were concerned that the father would be left out. One woman said that she had been spat at and her children had been bullied.

It's an important reminder of the view of gay parents that prevailed when the current generation of grandparents were growing up and had young children themselves, and how that might linger as a certain nervousness about same-sex families. After all, same-sex marriage has only been legal since 2014. Gay people immediately become more alert to homophobia when they have children, and painfully sensitive to negative comments about kids who grow up without a dad. But on the whole, attitudes have changed for the better. Stella says, 'There probably is some tiny part of me that thinks how tidy it would be if my daughter was married to a man rather than a woman, but I know I get quite a lot out of the fact that she's not. My daughter and her wife belong to a lesbian mums' group, and there's a whole gang of them, whereas when my friend had children 25 years ago they were the only same-sex family at the school. The hospital were totally fine about it too.'

WHEN FERTILITY TREATMENT IS SUCCESSFUL

When fertility treatment is successful, grandparents and parents may still feel anxious as well as ecstatic. There's no reason why the pregnancy and birth should be more difficult, but it's natural to be on high alert for problems, simply because there is so much at stake. Grandparents need to take the lead from their adult child and be prepared to stand back patiently unless they're needed. Ellen Glazer says, 'I always say, these pregnancies don't just have three trimesters, they also have all these pre-mesters leading up to it. So by the time there's a positive pregnancy test, the couple already feel like they're six months pregnant. It crawls along. It's hard for them to feel they have to report on every single iteration, so it's best for grandparents to say they'll wait until there's some news.'

When the baby finally arrives, new parents who have been through fertility treatment may be reluctant to acknowledge that they're struggling at times. Having longed for a baby so much, they may feel guilty if they're at the end of their tether with sleepless nights and exhaustion. It's clearly helpful if grandparents can be sensitive to this, and offer support when it's needed. Even something as simple as babysitting can make all the difference. Ellen Glazer is reassuring: 'There are going to be moments when your son or daughter wonders why they ever did this, when the baby is driving them crazy. And those moments are going to be fleeting, and it's OK. I always tell couples that infertility doesn't make you a martyr, and you don't have to hold yourself to a different standard. It's liberating if they can admit how they feel, and that they're just like everybody else.'

HOW TO SUPPORT YOUR SON OR DAUGHTER THROUGH FERTILITY TREATMENT

- The best way to be supportive is just by being there and ready to listen, on the other end of the phone.
- You will be better placed to offer support if you have a good grasp of the different options and understand what each cycle of treatment involves. Do your research from reliable sources, like the HFEA or the Fertility Network.
- Remember that sons need support too, even if they don't talk about it.
- Make it clear to your daughter or son that you want to be supportive, but accept that it's up to them how involved they want you to be.
- Don't dismiss the problem by saying it's only a matter of time or advising them to relax. It's important to acknowledge that the problem is real.

- Avoid telling anecdotes about friends of friends' success stories. Each case is individual.
- Respect your adult child's privacy, and whether they want to be open about infertility, or only want certain people to know.
- Let your adult child control the communication. They are more likely to talk about how they're feeling if they know that it's OK to be silent when they want to be.
- Don't expect constant updates. Make it clear that you'd like to be kept in the loop, but wait for them to give you news.
- Keep an open mind. If your child is considering different options, such as egg or sperm donation, or surrogacy, or adoption, let them know that you're OK with it.
- Try to keep your feelings under control: the last thing your adult child needs is to deal with your emotions as well as their own.
- Talk to someone you can trust about what you're going through: you need support too.

10

If Your Child Divorces or Your Own Marriage Ends

An advert caught my eye on the escalator going down to the Elizabeth Line yesterday. It showed a smiling granny with her grandson and the caption, '"Don't let Sam take my grandkids away" . . . Let Amicable help your son with his divorce.' It taps into one of grandparents' biggest fears. They know that if their adult child divorces it will have a huge impact on the grandchildren, and not least on how much they see them. They might even lose contact completely.

It's a fear that too often comes true. Currently, the Office for National Statistics (ONS) estimates that 42 per cent of marriages in England and Wales will end in divorce, and divorce rates peak when couples are in their forties and most likely to have children. But it doesn't matter how commonplace divorce becomes, it's still traumatic for each individual family. Grandparents have to bear multilayered sorrow and anxiety: for their grandchildren, for their adult child, for their relationship with their child-in-law, for the family unit they'd hoped would endure. Douglas, whose daughter Kate got divorced 13 years ago, says, 'It really does hurt, what's happened to Kate. I mean it hurts *us*. I think you feel more for daughters than you do for sons.'

But above all, grandparents, and especially paternal grandparents, worry about the huge impact it will have on their grandchildren. They know only too well that they have no legal rights. Suddenly, all those heartbreaking stories of grandparents being denied access feel uncomfortably close to home; research consistently shows that paternal grandparents have less contact with their grandchildren after divorce. Karen Woodall, a psychotherapist who runs therapeutic circles for grandparents in families who are going through difficult break-ups, says, 'The grandparents I see are in enormous grief. They are terrified that they'll never see their grandchildren again. They haven't done anything to cause the onset of that, and they are totally helpless. That is quite an existential terror for all grandparents, that they may lose such a precious relationship.'

Of course, by 'marriage' I also mean civil partnerships and cohabiting, and by 'divorce' I include separation. In 2021, for the first time ever, more babies in England and Wales were born outside a marriage or a civil partnership than within one. This makes many grandparents extra anxious. If it's your daughter, the burning practical concern is more likely to be the threat to her financial security and home, because mothers with young children are still more likely than fathers to have a lower paid income, and because cohabiting partners have no automatic rights to ownership of each other's property. If it's your son, his rights to custody of his children are likely to be the biggest concern. Parents of gay couples also worry, whether they're married or not. Stella says, 'If my daughter and her wife were to break up it would be more complicated, simply because they're gay. I know gay families who have split down biological lines, and that's heartbreaking. So I desperately need them to be fine. A divorce would throw everything up in the air.'

If grandparents themselves get divorced, it can also have a huge impact on grandchildren. Adult children are deeply affected, and are often desperately unhappy, when their parents' seemingly rock-solid relationship ends, and that can affect how much grandchildren see at least one of their grandparents. I've just read a compelling novel by Roxana Robinson called *Leaving*, an unusually sympathetic portrait of a man who loses his relationship with his daughter and his grandchild when he tries to leave his wife. His daughter is both powerful and unforgiving, as adult children can be when their parents separate. There are added complications if a grandparent introduces a new partner into the family. (More about grandparents' divorce on pages 228–234.)

When an adult child divorces, grandparents should have three top priorities: supporting their grandchild, staying on good terms with their former child-in-law, and supporting their adult child. They are all interlinked: you can't help your grandchild unless you have a workable relationship with both parents, especially the one they live with. Grandparents provide stability and continuity for the whole family during a period of bewildering upheaval and chaos. They babysit, contribute financially and help with housing. It's not uncommon for one parent to move back home for a while, with or without their children. 'Grandparents play a powerful role in supporting the children's long-term psychological welfare,' says Karen Woodall. 'When grandparents really embrace that role I've seen a huge shift in their grandchildren's health and well-being. And there's a corresponding shift in the grandparents, because they know their place in the family, so they relax, they're not traumatised by the fear of loss of their grandchildren.'

SUPPORTING YOUR GRANDCHILD

It's widely recognised that grandparents can make a hugely positive difference to how well grandchildren cope with divorce or separation, both during the immediate crisis and in its aftermath.

Research at London's Institute of Psychiatry and elsewhere found that grandparents are key to young children's adjustment to divorce, and that children of all ages value talking to grandparents about their parents' divorce. Of course, it helps if the relationship is already close. The psychologist Professor Peter Smith says, 'Grandparents can be a real support to grandchildren when their parents separate, not least because they are not directly involved in the acrimony of the divorce. They can be a constant figure in the grandchildren's lives, which is often hugely beneficial. They can also be a confidant, particularly for adolescent grandchildren.'

So how can grandparents support grandchildren whose world has been turned upside down? The best way to find out is to ask grandchildren themselves. Dr Jordan Soliz at the University of Nebraska-Lincoln asked young adults, whose parents had divorced earlier in their lives, to look back on how their grandparents had helped them. They came up with six main kinds of support:

1. Being empathetic and non-judgemental;
2. Providing a stable family context by acting normally and staying positive;
3. Reducing conflict between the separating parents by maintaining a relationship with them both;
4. Talking about the divorce and explaining what happened;
5. Helping the child realise that they can't change the situation;
6. Supporting the parents.

It's not surprising that these young adults placed great value on having an empathetic grandparent, particularly a grandmother, who was there for the grandchildren and made them feel that everything was going to be OK. The young adults in the study also talked about what got in the way of support: a distant relationship and grandparents who were critical or refused to talk about the divorce. Pearl's parents divorced when she was a toddler, and her grandparents provided the reassurance and continuity she and her mum, Kate, desperately needed. They remain a big presence in Pearl's life now that she's a teenager. Kate says, 'My mum has been a constant to my daughter through lots of chaos, and she provided the stability that she needed all the way through. Nothing else was easy in our lives. Not only had her dad gone, we were living in a new area, she was never settled, and it was hard for her. My parents completely protected her and made sure she still saw her father.'

It's been suggested that the unique bond grandparents have with grandchildren, and the grief they share about the divorce, makes them perfectly placed to give them the support they need. The stability and continuity they offer helps grandchildren cope with the emotional upheaval in their lives. Everything changes for grandchildren when their parents live in separate homes, and all the things they took for granted are different. They may move to a different area, change schools, or start living with a step-parent and step-siblings (more on this on p. 223). The grandparents' home itself can provide a familiar, cosy haven, a place where things are just as they've always been, and grandchildren can be themselves. Kate says, 'Pearl feels very secure and relaxed with my mum and dad, she doesn't have to put on a show. If she's in a bad mood, she shows it.' If grandparents are still together as a couple themselves, as Pearl's are, they provide reassurance that relationships can last.

It's quite common for grandchildren to confide in their grandparents, because they're outside any conflict at home and the relationship is less emotionally intense. They may feel able to ask grandparents questions about the divorce that they're nervous of broaching with their parents. An unbiased, straightforward response can help grandchildren make sense of a break-up and accept that their parents aren't going to get back together. Pearl's grandmother

Jean says, 'Pearl is interested to know about what happened with her mum and dad, because of course she doesn't recollect anything. Things gradually filtered through to her in the way kids learn about things. A lot of her friends have a different father. When she comes to stay and we're having a chat, I always give her an opening to see if she wants to go further, and sometimes something will come out. I've always believed in answering the questions she asks and no more.'

Coping with challenging behaviour

Each grandchild has a different experience of divorce, even within the same family. Age, personality, position in the family, and how they get on with their siblings, all play a part. It's important to keep this in mind when one grandchild gets stroppy or sulky. Difficult behaviour is totally understandable, but it's annoying and wearing, and it's hard for grandparents to know how best to deal with it. As one grandmother put it, 'My step-grandchildren's behaviour became impossible when their parents were splitting up. There's no way I could look after them on my own.' Grandparents want to be kind, not cross, when grandchildren are going through a tough time. And because they don't have the authority of parents, it can be harder to hold the line.

But grandparents have a considerable advantage in that they can be more objective than parents, who don't always have the bandwidth to deal with their children's emotions on top of their own. Grandparents are well placed to notice if one child seems withdrawn or anxious, or another goes into parent mode with younger siblings. If a child is getting a bit bossy with the others, Karen Woodall advises grandparents to gently show that they don't need to, because they are there to provide the structure, discipline and routine that's necessary. If grandchildren's behaviour gets challenging or difficult, she advocates an approach called PACE: 'Playfulness, Acceptance, Curiosity and

Empathy'. It was developed by an American psychologist, Dr Dan Hughes, who works with traumatised children, and it features on a number of local authority websites in the UK. Karen Woodall explains how it works: 'You divert the children playfully and with curiosity, rather than any sort of authoritarian approach. It's very simple and it's really useful for grandparents in this position, who need to provide some structure in the grandchildren's lives without being authoritarian.'

Don't dis your grandchild's other parent

One of the most common mistakes that grandparents make is to bad-mouth the other parent when they think their grandchild isn't listening. It puts grandchildren in an impossible position, and sometimes kids imitate what they've heard just to stay in with the adults. Grandchildren need to feel that it's absolutely OK for them to love everybody and that everybody loves them. Dee Holmes, a family counsellor for Relate, says, 'It is difficult for grandparents. They find it so hard not to involve the grandchildren. But for grandchildren it is really tricky when they pick up on the fact that their parents and grandparents don't like each other, because the grandchildren still love all those people the same. They're still their parents and grandparents, and they don't want to have to defend their mum or dad to Granny.'

And in the long term, this kind of outspoken criticism can backfire. As grandchildren get older, they feel more confident about having opinions that are different from their parents' or grandparents'. Pearl was furious with her dad for cutting her grandparents dead when they met by chance. Her mum, Kate, remembers, 'Pearl once said to me, "Dad's always made it clear to me that he's not keen on Grandma and Grandpa." I think it's made Pearl feel pretty angry with her dad and protective towards her grandparents.'

STAYING ON GOOD TERMS WITH YOUR FORMER CHILD-IN-LAW

Grandparents may well want to have nothing more to do with their child-in-law and feel that they already get quite enough support from their own family. They understandably want to focus all their attention on their own adult child and grandchild. But it helps grandchildren if grandparents can stay on reasonable terms with the ex, who may be a former partner but will always be the parent. Paternal grandparents in particular have to stay on good enough terms with their daughter-in-law in order to see their grandchildren. Experts are unanimous about the need for grandparents to remain as neutral as they possibly can, for the grandchildren's sake if nothing else. Children hate conflict. In a study of grandparenting in divorced families at Cardiff University, grandchildren as young as eight remained loyal to both parents and they gave little away when asked about what they did when they spent time with the other parent or grandparent.

The problem is that there's almost an expectation that grandparents will feel alienated from their former child-in-law. Over half the grandparents interviewed in the Cardiff study expressed resentment towards their adult child's former partner. Some seemed angrier and more bitter than the adult child who was actually going through the divorce. Many of these grandparents saw their antagonism as perfectly normal, and felt that it would be strange to be on good terms. Most didn't think about the long-term implications for the relationship.

Bad feelings aren't surprising. Staying impartial might sound sensible in theory, but when the chips are down we all fight our children's corner, even when they're grown up, and especially when they're up against it. That's true even if they initiated the break-up. Family counsellor Dee Holmes says, 'Too often when there's a separation or divorce it becomes about one person being all bad or all wrong. Yes, people do terrible things. But there is a whole story attached to the couple relationship breaking down. Ideally, grandparents should try to be as neutral as they can, and not get caught up in thinking, "My son-in-law is a complete swine, or my daughter-in-law only ever thinks of herself", because that can lead to them colluding with their own child against their ex when it comes to the grandchildren going to the other parent's. If grandparents can maintain a good relationship with both their own adult child and their child's ex-partner, that is only going to benefit the children. Grandparents should be doing their best to ensure that the children are able to ride the storm the best they can.'

How you got on in the past

A great deal depends on how well grandparents and children-in-law got on in the past. Many grandparents see their children-in-law as friends and miss the closeness, while others just put up with each other. If the relationship was cordial it stands a good chance of weathering the storm, when emotions are off the scale and bad feeling runs high. Indeed, one study found that the connection between paternal grandmothers and ex-daughters-in-law continued *only* if the relationship was 'satisfactory and friend-like' before the separation. Even so, all it takes is a well-meant remark that gets taken the wrong way, or a perceived lack of moral support from the grandparents, to create bad feeling. Pam, whose daughter-in-law and grandson have moved back to China, says, 'I'm very fond of my daughter-in-law and she's very fond of us. It has been difficult since the split and although we are still on good terms with her, when I look back on how we used to WhatsApp each other, that closeness has gone, which is a huge sadness to me. She was good for Patrick, she brought him out of himself, and that's another reason I was so sorry they split up. She made a huge sacrifice in moving here to live with him; in England she was like a fish out of water, and that can't have helped their relationship. The Covid pandemic didn't help either, because it meant that her mum couldn't come over and they were so isolated.

'The other grandparents have heard a slightly distorted view of what happened from their daughter. She remembers things in a certain way and some things I know didn't actually happen. But I'm not going to point any fingers. I put myself in the other grandparents' shoes. If you had a daughter on the other side of the world whose husband left her with a small baby, I don't think you'd be very happy, would you?'

It's obviously much harder to be civil if there was not much love lost in the past, particularly if one partner is blamed for triggering the divorce. Douglas and Jean always did their best to get on with their son-in-law, despite their reservations, until the break-up of the marriage changed everything. Douglas says, 'I always worried about Ollie, from the minute I met him. Something in his attitude didn't quite chime with us as parents and grandparents. Let's put it this way: his interests always came first. Jean and I really did work hard at the relationship with him, and to be fair he was never standoffish or anything.' Jean adds, 'When we went to the divorce court with Kate, he blamed us for encouraging her to go through with the divorce. In fact we were just giving her moral support.'

It's not easy to show support for one parent without upsetting the other. You want to help your child-in-law and keep them on side, but that may well put your adult child's nose out of joint because they expect your undivided loyalty. It's an incredibly difficult balancing act, but some grandparents manage to maintain good relations with their child-in-law, even when extreme conflict exists between the couple. It really helps if grandparents can make it clear that the former partner is still part of their family. In some cases, the grandparents' diplomacy even prevents their son being excluded from his children's lives. While Pam's daughter-in-law refuses to speak to Pam's son, Patrick, she still has a good relationship with Pam, even though Pam made it clear from the outset that her son was her priority. 'During one of the many conversations I had with my daughter-in-law I told her that for me Patrick will always come first, because he's my son. Not even my grandson will come before him, because there are other people to look after him. I said, your mother would probably say exactly the same thing. She didn't really react. It sounds harsh but I don't regret saying it because it is absolutely true, and I think most parents would say the same.

'When things originally kicked off between them it was all very emotional and high tension. On one occasion when we got to the flat it was horribly tense, and my daughter-in-law had gone off to walk round the park with the baby. In the end I had to comfort this poor girl and drive her back to our house, while my husband stayed overnight with our son. Then there was another big ding-dong during our last visit recently. Patrick told me afterwards that she had got very annoyed and upset about us arriving before him, although she had said it would be fine. What makes it so difficult is that I can't explain, because if I said I was sorry to have upset her she might be annoyed with Patrick for talking to me about her.'

Take the long-term view

The iciness between former in-laws can thaw in time, however impossible that seems when emotions are so raw. Of course, when this doesn't happen it is incredibly painful for grandparents who see less of their grandchildren than they would like, or who are prevented from seeing them at all (more on this on p. 218). But things can calm down even after the bitterest divorces, like Kate's. Thirteen years on, she says, 'Time is a great healer in in-law relationships. The last time I saw my former mother-in-law she was very chatty, having been so cold and horrible to me at the time of the divorce. In fact, she even embraced me, which I wasn't expecting, and it was a bit awkward to be honest! She was grateful because I had encouraged my daughter to go on holiday with them without her dad when he cancelled at the last minute. I always wanted my daughter to have as much love and involvement as possible from every person in her family.'

MAINTAINING LINKS WITH YOUR FORMER DAUGHTER- OR SON-IN-LAW

- Think of your child's ex-partner as your grandchild's mother or father, not your child's ex.
- Above all, keep a clear vision of what's best for your grandchild at the forefront of your mind.
- One of the easiest ways to maintain the connection is by offering to help with babysitting or by contributing to specific expenses like swimming lessons or school trips.
- Don't wait to be asked: your child-in-law might feel awkward about asking for help, even if you've made it clear that you want to support them.
- Grandparents can't help being biased, but try not to take sides. Grandparents are wise enough to know that there are always two sides to the story when a couple breaks up, even if they're outraged on their own child's behalf.
- Make sure your child-in-law feels that they are still part of the family, by inviting them to gatherings and celebrations.
- When you see the ex with your grandchild, be friendly or at least polite.
- Be clear that while you'll support them, your primary loyalty is to your adult child.

> - When things begin to settle down after the immediate crisis has passed, it should be possible to reduce how much help you give, if that's what you want.
> - If they want nothing to do with you, try to keep some kind of connection going, even if it's just by remembering their birthday (not just your grandchild's).

SUPPORTING YOUR ADULT CHILD

When their marriage breaks down, adult children often need their parents in a way they haven't for years. They may even move back home while they sort themselves out, with or without the grandchildren. Jean and Douglas uprooted themselves from a different part of the country so that they could help their daughter with childcare and could be on hand whenever she needed them. 'It was Kate who needed our support,' Jean remembers. 'Pearl was only eighteen months old when her parents separated; she was too young to understand. Kate suffered a lot. It's very difficult being left on your own with a young baby and trying to work and do everything else at the same time. She's always rung me if she's upset and told me what's going on. We were there for her.'

Grandparents often help compensate for the drop in family income, contribute to divorce costs, mortgages and rent, pay for holidays and buy toys and clothes. They offer advice, which may or may not be taken. They worry about how their adult child is coping with the heartbreak, whether they're eating properly or drinking too much, whether they're lonely or depressed. Pam remembers, 'My son was like a shadow of himself, unrecognisable, he didn't really engage. I was so worried about him that I made a point of making sure he was there every day and telling him, I'm here if you need me. So did his younger brother. I'm very conscious of him being on his own with no one to share things with.'

The natural response is to snap straight back into full-on parent mode. But grandparents need to be sensitive about how hard it can be for adult children to go back to being dependent, even for a short time. While they're grateful, it's uncomfortable, and not great for self-esteem, to be thrust back to being a child after years of leading a totally independent life. One woman said she felt that her parents' support came at a cost, and that she felt obliged to follow their advice. It can tip the balance of the relationship backwards, away from the equality of adulthood.

But during the crisis of family break-up, distracted parents need all the help they can get to keep family life on an even keel. Karen Woodall says, 'The experience of separation can create gaps in healthy parenting, as parents become more focused on their own emotional and psychological experience. Children can shift from being responsibilities that parents take very seriously to become weapons of war.' Grandparents can help to fill those temporary gaps not only by being there for their grandchildren, but also by supporting the parents. There was a period a few years ago when Bill had to focus his attention on his stepson Gus, whose relationship with his partner was slowly and painfully breaking down. 'It was a pretty miserable time,' Bill remembers. 'I wasn't able to do much for the grandchildren, because they were traumatised and very difficult. I did what I could to help. When things got really bad, my stepson used to ring me late at night and ask if I could come over. When I arrived there'd be a lot of shouting, and Gus and his partner would be having a big stand-up row. I would try to separate them so that Gus could deal with the kids and quieten them down. I'd spend time with his wife, who would often be drunk and very angry. Basically, I just let her talk.

'I was aware that whatever I did could never be enough. It was really upsetting to watch Gus being broken down; I thought he would never have the will or the energy to leave. But I couldn't advise him; it needed him to act, and eventually he did. He took the children to live near his own biological father. I felt he didn't need me so much after that. Things are definitely better for him and the kids now.'

Divorce is rarely a civilised 'uncoupling'. In most cases it's one partner who wants to end the relationship, leaving the other heartbroken. But it's often forgotten that divorce is painful for both sides, including the person who wants to end it. Whether your child is the leaver or the one being left, the key is to avoid driving a bigger wedge between the couple. That means listening, allowing them to vent, and not making comments or being judgemental. It's totally unhelpful to say 'I never understood what you saw in her' or 'I told you so'. The last thing your adult child needs is to question their own judgement.

Grandparents should also do their best to keep their own feelings out of the mix. Karen Woodall says, 'You need to be ready to be Mum or Dad when your adult child comes through the door, and not become too emotionally involved. If you tangle your own feelings with theirs you lose your capacity to provide wise guidance, because you are blurring the boundaries. If your child caused the split and you disapprove, you might tell them that what's going on is not something you approve of, but you will always try to find a way to support them. It's about giving your adult child the opportunity to slow down, reflect and make decisions with forethought rather than rushing into things.'

Part and parcel of this is to pay attention to your own physical and emotional health, which may well flounder: one grandmother I know ended up in hospital with suspected heart problems during her daughter's divorce, and it was put down to stress. So it's really important to find ways to manage your own stress, and to make time for the things you usually rely on to keep you on an even keel. Grandparents need support too: talk to a wise friend who won't gossip, or a therapist.

If your son or daughter triggered the break-up

Parents of the partner who triggered the break-up are likely to feel a whole range of conflicting emotions. However upset they are by their adult child's behaviour, they still worry about how they're coping and want to be there for them. They agonise about their adult child's relationship with his or her children. And they face the disapproval of the other grandparents, while at the same time empathising with their adult child and sticking by them. Pam says, 'It's bloody to be the parent of the child who instigated the split. My daughter-in-law, who I'm very fond of, was heartbroken. It was a harrowing time. I said to Patrick, "You're going to get a lot of flak for splitting up with your wife when she's just had a baby, it won't reflect well on you." Looking back, I think maybe that was too harsh to say to him, although I still think it's true.

'When our grandson was a year old, I flew out to Nanjing with Patrick for his birthday. My husband wouldn't go because he couldn't face the family. I thought, I'm not having Patrick going on his own, he needs support. So I went with him, and he did need it. We had a meeting with Patrick's father-in-law and brother-in-law, who said how upset they were that Patrick wanted to break the vows he had made, but they acknowledged that our family is important to their grandson and said that we would always be welcome. It's reassuring to have our daughter-in-law's family on side, because if she ever changes her mind about us, her parents would probably say that the child needs his father's family, because that is important in China.'

Long-term support

In the years after a divorce there are bound to be peaks of pain and unhappiness for the adult child, particularly when grandchildren go away for weekends and holidays with the other parent. It's even more painful if there's a new step-parent on the scene. Grandparents' support continues to be invaluable, as long as they are careful not to take sides or collude with their adult child against the other parent. They can help simply by acknowledging that it's tough, and letting their adult child know they're thinking about them, with a call, or a treat, or by taking them somewhere fabulous. Ryan Lowe, a child psychotherapist, says, 'This is a good example of where grandparents can definitely help their adult children because they are a little bit further out of the situation. They will have the same jealousies as a parent when they see their grandchild go off to some other woman's or man's house, but it won't be quite as acute. That's a good position, because they can understand the feelings without being quite as consumed by them as their adult child is.'

For sons who don't have custody of the kids, grandparents' support can be a real blessing when the grandchild comes to stay. They could be on hand to help out over the weekend, or pop in for a couple of hours. But grandparents need to be aware that their son also needs to have time on his own with his children. The chances are that fathers won't want their parents around every weekend the child visits them, and however grateful they are for their help they may feel that grandparents are eating into their limited time together. That's another good reason to maintain friendly links with your daughter-in-law, so that you don't always have to go through your son to see your grandchildren.

SUPPORTING YOUR ADULT CHILD THROUGH DIVORCE

- Put your own feelings to one side. Your role is to be objective, consistent and calm.
- Talk to a good friend who won't gossip or judge.
- Don't collude with your adult child against their ex. Resist joining in when they're having a good old bitch.

- Your grandchild needs to know that their other parent is respected in the family. Never bad-mouth them, and always ask how their mum or dad is doing.
- Come up with ways to support your adult child when the children go to stay with the other parent. It will be extra tough if there's a new partner on the scene.
- Don't try to come up with instant solutions or offer advice unless it's asked for. Adult children need space to work things out for themselves.
- Focus on practical ways to help, such as babysitting, or contributing to the first few months of a new place to rent. You could also ask if it would be helpful to be around when the children come for the weekend.
- Don't neglect your own health and well-being. It's impossible to stay grounded and supportive if you don't take time out to nurture yourself.

HOW GRANDPARENTS CAN MAKE THE BREAK-UP MORE DIFFICULT

Grandparents sometimes make the break-up more difficult for the whole family if they get so caught up emotionally that they stoke bad feeling, intentionally or not. Years of court work with divorcing families have taught Karen Woodall that it can be totally counterproductive, and grandparents even risk losing contact with their grandchild. She explains, 'Grandparents can be very positive but also very negative figures during the crisis of separation. What I tend to see going wrong with grandparents is that they become over-emotional and reactive, and overly invested in fixing things. Their terror of losing their grandchildren, or of having that relationship manipulated or changed in some way, can create a fixation on trying to manage the parents' relationship. Maternal grandparents are often very angry with the father and want to build walls around the grandchildren. They've stepped in front of their daughter as defenders and champions: "You're not coming near her again" kind of thing. I work with grandparents to step back to see how that affects the way their grandchildren see them, and how it puts them in the firing line for losing the relationship with their grandchildren further down the line if they are eventually seen as the cause of conflict.'

When Kate left her husband, the wrangling with his parents nearly culminated in a legal tug of war over her one-year-old daughter. Her parents had no previous experience of divorce in their family, and the bitterness came as a shock. Her mum, Jean, remembers, 'The other grandmother sent me a letter that really upset me. She blamed Kate for the break-up when it was her son who had the affair. Kate persuaded me not to reply, but I kept the letter.' Kate adds, 'If there is a way of *not* behaving well as a grandparent in that situation, I was definitely on the receiving end of it. I felt as if my life was falling apart; every day I found out something new about my husband's affairs. His parents made things worse, even though in the first few days they seemed relieved when I told them that I would always want to be friends with Ollie. After that my mother-in-law went on the defensive, which was a big mistake. She became very tribal and quite hostile. And because I started divorce proceedings very quickly, and she didn't want me to, she became quite threatening and said she was going to the European Court for grandparents' rights. That was a bit weird because I would *never* have stopped them from seeing their granddaughter.

'Communication broke down quickly until we had a very difficult meeting with his parents and my parents. By that stage I had zero compassion and empathy for them, because I was so shocked by his mother's reaction. It felt very cold to me. I had felt that we were close; I had made a big effort with them and I had built up a relationship with his whole family. But only my husband's dad showed any emotion. He sat quietly crying through the entire thing. I felt like my mother-in-law hated me, and at that point the hurt turns to anger and you just have to go, "I don't want you in my life anymore". But the whole way through I kept in mind that I loved my daughter more than I hated them.'

GRANDPARENTS NEED TO FACE THEIR OWN FEELINGS

To be genuinely supportive, grandparents need to deal with their own response to the break-up: their grief, sadness, anger, regret, and above all the fear that they might lose contact with their grandchildren. In the heat of the crisis, they may feel too overwhelmed to pay much attention to how they feel. Their natural instinct is to push their own upset to one side because it seems secondary. But they will be better equipped to look after the family if they can acknowledge and deal with their own emotions off-stage, by talking to their friends or their partner or even a counsellor. They need to be as neutral as they can to counteract the emotional turmoil that both their adult child and their grandchildren are going through. Karen Woodall says, 'It's important that grandparents think deeply about their own reaction because their adult child's divorce will trigger all sorts of feelings in them: of sadness, regret, maybe even jubilation. The grandparent can inadvertently show the grandchild what they really feel about the divorce and that can affect them greatly. So first of all it's important that the grandparent reflects on their own values, and what divorce means in their lives. If a grandparent has previous experience of traumatic divorces, or if they have seen poor outcomes where grandchildren have become estranged, that is going to rock their psychological world.'

Some grandparents beat themselves up for not doing more to support the marriage before it was too late or doing something that might have pre-empted the split. If they blame themselves for not realising how much the couple were struggling, it can exacerbate their grief and anger. But the truth is that adult children often keep their relationship problems from their parents, not because they're secret, but because they just don't discuss emotional stuff with them. Some families are more open in this way than others, and daughters are often more open than sons. There are many other reasons why adult children may put off telling their parents the bad news until they really have to. They may fear their parents' disappointment and upset, or worry about being judged. They may also feel they can't cope with their parents' feelings on top of their own.

If their son or daughter ended the marriage, as Pam's son did, they may question whether they contributed in some way, and even have doubts about the way they brought them up. Pam says, 'When your son and his wife separate when their baby is only tiny you do wonder if you could have done more. But it's a difficult line to walk between how much you get involved and how much you leave them as a family to bond. There's such emphasis nowadays on bonding as a family. And when the baby was born and Patrick was on paternity leave they seemed perfectly OK. My son did everything, everything. They were sleeping in the same bed, it was just a normal family. I went to stay a few times, but it's quite difficult when there are three of you. Looking back I think I should have done more for them after they had separated, and my daughter-in-law still seemed hopeful that they might get back together. We did try to say to Patrick, just wait, things can change, you may feel differently. You're not always going to be passionately in love but you will have the baby and maybe that will bind you. But he just said he didn't love his wife anymore.'

WHEN YOUR SON DIVORCES: PATERNAL GRANDPARENTS

Paternal grandparents in particular dread divorce, because they know that it could mean losing contact with their grandchildren. When a family breaks up, most grandchildren live with their mother, although in some countries, such as Finland, it's more common for children to divide their time between their parents' households. There are other obvious reasons why paternal grandparents see less of their grandchildren. Generally speaking, women are still more disadvantaged by divorce than men, both financially and socially, and often have to turn to their own parents for help with money and childcare. Anna Tarrant, Professor of Sociology at the University of Lincoln, says, 'Paternal grandparents are definitely more vulnerable to losing time with their grandchildren when there is a divorce. The mother often has a lot of sway over whether the grandparents can see the grandchild. If the divorce is acrimonious or the relationship with the father is problematic then there's often less reason why the mother would stay in touch. Paternal grandparents have to do more work to maintain the relationship with the grandchildren.'

What many families forget is that paternal grandparents can be just as important in helping grandchildren cope. Studies have shown that staying in contact with paternal grandparents is good for grandchildren's mental health and behavioural adjustment; unsurprisingly, it's good for grandparents too. But they do have to make more effort than maternal grandparents, particularly with their former daughter-in-law. Some paternal grandparents bend over backwards to help as a way of compensating for their own vulnerable position and because they feel guilty if their son initiated the split and left the mother struggling on her own with young children. The delicate task of negotiating usually falls to grandmothers, with their experience and understanding of tricky family relationships. It's grandmothers who get why it's important to include their daughter-in-law as well as their grandchild in family gatherings, so that she still feels part of the paternal tribe. In turn, this will hopefully mean that paternal grandparents get invited to sports days and birthdays. This matters to grandchildren. It's so reassuring to see their grandparents being friendly to both their parents at these occasions.

The tendency for grandchildren to be absorbed by the maternal side of the family is not just sad for paternal grandparents. In the long term, grandchildren may suffer if they don't spend time with both sides of the family, according to experts like Karen Woodall. She explains, 'If the maternal grandparents are heavily involved that creates a gravitational pull to their side of the family that can really unbalance things. My research indicates that over time this appears to unbalance the child's internal sense of self. When there is a very powerful psychological identification with the maternal family, the other self that relates to the paternal family is undeveloped. That can cause all sorts of difficulties as children grow up, particularly in relationships. There are parts of the self that are undeveloped and felt as loss and regret.'

ESTRANGEMENT

'It's physical: I just long to give him a hug'

It's estimated that one million grandparents in the UK have no contact with their grandchildren, and inevitably paternal grandparents are most at risk. Too often it is the tragic result of a bitter break-up. But divorce is not the only cause. A survey of Gransnet members found that common reasons also included personality clashes, frequent rows and disagreements, and their daughter- or son-in-law not approving of them. Websites that support grandparents who are denied contact tell heart-wrenching personal stories. Grandparents naturally worry that their grandchildren might think their grandparents don't want to see them or don't love them.

It seems so harsh that grandparents, who are so important in their grandchildren's lives, have no legal rights. In the UK they can apply for a contact order under the 1989 Children Act, but it can be a costly process. Besides, even if a contact order is granted it can be difficult to enforce; grandparents' support groups report that parents who break them rarely face consequences. But the real risk is of creating more bad feeling, and many grandparents give up because of this, and because they worry about the emotional toll on their grandchild. Karen Woodall, who was an expert court witness for 15 years, says, 'A small number of grandparents go to court if there are very determined parents or step-parents who are trying to oust them, but it's not common. It always makes me feel sad, because even when grandparents get a court order you can't stop the dynamic that created the need to apply for it in the first place.'

When Bill's daughter-in-law announced that she was moving to the US with his 12-year-old granddaughter seven years ago, it was a terrible blow. Bill's son Kai had been the main carer, and grandfather and granddaughter had always been close. She's 18 now and has chosen to move back to the UK, but it's still raw. Bill remembers, 'We had some discussions about Kai having a legal right to say that his daughter should not be taken out of the country, although he wasn't married to her mother. But in the end Kai decided that it would cause more problems, and obviously I supported him in that decision. I remember seeing him very distressed. He'd been his daughter's main carer for years, and it was really difficult for him. I understood what he was going through, but there was nothing I could do. While it's very hard for the grandparent in that situation, it's obviously not as hard as it is for the parent. I tried to make the most of my granddaughter living on the other side of the world. Kai managed to hang on to his relationship with her because of the wonders of modern technology, but I lost a lot of contact with her. It seemed such a shame to take her away from her family.'

Paternal grandparents like Bill are more vulnerable than maternal grandparents. It's estimated that one in eight divorced or separated fathers lose contact with their children, and so the chances are that the paternal grandparents will too. For grandparents who have built a close relationship with their grandchildren, it's tragic: one grandparent said it was like a bereavement. Research into the impact of separation on grandparents backs this up: one study found that 'losing contact with grandchildren was related to pronounced, long-lasting grief, poorer emotional and physical health, and reduced quality of life in grandparents, especially if the loss was through family conflict or divorce.' Pam, who is one of the most resilient women I've met, agrees that it was like grief when her former daughter-in-law took her baby grandson back to live in China. 'I was quite badly affected. I think I really was grieving, for the loss of my grandson and the failure of my son's marriage. I was genuinely depressed, not to the extent of needing medication, but it was certainly much more than feeling a bit down. Everything was just too much of a bother, and I got quite withdrawn. I found it quite difficult to get out of that frame of mind and pull myself up.'

For Pam, like Bill and indeed any grandparent whose child divorces, it was a double grief, for both the loss of her grandson, and for the devastating impact on her son. Now three, her grandson still lives with his mum and his other grandparents on the other side of the world. Pam says, 'I miss my grandson desperately. It's a physical thing, I just long to give him a hug. And I worry about him growing up in a three-adult household with no siblings. But what's more heartbreaking than me not seeing my grandson – I shall get wobbly now – is my son not being with him. That's way more painful. When Patrick thought of moving to China to be closer to his son, although I was upset, I thought it was a good idea as Patrick would see more of his son. But it never happened because his ex-wife wasn't keen on the idea.'

Divorce often leads to families moving to a different area, and if one side isn't that bothered about keeping up the connection, or actively resists staying in contact, the other side has to work hard to maintain it. If the family moves to the other side of the world, as Pam's daughter-in-law did, it's a heartbreaking emotional and logistical nightmare, as well as beyond the reach of many families financially. Pam describes the first time she saw her grandson after the divorce: 'Yuanyun didn't know his dad or me. It was a bit like those shared access meetings where you go somewhere neutral and the parent hands over the child. My daughter-in-law refused to speak to my son, but she did speak to me. In fact she was very good in that once she could see that Yuanyun was all right, she just left him with us. We met her every day at about ten and kept him until six. The most difficult thing is that he doesn't speak English, so you're just mouthing like a goldfish, basically.'

How to cope with estrangement

Grandparents find all kinds of ways to cope with not seeing their grandchildren. They send letters and birthday presents, although some parents don't even allow that. They keep a diary or compile a box or scrapbook of memories that they hope their grandchild will see when they're older, and realise how much they were loved. Or they set up a savings account in their grandchild's name and top it up regularly. These are all ways to keep the grandchild in mind, and to support them at a distance. Another is to send regular packages of things your grandchild enjoys: a book to read, a toy or game, a T-shirt that they might like, and so on. And always with a little card that says, 'I'm thinking about you'. Because the major thing for grandchildren is to know that they are being held in mind by their grandparents.

This is a great idea for all grandparents who, for whatever reason, don't see their grandchildren as often as they'd like to.

Of course, if you haven't seen your grandchild for a long time, it's really difficult to choose presents they'll like. Interests and passions rollercoaster as they get older, and you have no idea whether they're still obsessed with dinosaurs or Manchester United, or whether their favourite colour is pink or green. One way to tune in, and to feel connected, is to learn about the different stages of child development, and how they constantly change. Karen Woodall, who works with grandparents who can't see their grandchildren, suggests that all grandparents should become 'psychologically minded' so that they can understand their grandchild's developmental processes, to make it easier to relate to them, whether or not they see them regularly. She also recommends being creative with whichever social media platform a teenage grandchild uses. A WhatsApp group for the grandparents and grandchildren is ideal, unless it causes friction with the parents. She says, 'It's really important for grandparents who don't see their grandchildren that there is a public place where they can post thoughts and memories and happy pictures and cartoons, a place which signals security, continuity and permanence to the grandchild. Always do it in a fun way. As the grandchild gets older they know it's there and know how to contact the grandparent.'

Finally, while grandparents need to feel they are doing everything they can to repair relationships and will always hold their grandchild close to their heart, it's equally important to come to terms with the reality that is so different from their hopes and dreams. Counselling and therapy can help; so can genuinely empathetic friends who won't go on about their own grandchildren. Pam says therapy helped up to a point: 'I wept buckets. But after a few sessions I felt we were just going round in circles so I stopped. I just thought, I've got to not feel sorry for myself. This isn't helping. I thought, that's just the way it is, so just keep busy, do lots of volunteering and concentrate on the dog! I remembered how resilient my mother was when things got really tough. The last thing I want is people feeling sorry for me because I'm not a granny – well, I am a granny, it's just that my grandchildren are not close by.'

BECOMING A STEP-GRANDPARENT

Supporting your grandchild in their new family

Many grandchildren face another huge change: sharing their lives with a new step-parent and perhaps new step-siblings too. It may involve moving to a new house, and stepping into their stepfamily's territory, or relative strangers invading their home environment. All the things children usually take for granted are different: the smells, the routines, the boundaries. There's an assumption that kids just muck along together, but they need support and understanding to get through what is a massive adjustment for any child, whatever their age. They're not only dealing with the absence of one parent, but also getting to know a new step-parent, and it doesn't happen overnight.

Meanwhile, the grandparent has to make their own parallel adjustment to becoming a step-grandparent, and in some situations that's easier than others. Grandparents want to treat all their grandchildren fairly and support the new family, but they're navigating uncharted waters. At the same time, they are building their own new relationship with their grandchildren's new stepfather or stepmother, while hopefully maintaining a good connection with the ex. Keeping both sides happy without upsetting the other can be a difficult balancing act, and it's even more complicated if your grandchildren don't live with your adult child.

In Karen Woodall's experience, grandparents can make a huge difference to how well their grandchildren cope with becoming part of a new stepfamily, particularly during the early days. 'The grandparents' home offers respite from the constant need to adjust, and allows the grandchild to recover some of the settled ways of being that they are very much in need of. When parents move in with a new partner, grandparents can be on standby to provide that respite. They don't have to do anything in particular; they just have to be there. To put it simply, grandparents can provide familiarity in an uncertain world, and regular stays can allow the child to make adjustments over time.'

Grandparents can also play a really important role in making the new members of the family, both children and step-parent, feel welcome and loved, and part of the extended network of support. They can help the whole family create their own new memories and traditions that help to bind them as an enduring unit. The obvious way to do this is by getting everyone together, not just at Christmas and birthdays, but at more everyday family gatherings like barbecues or Sunday lunch. Teenage step-grandchildren might have better things to do, but it's important to keep inviting them and giving them the opportunity to feel part of the extended family.

If ex-partners can be included, that can also help grandchildren to adjust. When the other parent is not present, it's a golden principle that they should be respected and spoken about kindly. Grandparents should never feel awkward about asking the grandchildren how their mum or dad is in front of their step-parents; it doesn't need to be hidden or private. It's important for everyone in the family, including the new partner, to know that the other parent is still valued. Yet many grandparents don't think twice about making unkind remarks about the other parent and their family in front of their grandchild, and that's unfortunate. They may assume that the child is preoccupied or doesn't understand, but even young children read tiny clues from the familiar adults in their lives. Brigid remembers how painful it was for her teenage stepson when his grandmother was rude about his mum at family get-togethers: 'Logan would say something and his gran would say "Is that what your nutty mum or one of her nutty friends said?" Or if his mum FaceTimed him when we were on holiday together, his gran could not hide her hostility. It was really bad grandparenting.'

Biological and step-grandchildren

I've always assumed that grandparents ought to treat biological and step-grandchildren the same, and wondered how on earth they could manage it. Surely grandparents can't help being biased? 'Some people have more of a capacity to expand their family and the people that they love than others, and it's definitely supportive if they can. But you can't make it happen,' says Ryan Lowe, a child and adolescent psychotherapist. The step-grandparents I've spoken to all do their best to be scrupulously fair, while acknowledging the different relationship with a grandchild who shares their DNA. Jean has three step-grandsons, and she was thrilled that they all made a big effort to come to her 60th wedding anniversary celebrations. She sees her eldest step-grandson, Sam, the most. 'When Sam first called me Grandma, it made me feel very emotional,' Jean says. 'Having a step-grandchild is different, but I don't think any of our grandchildren would be aware of that. I've always treated them the same at Christmas and on birthdays and I always sign cards "Grandma and Grandpa". Sam is 16 now. We talk to him on Zoom and he's always been happy to come and stay with Kate and Pearl.'

Being fair doesn't mean treating everyone exactly the same. It's fine for grandparents to take their grandchildren on outings, and have them to stay, without their step-siblings. Step-grandchildren also have the love and support of their own grandparents, after all. Karen Woodall says, 'I always say to grandparents, honour your biological grandchildren and honour your step-grandchildren. But be aware of the difference, because your grandchildren feel it keenly. People assume that blended families should be blended all the time. That's an absolute denial of reality, and grandchildren will struggle against that. Yes, you will have some times when all the grandchildren in the family spend time with grandparents. But children also need time with their biological family, particularly in the early stages of separation. Biological family ties are very different to stepfamily ties, because attachment is in our bodies, our bones and our brains. The idea that if you just stick kids together it will all wash out doesn't work. I ask children a lot about this in my work, and they say that their step-sibling feels different to their true sibling.'

There are many different routes to becoming a step-grandparent. Some grandparents have been step-parents themselves for years, and becoming a step-grandparent is the natural next step. There's not the same radical adjustment that grandparents whose adult children divorce and remarry have to make. Grandparents who get divorced themselves may also become step-grandparents to their new partner's grandchildren. Some step-parents don't have children of their own and may struggle to work out where they fit in the family, although they often make brilliant grandparents. Extra sensitivity is required if only one partner is a step-grandparent, when both sides need to be open to the other's perspective, and be prepared to compromise. The step-grandparents I've spoken to tend to be more objective, and less indulgent, than the biological grandparent, and they're more likely to get prickly about too many babysitting requests.

Whatever the circumstances, being a step-grandparent is always complicated. Karen Woodall's personal experience with her biological grandchild and two step-grandchildren shows that the best way through the minefield is to be straightforward. 'I spend time with my husband's biological grandchildren, but he also visits them on his own. That allows the honouring of something that I feel for my grandchildren, and he feels for his grandchildren, that I can't possibly feel for his. You just can't. They are not the same: they don't look the same, they don't have echoes of your DNA. And all of those things impact on the way relationships work.'

Bill isn't so sure. He has three step-grandchildren and four biological grandchildren, and remembers, 'When I was bringing up my sons and my stepson, there definitely was a difference: it wasn't conscious at all, it was just felt deep within me. But when it comes to my grandchildren and step-grandchildren, I'm not sure there is such a difference. Certainly I don't notice it so much. Having said that, when I spent two weeks with my son's daughter recently there really was something I could identify with. I could see her through my son, so that felt like a bond quite quickly.' When Bill's youngest step-grandson had to move out of his bedroom to make way for his new step sister, Bill stepped in with practical help as well as moral support. 'My stepson has a new partner with a four-year-old daughter, and they've moved in with his three children. My middle step-grandson was miffed because he had to move into a smaller room. So over the summer I went to stay and built him his own platform bed, with a desk and cupboard underneath. It was a really nice week with them.'

If grandparents feel their grandchild is being unfairly treated, either by a step-sibling or a step-parent, it's hard to know what to do. Broaching your concerns with your adult child seems like the obvious solution, but it might not be the best thing for your grandchild. If you think you'll be ignored, or that what you say might be used against the grandchild or disturb the equilibrium in some way, then it's best to think twice. Instead, you could make sure your grandchild has an opportunity to talk if they want to, and acknowledge that it's difficult being a step-sibling. That does *not* mean criticising the parents or the step-sibling. It just means noticing that it's a big change, and that it's not easy, and it's difficult having to share a bedroom or whatever they're fed up about. And always make it clear that if they need a bit of space, they can always come to yours for a bit.

Long-term support: ups and downs

Even when the family settles down into its new normal, life never follows a smooth path: there are always hiccups along the way. Grandparents need to be open to constant change. Fortunately, grandparents are much more flexible than people think, because sometimes the hiccups feel pretty seismic. After years of disruption, things seemed finally to be on an even keel for Jean's beloved granddaughter, Pearl, who lives with her mum and stays with her dad's new family every other weekend. Then one Saturday, out of the blue, Pearl announced that she wanted to live with her dad. Jean was devastated. She'd had no contact with her former son-in-law, Pearl's dad, since the divorce and there's not much love lost between them. Jean remembers, 'It was a terrible blow. We knew we would see much less of Pearl. Douglas and I talked about it, and we said, we mustn't make Pearl feel guilty or resentful. All we can say is "We just want you to be happy, it's your decision, and we're always here for you". Anyway, the next time Pearl stayed with her dad, she rang and said she'd come to the decision too quickly and wanted to carry on living with her mum. We were all so relieved!'

WHEN GRANDPARENTS DIVORCE

'I thought Granny and Grandpa would always be together'

So far in this chapter I've talked a lot about how crucial grandparents are as a reassuring, stable presence for grandchildren whose parents are splitting up. They can also be important models of marriages that last. So what happens if grandparents get divorced themselves? More grandparents are divorcing than ever before. According to the ONS, divorce in the over-sixties increased a staggering 85 per cent between 1990 and 2012.

In many families, grandparents are seen as rock-solid. So if they separate, the whole family feels like the carpet has been pulled from under them as the shock and sadness ripple down through the generations. Even very young grandchildren can pick up on moods and emotions, and react to stress in the family. Paige, who was 13 when her grandparents divorced two years ago, says, 'It didn't really sink in when Mum first told me. I was very surprised that Gramps had a girlfriend; I thought he and Granny would always be together. My first thought was that Granny will be sad, and I didn't think I'd see as much of Gramps anymore. That worried me because he's always been really fun and I like him a lot. He's been round a couple of times since they split up, but I was quite busy so I didn't see that much of him. The other day I saw Granny crying. I'd never seen her cry before and I didn't know what to do. She mentions Gramps occasionally, like where he's going to be living, but it's not something I would take into a discussion.'

Meanwhile, adult children are caught in the middle, and their sadness may well affect their children. Ian, who was 38 when his parents divorced, likened it to a kind of grief that derailed his life in all kinds of painful ways. His is a very common reaction, yet it's not what anyone expects. It's assumed that adult children who have left home and have their own families won't feel it in the way younger kids do. In fact, grown-ups are just as upset as children when their parents separate: it really doesn't matter whether they're 3 or 43. As always, what happens with the grandchildren is largely determined by the way adult children react. Petra was shell-shocked when her father left after being married to her mum for over 30 years. She kept putting off telling her sons, until she felt she had to explain why Nanny was upset. 'The divorce was absolutely horrible. My parents were an institution; you think, if that's gone, anything could go.

They spent a lot of time with our boys and had a great relationship with them. When I told the boys they immediately wanted to know if they would still see Nanny and Grandad. It was terrible to see Mum so sad, and I really appreciated how hard she tried to be brave in front of the kids. For a while I felt angry with Dad, and didn't want to see him. I don't think he ever thought about us or his grandchildren when he decided to end the marriage. I think he just thought about my mum and how it would affect her.'

Adult children tend to take sides, even when they've been divorced themselves and probably should know better. They're often furious with the grandparent who is leaving, especially if it's for a new lover. There might be some underlying anxiety about their inheritance, and even a slight queasiness about the idea of their parent having sex. If grandparents have childcare responsibilities, parents may also worry about the impact on an arrangement they rely on. Meanwhile, most adult children feel protective towards the left-behind parent, who suddenly becomes an individual they have to worry about, rather than part of a double act who took care of each other.

'You know Grandpa who's not our Grandpa anymore?'

Sometimes the rift that opens up feels unbridgeable. I've spoken to adult children who refuse to speak to the parent who left, and that inevitably rules out seeing the grandchildren. Ian, who I originally interviewed for my book on adult children, told me, 'I didn't speak to Mum for two years. She attempted to make contact a few times after she divorced Dad but I just wasn't ready. And then, when my daughter was a toddler, I realised that in spite of my ambivalence I couldn't refuse to let my mother have a relationship with her granddaughter.' The emotions and loyalty of the middle generation filter down to the grandchildren like osmosis, even when nothing's said. However, some adult children make no bones about spelling out how angry they feel. Daphne, whose grandchildren were four and seven when she divorced, remembers, 'My daughter told her dad she didn't want to have any more to do with him. She said to her children, "Grandpa was horrible to Grandma, so we don't speak to him". That's not the way I would have dealt with it. My grandchildren adored my ex-husband, but they don't see him at all now, although I think that's partly because he doesn't make the effort. They used to say, "You know Grandpa who's not our Grandpa anymore?" . . . but they don't mention him now.' Some grandparents, like Brian, feel duty-bound to set the record straight. 'My grandchildren see their Granny Sharon as the villain of the piece, because they get more information from their mothers, who are very protective of me. In the end, I had to sit everyone down and tell them to cool off. I felt they needed to understand that it wasn't all my ex-wife's fault.'

Adjusting to being a divorced grandparent

Breaking up after years of marriage is in many ways much tougher than it is for younger couples. Reinventing yourself as a singleton after being joined at the hip as a couple feels overwhelming. Expectations about the future come crashing down, self-esteem takes a terminal hit, jealousy eats your heart out. Grandchildren are the one light in the darkness, the biggest comfort, a reason for optimism about the future. But grandparenting is bitter-sweet without a soulmate to share the joys, dilemmas and hard work. It's excruciating if your place is usurped by a step-grandparent.

For the grandparent who is left out in the cold by unforgiving adult children, it's very different. Contact with grandchildren depends on whether it's possible to repair that bruised relationship, and that inevitably gets more complicated if one grandparent has a new partner. Parents with young children may feel torn between wanting their children to see their grandparents, but not if the new partner is there as well. I've met adult children who are quite suspicious and refuse to welcome a potential step-parent into the family or allow them to spend time with the grandchildren. There are reasons why a degree of suspicion is understandable at first. But it's incredibly painful and difficult, particularly for the biological grandparent who is stuck between their love for both their adult child and the new love of their life. It takes time and patience for any initial suspicion to be dissolved by trust.

It's often the relationship with the grandfather that suffers most. According to Professor Anna Tarrant, who has done extensive research into grandfathers, divorced men are often at a disadvantage, simply because they're a bit lost when it comes to maintaining family relationships. 'Men don't necessarily do the intergenerational work that women do, and that's when the relationships with grandchildren are more likely to break down or become less secure. Grandfathers often end up isolated or very much invested in their new partner and the new family relationships that that might create.'

Some grandmothers take this on board, even when they're in pieces about the break-up; they must be saints! They make an effort to overcome their own feelings because they appreciate the importance of their grandchildren staying in contact with both grandparents, although their generosity rarely extends to their ex's new partner. Roni says, 'I'm often tempted to say something mean, especially about the other woman. But I've made it clear to my kids that they're all to keep up with their dad, and that I want the grandchildren to keep seeing him. I think that has been a great relief to them, and I'm proud of myself for that.'

Family celebrations become fraught with complication. It's impossible to please everyone. One grandparent refuses to be in the same room with their ex, while another is desperate to bring their new partner into the family and can't see what the problem is. It's not uncommon for families to end up holding two separate celebrations as a result. Negotiations with adult children, who want to include both their parents but don't want a joyous occasion to be tainted either by a heavy scene or by one grandparent's glaring absence, require tact and diplomacy. Grandparents need to remember that adult children have to make impossible decisions about who is, and isn't, on the guest list. It's best not to have expectations, and to be prepared to compromise if necessary. When Angie's son invited his dad's new partner to her twin grandsons' christening, she reluctantly decided not to go. 'I just couldn't face seeing her with him. I felt that it was a family occasion and the boys aren't her grandchildren. I could see that my son was in a difficult position, and that he was trying to be fair to both of us, but I was very upset; I'd bought a new dress and everything. Afterwards, I heard that the grandchildren asked where I was, and that still makes me feel terrible.'

How much do grandchildren need to know?

How much grandchildren need to know about their grandparents' divorce depends a lot on their age. Even very young children will be aware that something's wrong, and wonder why one grandparent is around less, or not at all. It may make older children question their trust in long-term relationships. So above all, they need reassurance that both grandparents will always love them just the same, and that their relationship with them will continue. Grandparents often leave it up to their adult children to explain. But it's important that grandchildren aren't left thinking their grandparents are upset because of something they've done. Saying something simple and direct like 'I'm sad and upset and I'm feeling a bit cross towards Grandpa, but I'm not cross with you' should help. Roni says, 'My granddaughter, who is four, often talks about Grandpa and asks when he's coming, I just say, "Grandpa will come to see you soon." She's too young to understand what's going on now, and she'll just become aware of it in time. I can see that the older ones feel sad, and they don't know what to say to me, but I can't talk to them about the divorce because it makes me cry.'

WHEN GRANDPARENTS DIVORCE

- Even if you are heartbroken, you need to keep in mind that you are still the parent and grandparent.
- Don't expect your adult child to take sides. Respect their loyalty to both of you.
- Make it clear that you want your grandchildren to keep in touch with both their grandparents.
- Adult children will have their own anxieties about the future, so it's important to listen and answer questions directly.
- If young grandchildren respond by being cross or difficult, give them plenty of attention, affection and reassurance.
- Be straightforward when talking to older grandchildren about what's going on. Don't try to second-guess how they'll respond. They just need to know the facts, and then you can answer their questions.
- Try not to cry in front of your grandchildren. Just say you're feeling upset, but make it crystal clear that you're not upset or angry with them.
- When it comes to family celebrations, don't make assumptions or demands about who will or won't be invited, and be prepared to compromise.
- If you shared childcare responsibilities with your partner, think about how they will be affected.

Conclusion

I have found it almost impossible to put the finishing touches to this book, simply because I keep meeting grandparents who've got something new to say or some new experience to share, and these fresh insights are just too good to leave out. Yet when I first set out to write this book two years ago the prevailing message about grandparenting was that it was bliss, pure and simple. I had four grandchildren by then, and I knew it wasn't that straightforward, yet no one seemed to talk about the complications and dilemmas, apart from people who *weren't* grandparents. Oddly enough, they were the ones with the strongest views about how exploited their friends were, and told tales of tensions with sons, daughters and children-in-law. Meanwhile, grandparents themselves tended to stick to the script. Then one day, out of the blue, an old friend emailed me. 'I LOVE my grandchildren but I am equivocal about being a grandparent,' she wrote. 'It's my observation that many are, but we can't say so.'

Things are very different for our adult children, who have carte blanche to discuss the ups and downs of parenting without being accused of selfishness. Meanwhile these days it's almost a badge of pride to declare how useless you are at parenting. Grandparents don't have the same luxury. They don't have enough safe spaces to air their complicated feelings. I don't mean a place to share cute videos and discuss how clever their grandchild is; there's quite enough of that. This generation of grandparents is approaching the whole thing in a very different way from their own grandparents, and even their own parents. That's especially true for grandfathers. Generally speaking, grandparents are more closely involved, for a start. Yet there's no road map, so there's a real need to discuss new ideas and approaches and talk things through. The challenges are universal but the complications are highly individual. There's never a one-size-fits-all when it comes to families.

So my mission was to find out how other grandmothers and grandfathers really feel, and I spent hours chewing the fat with people with a multitude of different experiences: one became a granny in her thirties, another in her seventies; their adult kids were straight, gay, single, divorced, and so were they; and they had step-grandchildren as well as biological grandchildren of all ages. I met one grandmother whose autistic granddaughter required much more devoted care than she could possibly have anticipated, and a grandfather whose daughter was jealous of any childcare he offered her sister. The saddest grandparents didn't get to see their grandchildren enough, either because they lived on the other side of the world or because contact became difficult when the parents split up. They mulled over everything, from possessive daughters-in-law to babymoons, from the differences between men and women as grandparents to childcare, and why so many people willingly give up their precious time without being paid.

I was also keen to find out what the middle generation think: the sons who've become fathers, the daughters who've become mothers, and of course their partners. The relationship with sons- and daughters-in-law goes on to another level when they have kids, and it's really useful to hear their side of the story. They gave me such good advice on managing the reversal of roles that looking after grandchildren entails, as well as insights into what it's like to have to tell your parents (or even worse, your parents-in-law!) what to do – and not to do.

But by far the biggest theme in both generations was ambivalence: grandparents' longing to build an enduring bond with grandchildren, which requires time and care, versus the desire to do their own thing before it gets too late. In my book on retirement, *Not Fade Away*, I warned readers that while grandchildren can fill the chasm left by work so richly, they can also hold grandparents back from exploring their own new direction in life. That was written before I had grandchildren myself, but even then I could see that they're a powerful force that can distract people from following their dreams and achieving their own goals.

And then real life stepped in in the shape of Lena and Gabriel, swiftly followed by Luke, Justin, Jem and Rosa, and I happily put my bucket list on hold to help look after my grandchildren two days a week and write this book. I've had no regrets and only a few reservations: there are times when it feels like I've gone back to the juggling of early motherhood, and I wish there were eight, or preferably nine, days in the week. There have been times when I wonder if I'll ever get to Kerala or reach Grade 8 on the flute. I get a pang when I meet people who've upped sticks to a lovelier part of the country, until I remember how important it is for me to be near my grandchildren. The bottom line is that it's my choice; no one's making me do it and I absolutely love it. Mixed feelings are par for the course.

Now that my eldest two are at school I understand something that I didn't fully take on board when they were babies: the first five years are crucial, and they go in a flash. That made me quite regretful until I spoke to a friend with older grandchildren, who described the lovely phase between 8 and 11, when they are independent enough to do stuff on their own, but they're not yet shy of a cuddle. Then my sister told me about a wonderful holiday she'd recently spent with her 20-year-old granddaughter, sharing a cabin on a boat sailing round the Summer Isles of Scotland. Last weekend I had my eldest granddaughter to stay on her own for the first time, which was brave of both of us! It was a happy glimpse into the future and changing relationships. Nothing stays the same, and grandparents need to be open-hearted and ready for the next new phase. Luckily, with so much experience of family life under their belts, that's exactly what they're good at.

Resources

GENERAL

Association of Child Psychotherapists
Publishes a very helpful leaflet: *Grandparents & The Extended Family: Understanding the Importance of Wider Family Relationships for Children and their Parents.*
childpsychotherapy.org.uk

Child development
These two online leaflets on children's emotional, physical and brain development, compiled for the NHS by Solihull Approach health professionals, are very useful.

'Brain development through childhood', NHS. Available at: inourplace.co.uk/brain-development-through-childhood-leaflet

'Developmental and emotional milestones 0–18 years', NHS. Available at: inourplace.co.uk/developmental-and-emotional-milestones-0-18y-leaflet

Gransnet
Online articles, information and forums for grandparents.
gransnet.com

Kinship
Offers free support, workshops and advice for all kinship carers: friends or family who raise a child when their parents aren't able to. Grandparents are the most common kinship carers, but other relatives and people who know the child well can also take on the role.
kinship.org.uk

Noisy Book Club

Created by primary school teacher Becca Ehrlich to help parents support their children's learning, both educational and emotional. It offers really useful insights for grandparents into current parenting ideas.
noisybookclub.com

Relate

Offers counselling for individuals, couples, families and children, and 'relationship toolkits' on a range of issues.
relate.org.uk

COURSES FOR GRANDPARENTS

Grandparents Antenatal Classes (online) run by Happy Parents Happy Baby

An online course all about brushing off the cobwebs and refreshing yourself with all the latest knowledge, ahead of the baby's arrival.
happyparentshappybaby.com

Grandparents' Refresher Course

An online course by midwife Freya Mahal with the latest research and advice on how grandparents can make a positive difference to pregnancy and parenting.
expectingclasses.co.uk

Grantenatal Workshops

Live, interactive online classes to give prospective and new grandparents the latest research and information. The sessions are also a chance to swap notes with other grandparents.
thebabyexperience.co.uk

Mini First Aid

Baby and child emergency first-aid classes for parents, grandparents and carers. Both in person and online.
minifirstaid.co.uk

St John Ambulance

An assessed two-day online and face-to-face course, 'Paediatric First Aid', for people who work with young children and care for them at home.
sja.org.uk

DIVORCE

Family Separation Clinic

Offers specialist services to families experiencing divorce or separation and, in particular, those where children have rejected a parent or are at risk of doing so.
familyseparationclinic.com

Happy Steps

The only research-based stepfamily resource centre in the UK.
happysteps.co.uk

National Family Mediation

Has an information leaflet specifically for grandparents, 'Grandchildren need grandparents'.
nfm.org.uk

Pace (Playfulness, Acceptance, Curiosity, Empathy)

ddpnetwork.org/about-ddp/meant-pace

ESTRANGED GRANDPARENTS

Grandparents Apart UK
Aims to help grandparents keep in touch with their grandchildren following divorce or separation of the children's parents. The focus is on putting the children first and conflict second.
grandparentsapart.co.uk

Local groups
There are local support groups all over the UK for grandparents who are separated from their grandchildren, such as the Bristol Grandparents Support Group.
bristolgrandparentssupportgroup.co.uk

Stand Alone
Supports people who are estranged, not just grandparents.
standalone.org.uk

FERTILITY

Fertility Network UK
Publishes a series of helpful factsheets, including: *A guide for friends and relatives of people with infertility problems.* Its 'Unspoken' podcast also shares real stories of individuals and couples.
fertilitynetworkuk.org

FFLAG
Information on LGBT+ parenthood for family and friends and their LGBT loved ones.
fflag.org.uk/portfolio-item/lgbtplus-parenting

Human Fertilisation & Embryology Authority (HFEA)

Information on the different kinds of fertility treatment, as well as sources of emotional support for men and women. Includes detailed information on egg freezing.
hfea.gov.uk

Miscarriage Association

Publishes a really helpful leaflet: *Supporting Someone You Know.*
miscarriageassociation.org.uk

NHS

The NHS website has a comprehensive section on infertility.
nhs.uk

Surrogacy UK

Supports people throughout their surrogacy journey with expert help and advocacy.
surrogacyuk.org

Bibliography

NOTE: This list is divided according to subject, in chapter order. The quotes in bold refer to the main text of this book.

GENERAL BOOKS AND RESEARCH

Sara Arber and Virpi Timonen (Eds), *Contemporary grandparenting: Changing family relationships in global contexts* (Policy Press, 2012)
This book includes a chapter that was a light-bulb moment for me: 'Being there yet not interfering: the paradoxes of grandparenting', by Vanessa May, Jennifer Mason and Lynda Clarke. It's a revised version of an earlier paper, 'Ambivalence and the paradoxes of grandparenting', *Sociological Review*, 55(4) (2007).
This paper was based on data collected by the London School of Hygiene and Tropical Medicine, 'Grandparenthood: its meaning and its contribution to older people's lives', ESRC L480254040, 1999–2002, Lynda Clarke, Ceridwen Roberts, Francis McGlone, Helen Cairns.

'In 2000, one in 1,000 fathers were the primary caregiver of nine-month-old babies; now it's 1 in 14': Marialivia Bernardi, Laurel Fish et al., 'Children of the 2020s: first survey of families at age 9 months', Department for Education, November 2023
Ann Buchanan and Anna Rotkirch (Eds), *Grandfathers: Global Perspectives* (Palgrave Macmillan, 2016)
John Burnside, 'A leap of faith', *The Tablet*, 18 November 2023
Karen Fingerman, Cynthia Berg, Jacqui Smith, Toni Antonucci (Eds), *Handbook of Life-Span Development* (Springer, 2010)
Geoffrey Greif and Michael Woolley, *In-law Relationships: Mothers, Daughters, Fathers, and Sons* (Oxford University Press, 2021)

Geoffrey Greif and Michael Woolley, *Adult Sibling Relationships* (Columbia University Press, 2015)

'7 in 10 families have taken grandparents on holiday, poll suggests', The *Independent*, 18 April 2019. Available at: independent.co.uk/travel/news-and-advice/family-holiday-grandparents-multi-generational-beach-a8876381.html

The American psychiatrist Arthur Kornhaber has written several books on grandparenting informed by the long-running Grandparent Study, which he initiated in 1970:
Contemporary Grandparenting (Sage, 1996)
Grandparents/Grandchildren: the vital connection (with Kenneth Woodward; Doubleday, 1981)
The Grandparent Guide (McGraw-Hill Education, 2002)

Vanessa May, *Families*: Key Concepts Series (Polity, 2023)

Vanessa May, 'On being a "good" mother: The moral presentation of self in written life stories', *Sociology*, 42(3) (2008), pp. 470–486

Susan Moore and Doreen Rosenthal, *Grandparenting: Contemporary Perspectives* (Routledge, 2017)

Margaret Mueller and Glen Elder, 'Family contingencies across the generations: Grandparent-grandchild relationships in holistic perspective', *Journal of Marriage and Family*, 65(2) (2003), pp. 404–417

'Grandparent-grandchild relationships seemed to be naturally easier and less tense': Alfred Radcliffe-Brown, 'On Joking Relationships', *Africa*, 13(3) (1940), pp. 195–210

'Help often comes with a negotiation about how the money is used': Karen Rowlingson, Ricky Joseph and Louise Overton, *Intergenerational Financial Giving and Inequality: Give and Take in 21st Century Families* (Palgrave Macmillan, 2017)

Anna Tarrant, 'Constructing a social geography of grandparenthood: a new focus for intergenerationality', *Area*, 42(2) (2010), pp. 190–197

Anna Tarrant, '(Grand)paternal care practices and affective intergenerational encounters using Information Communication Technologies', *Intergenerational Space*, Robert Vanderbeck and Nancy Worth (Eds), (Routledge, 2015)

Peter Smith (Ed), *The Psychology of Grandparenthood: An International Perspective* (Routledge, 1991)

Peter Smith and Lauren Wild, 'Grandparenting', in Marc Bornstein (Ed), *Handbook of Parenting, Volume 3: Being and Becoming a Parent* (Routledge, 2019), pp. 232–270

Maximiliane Szinovacz (Ed), *Handbook on Grandparenthood* (Greenwood, 1998)

'Missing Pieces: The Lesbian Mothers Scandal', produced by Sophie Wilkinson, BBC Radio 4, 8 December 2024

BRAIN FUNCTION AND MENTAL HEALTH

'Up to a day's grandchildcare a week had a positive effect on cognitive function': Katherine Burn and Cassandra Szoeke, 'Grandparenting predicts late-life cognition: Results from the Women's Healthy Ageing Project', *Maturitas*, 81(2) (2015), pp. 317–322

Jennifer Caputo, Kathleen Cagney and Linda Waite, 'Keeping Us Young? Grandchild Caregiving and Older Adults' Cognitive Functioning', *Journal of Marriage and Family*, 86(3) (2023), pp. 633–654

'Childcare is associated with a reduced risk of dementia': S. E. Choi, Z. Zhang and H. Liu, 'Gender differences in the protective role of grandparenting in dementia risk', *The Journals of Gerontology: Series B*, 79(6) (2024), pp. 337–351

John Condon, Mary Luszcz and Ian McKee, 'The transition to grandparenthood: a prospective study of mental health implications', *Aging & Mental Health*, 22(3) (2016), pp. 336–343

Abigail Fagan, 'Is Grandparenting Good for Our Brains? The cognitive benefits of being an active grandparent', *Psychology Today*, 5 November 2024

Helen Kivnick, 'Grandparenthood and the Mental Health of Grandparents', *Ageing & Society*, 1(3) (1981) pp. 365–391, published online by Cambridge University Press, 2008

Niina Metsä-Simola et al., 'Grandparental support and maternal depression: Do grandparents' characteristics matter more for separating mothers?' *Population Studies*, 78(3) (2024)

'Grandmothers are geared toward feeling what their grandchildren are feeling': James Rilling, Amber Gonzalez and Minwoo Lee, 'The neural correlates of grandmaternal caregiving', *Proceedings of the Royal Society B*, 17 November 2021. Professor Rilling was interviewed by Linda Geddes for the *Guardian*, 'Study of women's brain function finds more empathy activation when looking at pictures of grandchildren', 17 November 2021

TEENAGE GRANDCHILDREN

'Over a third of 11- to 16-year-olds said their closest grandparent was the most important person in their life outside the immediate family': Shalhevet Attar-Schwartz, Jo-Pei Tan and Ann Buchanan, 'Adolescents' perspectives on relationships with grandparents: The contribution of adolescent, grandparent, and parent-grandparent relationship variables', *Children and Youth Services Review*, 31(9) (2009), pp. 1057–1066

S. A. Ruiz and M. Silverstein, 'Relationships with grandparents and the emotional well-being of late adolescent and young adult grandchildren', *Journal of Social Issues*, 63(4) (2007), pp. 793–808

Jeremy Yorgason, Laura Padilla-Walker and Jami Jackson, 'Nonresidential grandparents' emotional and financial involvement in relation to early adolescent grandchild outcomes', *Journal of Research on Adolescence*, 21(3) (2011), pp. 552–558

LIVING WITH GRANDCHILDREN

'Under One Roof: Experiences of multigenerational living in the UK,' Legal & General, 2020. Available at: legalandgeneral.com/insurance/over-50-life-insurance/under-one-roof/?tduid=4e78a8cea0dbf7757b123e171448ea84

Angela Neustatter, *A Home for the Heart: Home as the key to happiness* (Gibson Square, 2012)

RELATIONSHIPS WITH IN-LAWS

Terri Apter, *What do you want from me? Learning to get along with in-laws* (Norton, 2009)

Lucy Rose Fischer, 'Mothers and Mothers-in-law', *Journal of Marriage and Family*, 45(1) (1983), pp. 187–192

Geoffrey Greif and Micah Saviet, 'In-law relationships among interracial couples: A preliminary view', *Journal of Human Behavior in the Social Environment*, 30(5) (2020), pp. 605–620

Geoffrey Greif and Michael Woolley, 'The father-in-law's relationship with his son-in-law: A preliminary understanding', *Smith College Studies in Social Work*, 88(2) (2018), pp. 152–173

Geoffrey Greif and Michael Woolley, 'Sons-in-law and their fathers-in-law: Gaining a preliminary understanding of an understudied family relationship', *Journal of Family Social Work*, 22(3) (2019), pp. 292–311

Geoffrey Greif and Michael Woolley, 'Women and their mothers-in-law: Triangles, ambiguity, and relationship quality', *Social Work Research*, 43(4) (2019), pp. 259–268

Geoffrey Greif and Michael Woolley, 'A preliminary look at relationships between married gays and lesbians and their parents-in-law: Five case studies', *Journal of Gay & Lesbian Social Services*, 31(3) (2019), pp. 290–313

Deborah Merrill, *When Your Gay or Lesbian Child Marries: A guide for parents* (Rowman & Littlefield, 2016)

Deborah Merrill, *Mothers-in-Law and Daughters-in-Law: Understanding the relationship and what makes them friends or foe* (Praeger, 2007)

CHILDCARE

'5 million grandparents take on childcare responsibilities', Age UK, September 2017

'One in four working families rely on grandparents to look after the kids': *Looking after the grandchildren? make sure it counts towards your state pension*, Department for Work and Pensions. Available at: gov.uk/government/news/looking-after-the-grandchildren-make-sure-it-counts-towards-your-state-pension, July 2013

Karen Glaser et al., 'Grandparenting in Europe: Family policy and grandparents' role in providing childcare', A study of grandparenting in Europe by King's College London for Grandparents Plus, 2013

Greg Heffer, 'Ministers told they should consider paying grandparents who help out with childcare', *Mail Online*, March 2023. Available at: dailymail.co.uk/news/article-11885529/Ministers-told-consider-paying-grandparents-help-childcare

Sonja Hilbrand et al., 'Caregiving within and beyond the family is associated with lower mortality for the caregiver: A prospective study', *Evolution and Human Behavior*, 38(3) (2017), pp. 397–403

Erin O'Connor, 'The Case for Grandparent Paid Leave', *Psychology Today*, January 2025. Available at: psychologytoday.com/gb/blog/scientific-mommy/202501/the-case-for-grandparent-paid-leave

Anna Rönkä et al., 'Positive Parenting and Parenting Stress Among Working Mothers in Finland, the UK and the Netherlands: Do Working Time Patterns Matter?' *Journal of Comparative Family Studies*, October 2018, 48(2), pp. 175–196. DOI: 10.3138/jcfs.48.2.175

'Grandparent Army Report', International Longevity Centre, February 2017

'Grandparents "save summer" with two and a half weeks of childcare, totalling nearly £1,000 per child': Saga, September 2023. Available at: saga.co.uk

'Parents and Carers: Looking After Grandchildren?' Usdaw, 2017

Melissa Verhoef et al., 'Childcare and parental work schedules: A comparison of childcare arrangements among Finnish, British and Dutch dual-earner families', *Community, Work & Family*, 19(3) (2016), pp. 261–280

Sarah Wellard, 'Doing it all? Grandparents, childcare and employment: An analysis of British Social Attitudes Survey Data from 1998 and 2009', Grandparents Plus, December 2011

Francesca Zanasi et al., 'The prevalence of grandparental childcare in Europe: a research update', *European Journal of Ageing*, 20(37) (2023)

GRANDFATHERS

M. C. Baranowski, 'The grandfather-grandchild relationship: Meaning and exchange', *Family Perspective*, 24(3) (1990), pp. 201–215

James Bates, 'Generative Grandfathering: A conceptual framework for nurturing grandchildren', *Marriage and Family Review*, 45(4) (2009), pp. 331–352

James Bates and Alan Taylor, 'Grandfather involvement and aging men's mental health', *American Journal of Men's Health*, 6(3) (2012), pp. 229–239

'Divorced grandfathers are less likely to see their grandchildren': Mirkka Danielsbacka and Antti Tanskanen, 'Grandfather Involvement in Finland: Impact of Divorce, Remarriage, and Widowhood', in *Grandfathers: Global Perspectives*, Buchanan and Rotkirch (Eds), pp. 183–197

Judith Davey and Cherryl Smith, '*Maori Grandfathers in Aotearoa (New Zealand)*', in *Grandfathers: Global Perspectives*, Buchanan and Rotkirch (Eds), pp. 105–124

Mary Lee Hummert, 'Physiognomic associations with stereotypes of the elderly', paper presented at meetings of Gerontological Society of America, San Francisco, 1991

Vira Kivett, 'The grandparent-grandchild connection', *Marriage & Family Review*, 16(3–4) (1991), pp. 267–290

'Grandparents, especially grandfathers, are more likely to be involved with their grandchildren if they're part of a couple': Knud Knudsen, 'European grandparents' solicitude: Why older men can be relatively good grandfathers', *Acta Sociologica*, 55(3) (2012), pp. 231–250

Robin Mann, Anna Tarrant and George Leeson, 'Grandfatherhood: Shifting Masculinities in Later Life', *Sociology* 50(3) (2015)

'Teenage boys in one study were more likely to nominate their maternal grandfather as the grandparent they got on with best': Robin Mann, Hafiz Khan and George Leeson, 'Age and gender differences in grandchildren's relations with their maternal grandfathers and grandmothers', *Oxford Working Paper Series* 209 (February 2009)

Rosenthal and Moore, Unpublished grandfather interviews, (see *Grandparenting: Contemporary Perspectives*, Moore and Rosenthal)

Jo-Pei Tan and Ann Buchanan, 'Links between grandfather involvement and adolescent wellbeing in England and Wales', in *Grandfathers: Global Perspectives*, Buchanan and Rotkirch (Eds), pp. 229–247

SINGLE GRANDPARENTS

'The obstacles you faced as a single parent have now just grown exponentially': 'Single Grandma Talks Straight From the Heart', *Grandparents Link*. Available at: grandparentslink.com/experts-corner/single-grandma-talks-straight-from-the-heart
Sara Pascoe (guest), *Young Again with Kirsty Young*, BBC Radio 4, 14 January 2025

MATERNAL AND PATERNAL GRANDPARENTS

Floella Benjamin, illustrated by Margaret Chamberlain, *My Two Grannies* (Frances Lincoln, 2009)
'Not only are the middle generation of mothers likely to have closer ties to their own parents than to their parents-in-law, but…': Christopher Chan and Glen Elder, 'Matrilineal Advantage in Grandchild-Grandparent Relations', *The Gerontologist*, 40(2) (2000), pp. 179–190
Mairi Hedderwick, *Katie Morag and the Two Grandmothers* (Red Fox, 2010 – reprint)

FERTILITY

Zoë Clark-Coates, *Pregnancy After Loss* (Orion Spring, 2020)
Ellen Glazer, *The Long-Awaited Stork: A guide to parenting after infertility* (Prentice-Hall, 1993)

Ellen Glazer, *Infertility: Grandparents in waiting*, Harvard Health Blog, Harvard Medical School, 17 December 2019

Ellen Glazer and Evelina Sterling, *Having Your Baby Through Egg Donation* (Jessica Kingsley, 2013)

Sheila Lamb, *This is . . . Pregnancy after Infertility and Loss* (MFS Books, 2022)

Beth Lewis, 'I wasn't her father, and the world didn't see me as her mother, either. So who was I?' *Daily Mail*, 15 May 2023

'LGBT+ Parents Report', Just Like Us, 2024

M. S. Oud et al., 'A de novo paradigm for male infertility', *Nature Communications* 13 (2022)

'It's been estimated that as many as one in three couples undergoing IVF get financial help from would-be grandparents': Alice Smellie, 'Greatest gift of all from the bank of mum and dad', *Daily Mail*, 19 April 2015. Available at: dailymail.co.uk/femail/article-3046128/Greatest-gift-bank-mum-dad-modern-trend-parents-help-fund-cost-IVF-grandchildren.html

DIVORCE

C. Duran-Aydintug, 'Relationships with former in-laws: Normative guidelines and actual behavior', *Journal of Divorce and Remarriage*, 19 (1991), pp. 69-82

Shalhevet Attar-Schwartz et al., 'Grandparenting and adolescent adjustment in two-parent biological, lone-parent, and step-families', *Journal of Family Psychology*, 23(1) (2009), pp. 67–75

Joan Barth, 'Grandparents dealing with the divorce of their child; Tips for grandparents and therapists', *Contemporary Family Therapy*, 26 (2004), pp. 41–44

J. H. Bray and S. H. Berger, 'Noncustodial father and paternal grandfather relationships in stepfamilies', *Family Relations*, 39(4) (1990), pp. 414–419

L. J. Bridges et al., 'Children's perspectives on their relationships with grandparents following parental separation: a longitudinal study', *Social Development*, 16(3) (2007), pp. 539–554

Lillian Carson, *The Essential Grandparent's Guide to Divorce: Making a difference in the family* (Health Communications Inc, 1999)

L. A. Drew and M. Silverstein, 'Grandparents' psychological well-being after loss of contact with their grandchildren', *Journal of Family Psychology*, 2007, 21(3), pp. 372–379

L. A. Drew and P. K. Smith, 'The impact of parental separation/divorce on grandparent-grandchild relationships', *The International Journal of Aging and Human Development*, 48(3) (1999), pp. 191–216

'Losing contact with grandchildren was related to pronounced, long-lasting grief': L. M. Drew and P. K. Smith, 'Implications for grandparents when they lose contact with their grandchildren: Divorce, family feud, and geographical separation,' *Journal of Mental Health and Aging*, 8(2) (2002), pp. 95–119

J. Dunn, 'Understanding Children's Family Worlds: Family Transition and Children's Outcome', in Merrill-Palmer Quarterly, 50(3) (2004)

J. Dunn, et al., 'Family lives and friendships: the perspectives of children in step-, single-parent, and nonstep families', *Journal of Family Psychology*, 15(2) (2001), pp. 272–287

J. Dunn and K. Deater-Deckard, 'Children's views of their changing families', Joseph Rowntree Foundation (2001)

'Grandchildren as young as eight remained loyal to both parents': Neil Ferguson et al., *Grandparenting in Divorced Families* (Policy Press, 2004). Based on a two-year research study at Cardiff University.

'Estrangement: 14% have no contact with their grandchildren', Gransnet survey, 2019. Available at: gransnet.com

Craig Henderson et al., 'Grandmother-grandchild relationship quality predicts psychological adjustment among youth from divorced families', *Journal of Family Issues*, 30(9) (2009), pp. 1245–1264

Gretchen Lussier et al., 'Support across two generations: Children's closeness to grandparents following parental divorce and remarriage', *Journal of Family Psychology*, 16(3) (2002), pp. 363–376

Jordan Soliz, 'Intergenerational support and the role of grandparents in post-divorce families: Retrospective accounts of young adult grandchildren', *Qualitative Research Reports in Communication*, 9(1) (2008), pp. 72–80

'The connection between paternal grandmothers and ex-daughters-in-law continued *only* if the relationship was "satisfactory and friend-like" before the separation': Maximiliane Szinovacz (Ed), *Handbook on Grandparenthood* (Greenwood, 1998)

Virpi Timonen, Martha Doyle and Ciara O'Dwyer, with contributions from Elena Moore, 'The Role of Grandparents in Divorced and Separated Families in Ireland', School of Social Work and Social Policy, Trinity College Dublin, 2009

Karen and Nick Woodall, *The Guide for Separated Parents: Putting your children first* (Piatkus, 2009)

FICTION & DRAMA

Jen Brister, *The Other Mother* (Vintage, 2021). A memoir of same-sex parenting.

'Ecce Puer', James Joyce's poem on the birth of his grandson (the words are also sung by Joan Baez).

Chimamanda Ngozi Adichie, *Dream Count* (Fourth Estate, 2025). This novel features a short but unforgettable exploration of the way relationships change dramatically overnight, with the transformation from mother to grandmother and adult daughter to new mother.

Roxana Robinson, *Leaving* (Magpie Books, 2024)

Bijan Sheibani, *The Cord* (play) (Nick Hern Books, 2024)

Susan Spindler, *Surrogate* (Virago, 2021). A novel about IVF and surrogacy from the grandparents' point of view that offers insights into the experiences and emotions of the whole family.

Francis Spufford, *Light Perpetual* (Faber & Faber, 2021)

Colm Tóibín, *Long Island* (Picador, 2024)

Joanna Trollope, *Daughters-in-law* (Doubleday, 2011)

Salley Vickers, *Grandmothers* (Penguin, 2009)

Acknowledgements

This book would be nothing without the contributions of the grandmothers, grandfathers and adult children who agreed to be interviewed. They were so generous with their time, and so open and articulate about painful and difficult experiences, as well as the happy ones. I'm also hugely grateful to the psychologists and sociologists who were willing to discuss their research on so many different aspects of grandparenting and family life, as well as the psychotherapists, family therapists and other experts on grandparenting who spoke to me. Sadly, the eminent psychologist Professor Peter Smith, who wrote comprehensively about grandparents, has died since our interview, in 2025. His knowledge and insights are invaluable.

A big thank you to the brilliant team at Bloomsbury, especially Charlotte Croft, who always goes the extra mile. Thanks also to my editor Caroline Hewlett for her patience and support, the copyeditor Jenni Davis, and the proofreader Gina Rathbone.

Last, but definitely not least, thank you to all my family, especially Paul, Adam and my daughters-in-law, Frances and Chloë.

Index

A

adolescents *see* teenagers
adult children, relationship with your *see* relationships with adult children
age of grandparents   6–7, 12–13, 19–20, 38–9
agency and independence   23–5
ambivalence, feelings of   2–3, 23–4, 111, 125, 236–7
anxiety, childcare   134

B

babies and older siblings   41–2
babies, relationships with new   29–32
babysitting *see* childcare
'bewildered curiosity,' acting with   33
births, traumatic   169–70
boredom and childcare   134–5
boundaries   36, 101–2, 104, 105
brain function, human   27–8
Brister, Jen   191
Buchanan, Professor Ann   141
Burnside, John   23, 138–9

C

child-rearing disagreements   71–2, 73–5, 80–1, 123–4
childcare   3–5, 21, 26, 40–1
  benefits of providing   117–20
  boredom   134–5
  catching children's bugs   127–8
  considerations before commitment   122–3
  costs   3–4, 26, 110–11
  difficulty instructing and criticising grandparents   130
  exclusion from   116–17
  following parents' rules and routines   123–4, 128–9, 132
  grandparents' ambivalence   111–12
  grandparents' anxiety   134
  grumpy grandchildren   135–6
  guilt   131–2
  late parents and clocking-off time   124–5
  location – whose home?   136–7
  mess   78, 127
  parents' checking up   126

parents' perspective 112–13, 126–32
professional 113
providing for multiple grandchildren 120–2
provision and policy 113–14
saying 'no' to 114–16
short notice 125–6
television as entertainment 130–1
tips for making it work 132–3
unreliable grandparents 131
your health and wellbeing 127–8
communication, internet 49–50, 55
confidant role 35–7, 200–1
confidence, grandfathers' lacking 146–8
cost-of-living, increasing 110–11
courses, grandparenting 124

D

Daley, Tom 192
daughters-in-law and mothers-in-law
  see mothers-in-law and daughters-in-law
Davey, Dr Judith 14–15
descendants, comfort of having 16–17
disagreements, child-rearing 71–2, 73–5, 80–1, 123–4
disciplining grandchildren 123–4, 133, 135–6
distance, living 45–53
divorce/separation, impact of an adult child's 7, 196–8
  bad-mouthing your grandchild's other parent 202
  estrangement from grandchildren 218–23
  facing your own feelings 215–16, 222–3
  paternal grandparents 217–18, 220–1
  relations with former child-in-law 203–8
  step-grandparenting 223–8
  step-parents 211–12
  supporting your adult child 208–13
  supporting your grandchild 198–202, 204, 228
  when grandparents make things worse 213–15
  see also single grandparents
dreams and ambitions, your 21, 123, 237
dynamics, changing family 13–15, 69–78

E

estrangement from grandchildren 218–23

INDEX

F
FaceTime 50
fathers-in-law 106–8
fathers, new 68–9
favourite grandchildren 42–4
fertility treatment, your child's 183
  biological connection to grandchild 190–1
  cost of 185–6
  dealing with your own emotions 186–8
  egg freezing 189–90
  heterosexual couples 183–8
  how to be supportive 185–6, 188, 194–5
  raising the subject 183–4
  same-sex couples and singletons 189–93
  sperm donors and sperm banks 191–2
  supporting your son 184–5
  surrogacy 186, 189
  when it's a success 193–4
future, your view of the 16–17, 38–9

G
genetics 27
'gentle parenting' trend 73–4
gifts, giving 40, 43, 72–3
Glazer, Ellen 34–5, 182, 183, 186, 190, 193, 194

grandchild-less, accepting being 181–2
grandfathers 8, 24, 35, 118–19, 138–40
  care and concern 153–4
  a chance to do things differently 142
  feeling second best/underestimating their role 140–2, 146–8
  fun factor 152
  influence of own grandfather 143–5
  learning from their sons 145–6
  single 149–50, 154, 232
  strengths 150–1, 153–4
grandparent and grandchild relationships 5–6, 21–2, 27–9
  being fair — multiple children 39–41
  challenging behaviour 201–2
  confidant role 35–7, 200–1
  early years 31–4
  estrangement 218–23
  favourites 42–4
  grandparents and newborns 29–31
  grandparents' divorce 7, 162–3, 198, 228–34
  holidays with grandchildren 61–4

259

living with your grandchildren 58–60
long distance relationships 45–55
moving near your grandchildren 56–8
new babies and older siblings 41–2
non-binary grandchildren 38
older pre-teen children 34–5
step-grandchildren 223–8
support through a divorce 198–202, 233–4
teenagers 33–4, 35–7
tips for staying close over time 44–5
young adult grandchildren 37–8, 199–200
see also childcare
grandparent, becoming a
age limitations 19–20
being yourself 17–18
changing priorities 15–16
family dynamics 13–15, 20
identity change 11–13
impact of timing 19–20
influences of your elders 19
thinking about the future 16–17
your health and well-being 17
grandparenting and parenting, the difference between 21–3

grandparents, your own 19, 143–4
Greif, Professor Geoffrey 44, 75, 78, 88, 91, 94, 95, 96, 98, 106–7, 108, 117, 119, 166, 167, 168, 171

H

health and well-being, your 17, 21, 127–8, 137, 210
hobbies and pastimes, your 21, 112, 237
Hodson, Phillip 152
holidays with grandchildren 61–4
Holmes, Dee 86–7, 202, 203–4
house sharing, three-generation 58–60
Hughes, Dr Dan 202

I

identity change 11–13
illnesses/bugs 127–8
image of grandparents 11–13
in-laws/partners, relationships with 14, 78–84, 87, 89–92
accepting your differences 94
fathers-in-law 106–8
improvement over time 96–7
living with mixed feelings 93–4
mothers-in-law and daughters-in-law 97–105, 119

resentment 95
tips for successful relationships 108–9
see also divorce/separation, impact of
infertility, male 181
interference 25, 76–7, 100–1
internet and communication 49–50, 55
IVF *see* fertility treatment, your child's

J
Johnson, Sarah 30, 124

K
Kornhaber, Arthur 18, 63–4, 142

L
language barriers 48
Lask, Judith 111
learning from children, bonding by 33
legal rights, lack of grandparents' 219
Lewis, Beth 191
life expectancy 6, 38–9
living with your grandchildren 58–60
long-distance relationships 45–55, 220–1
Lowe, Ryan 37, 49, 212

M
Mahal, Freya 68–9, 82, 128, 165, 175
Maori culture 14–15
maternal *vs* paternal grandparents
 avoiding competition 172–4
 being confident paternal grandparents 174–5
 competitive grandparenting 164–7, 172–4
 insecurities of maternal grandparents 170–1
 maternal grandparent bias 167–70, 171–2
 paternal grandparents' vulnerability 171–2, 217–18, 220–1
 positive relationships with the other grandparents 176–9
May, Professor Vanessa 25, 26, 95, 100, 110–11, 113
McDermid, Val 192
Merrill, Professor Deborah 104
money issues 72–3
Moore, Susan 144, 148
mother-daughter bond 167–9
mothers-in-law and daughters-in-law 97–105, 119
 blurred boundaries 101–3
 helping out 102–3
 your son's role 103–5
mothers, new 67–8, 169–70

moving near your grandchildren 56–8
multigenerational households 58–60

N
names, baby 71–2
Neustatter, Angela 12, 22, 91
newborns 29–32

O
overseas relationships 48–50, 52–4, 220–1

P
parenting regrets 85–6
parents, new 67–9, 193–4
parents, your own 19
partners/in-laws, relationships with *see* divorce/separation, impact of an adult child's; in-laws/partners, relationships with
paternal grandparents 80, 89–90, 97–101, 197, 203, 216–18, 220–1
  see also maternal *vs* paternal grandparents
patience with young children 32–3
postnatal depression 68, 169–70
power balance shifts 69–71

pre-teen children, older 34–5
priorities and focus, changing 15–16, 21

R
racism 170
relationships with adult children 1, 4–5, 20, 26, 65–7, 87–8
  common complaints 77–8
  conflicting expectations 71–2, 73–5, 80–1
  first weeks and months with new parents 67–9
  grandfathers learning from their sons 145–6
  in-laws/partners 78–84, 87, 89–109, 203
  influence of pre-grandchild relationship 84–7
  money issues 72–3
  parenting style differences 73–5, 80–1, 87
  power balance shifts 69–71
  support or interference? 76–7
  see also childcare; fertility treatment, your child's
resentment 95, 203–4
  see also divorce/separation, impact of an adult child's; in-laws/partners, relationships with; maternal *vs* paternal grandparents

retirement   112, 113, 142
Rilling, Professor James   28
rivalry, grandparents' *see* maternal *vs* paternal grandparents
rivalry, sibling   42, 44, 121–2
Rosenthal, Doreen   148

S
Saga   114
school life, involvement in   44–5
siblings, new babies and older   41–2
Singh, Dr Reenee   23, 56, 74–5, 102, 114
single grandparents   7–8, 154–5
    babysitting solo   157–8
    bonds with ex-partners   162–3
    emotional challenges   160–1
    grandfathers   149–50, 161–2
    managing multiple grandchildren   158–60
    when grandparents divorce   162–3, 228–34
Smith, Professor Peter   13, 29–30, 199
Soliz, Dr Jordan   199
sons as new fathers   68–9
sons-in-law   90, 93, 95, 98, 106–8, 207
Specified Adult Childcare credits   114

step-grandparents   7, 223–8
stereotypes, grandparent   13
stress and childcare   137
support *vs* interference   76–7
Szinovacz, Maximiliane   172

T
Tarrant, Professor Anna   138, 139–40, 141–2, 145–6, 150, 217, 232
teenagers   33–4, 35–8, 224–5
titles/names, grandparent   11–12, 165
Toksvig, Sandi   192

U
Usdaw   112, 114

V
Vance, J.D.   113
visits, cross-country   50–2

W
Woodall, Karen   14, 33, 50, 197, 201–2, 209, 210, 213–14, 218, 219, 222, 223–4, 226–7

Z
Zoom   50